NINE MINUTES,
TWENTY SECONDS

NINE MINUTES, TWENTY SECONDS

THE TRAGEDY AND TRIUMPH
OF ASA FLIGHT 529

Gary M. Pomerantz

MICHAEL JOSEPH
an imprint of
PENGUIN BOOKS

MICHAEL JOSEPH

Published by the Penguin Group
Penguin Books Ltd, 80 Strand, London WC2R ORL, England
Penguin Putnam Inc., 375 Hudson Street, New York, New York 10014, USA
Penguin Books Australia Ltd, 250 Camberwell Road, Camberwell, Victoria 3124, Australia
Penguin Books Canada Ltd, 10 Alcorn Avenue, Toronto, Ontario, Canada M4V 3B2
Penguin Books India (P) Ltd, 11 Community Centre,
Panchsheel Park, New Delhi - 110 017, India
Penguin Books (NZ) Ltd, Cnr Rosedale and Airborne Roads,
Albany, Auckland, New Zealand
Penguin Books (South Africa) (Pty) Ltd, 24 Sturdee Avenue,
Rosebank 2196, South Africa

Penguin Books Ltd, Registered Offices: 80 Strand, London WC2R ORL, England

www.penguin.com

First published in the United States of America by Random House 2001
Published in Great Britain by Michael Joseph 2002

1

Printed in Great Britain by Clays Ltd, St Ives plc

A CIP catalogue record for this book is available from the British Library

ISBN 0-718-14435-X

For Leigh,
the little girl who makes my heart sing

*In honor of the 29 who flew that day,
those who lived, those who died*

Contents

SEAT 1B
DAWN DUMM
Teacher
40 years old
Abingdon, MD

SEAT 4B
JENNIFER GRUNBECK
Hotel Coordinator
28 years old
Bangor, ME

SEAT 5A
JIM KENNEDY
Engineer
62 years old
Germantown, MD

SEAT 5C
BOND RHUE
Federal Prosecutor
56 years old
Laurel, MD

SEAT 6C
ALAN BARRINGTON
Personnel Manager
35 years old
Roswell, GA

SEAT 7B
DAVID McCORKELL
Computer Trainer
37 years old
Northfield, MN

SEAT 7C
KEVIN BUBIER
Assistant Dockmaster
37 years old
Waterboro, ME

SEAT 8A
REV. STEVEN WILKINSON
Minister
34 years old
Biloxi, MS

SEAT 8C
DAVID SCHNEIDER
Engineer
28 years old
Centreville, VA

SEAT 9A
MICHAEL HENDRIX
Engineer
35 years old
Jamesville, MD

SEAT 9B
CHARLES BARTON
Deputy Sheriff
57 years old
Purcellville, VA

SEAT 9C
TOD THOMPSON
Deputy Sheriff
33 years old
Purcellville, VA

SEAT 10B
LUCILLE BURTON
Retired teacher
69 years old
Asheville, NC

SEAT 10C
LONNIE BURTON
Community Leader
69 years old
Asheville, NC

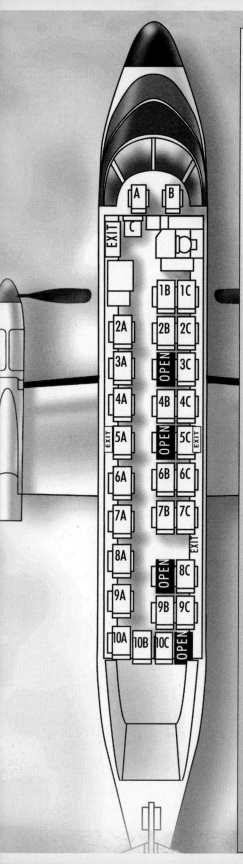

SEAT A
ED GANNAWAY
Captain
45 years old
Dublin, GA

SEAT B
MATT WARMERDAM
First Officer
28 years old
Warner Robins, GA

Rich Addicks/ASC

SEAT C
ROBIN FECH
Flight Attendant
37 years old
Macon, GA

"There is one spectacle grander than the sea, that is the sky; there is one spectacle grander than the sky, that is the interior of the soul."

Victor Hugo, *Les Miserables*

Part I

Propeller

1

CHRIS BENDER'S LIFE CHANGED when he saw a roomful of auto mechanics with big bellies. He was soft-spoken, courteous, earnest—and drifting. He wasn't sure what he wanted his world to be. One look around that room that day told him he didn't want to be one of those men. The thought scared him. He realized he might spend a lifetime working on cars and one day show up middle-aged and worn out to take an auto mechanic's certification test. He was too young to give up dreaming.

His dreams began with cars. A few years before, as a high-school student, blue-eyed, his straw-blond hair long, his weight lifter's torso shown off in muscle shirts, Bender ran a souped-up Camaro in North Carolina drag races. After graduation he'd found mechanic's work in a garage and later at an auto dealership in Charlotte.

But that day in that room with those men, their dreams gone, Bender knew he had to do something else. The question was, What?

It would be something with his hands. He knew that much. He loved working with his hands. They were a big man's hands on a man five-foot-eight. His father's decision had kept those hands out of bakery dough; Luke Bender was a third-generation baker, forced into the business by his father and determined not to impose his past on his son's future. This father would let his son find his own way.

So in the fall of 1993, Chris Bender checked the local newspaper's help-wanted columns, and there he saw an ad for aircraft technicians.

Aircraft. Now, that would be something.

A company named Hamilton Standard sought workers with a mechanical bent, a good work attitude, and good reading-comprehension skills. All that, Bender figured, he could handle. He'd attended a local two-year technical school in Fort Mill, South Carolina; he'd been an excellent auto mechanic, and though he would confess to knowing nothing about ultrasound techniques (he thought that was only for pregnant women), he would yet impress Hamilton Standard managers. They would sift through five hundred applicants in order to hire twenty workers. A battery of interviews and personality tests pared candidates from the list. Managers characterized Bender as inquisitive, careful, a team player willing to learn, and willing to work hard. The remaining job candidates trained four nights a week on scrapped blades. Managers scrutinized his work and it made Bender nervous.

But the managers liked what they saw. In January 1994, Chris Bender was hired to work in the company's maintenance facility at Rock Hill, South Carolina, a suburb of Charlotte.

Out of a grease monkey's garage, Bender found himself working for a multibillion-dollar, multinational aerospace corporation whose roots could be traced back to aviation's earliest days.

Ham Standard, as it was known, manufactured products as varied as microelectronics, advanced optical systems, and space suits for NASA. Its high-profile customers included Lockheed Martin, Bombardier, Rolls-Royce, and the United States government. Its eighty-five hundred employees circled the globe, from corporate headquarters at Windsor Locks, Connecticut, to Prague, Singapore, and Kuala Lumpur.

At Rock Hill, after several months' work replacing and repairing the propellers' exterior nickel sheath and fiberglass components, Bender moved to inspection and repair of the blades' hollow centers, the so-called "taper bores."

By all accounts, Bender was conscientious, did the taper-bore work well, and followed instructions to the letter. He took his role seriously, boning up on every detail and procedure. He wanted to know everything about the tools of his arcane trade: borescopes, ultrasound equipment, sanding instruments.

Some people around Rock Hill might not have liked working with the hollow centers of airplane propellers in a warehouse, in an industrial park, on the south end of the city. Bender loved it. Ham Standard paid him $9 an hour, plus insurance. He'd made more working on cars. But Ham Standard said, with good work, he could earn up to $12.50 an hour. Besides, Chris Bender was only twenty-three. He'd left behind those big bellies in that dreary room. Who'd have dreamed it, working on airplane propellers?

The first propellers were made of wood. They are distant cousins of the giant revolving arms on Europe's late-thirteenth-century windmills. Those arms were clumsy copies of birds' wings, the mysterious limbs that gave a bird the power of flight while man stood below, earthbound, confused. Great minds imagined means to match the birds'. In the fifteenth century, Leonardo da Vinci sketched propellers on helicopters and flapping ornithopter flying machines. French hot-air balloonists two centuries later used hand-turned propellers, or airscrews, in clumsy attempts to steer their balloons.

The Wright brothers, Wilbur and Orville, made the first powered, controlled, and heavier-than-air flights in December 1903, their longest flight of the first day 852 feet. Their airplane, the *Flyer,* used two propellers set behind the wings. These "pusher" propellers were more than eight feet long, made of three thin layers of spruce glued together, the tips covered with canvas and coated in aluminum paint.

Only after World War I did metal become the dominant material in the production of airplane propellers, including those used by Charles

Lindbergh on his historic trans-Atlantic flight in 1927. Carrying five sandwiches, working from a wicker porch chair, fighting sleep, Lindbergh made his thirty-three-hour solo New York–to–Paris flight aboard *The Spirit of St. Louis*. The plane's two composite metal "duralumin" propeller blades were made by the Standard Steel Propeller Company, which, through corporate evolution, would become Hamilton Standard.

By March 1994, there were fifteen thousand Ham Standard propeller blades on aircraft around the world.

And then, in that month, on separate commercial flights, two of those blades broke as a result of metal fatigue.

One blade shattered high in the sky over a frozen lake in Canada, the other at twenty-two thousand feet over Brazil. While both aircraft landed safely, two such incidents in a month were more than alarming. They constituted a corporate crisis.

The first blade's failure was particularly dramatic. Heavy metal components broke off the propeller assembly on the right wing of an Inter-Canadien airliner, an ATR-42. Metal pieces slammed through the ATR-42's fuselage, causing depressurization of the passenger cabin, damaging a third-row window seat, and leaving a vertical scar on the plane's skin forty-one inches long and an inch wide.

Not all metal-fatigue cracks are visible fault lines on the propeller's surface. Some faults lie within the propeller's metal itself, no less dangerous for being unseen, perhaps even more dangerous because they're hidden so well. In time, as with tectonic plates shifting under the earth, those faults may reach the surface and cause all hell to break loose.

Investigators decided that both propeller failures in March 1994 were the result of metal fatigue that started with bleached corks. The corks were used as plugs to hold lead wool in the blades' taper bores. The corks' bleach contained chlorine. (Cork manufacturers used chlorine to lighten the color of cork and also as an antiseptic agent for medical use.) The chlorine acted as a corrosive agent, creating pits in the aluminum lining of the blades' hollow cores.

Those pits were discovered by investigators studying the broken blades. They were confirming evidence of a metallurgical war, microscopic battles waged by corrosion against metal. If a propeller blade develops a weak point, the stresses of flight will cause it to break along that point. Once a crack reaches critical length and compromises a blade's stability, it is no longer a question of whether the blade will break, only when.

When the two blades broke in March 1994, Ham Standard's corporate hierarchy went into crisis management, notifying its offices around the world. Almost immediately, the Federal Aviation Administration ordered that all fifteen thousand Ham Standard blades be subjected to ultrasonic inspection. Any blade failing that on-site inspection was to be returned to the company for further assessment and repair if necessary.

Much of the work would be done in the shop at Rock Hill, South Carolina.

One returned blade carried the serial number 861398. It was style 14-RF-9, an instrument of aerodynamic beauty, its form perfect for its function, moving a twin-engine turboprop aircraft through the sky. The 14-RF-9 is five feet long and weighs about thirty pounds. It has a tapered aluminum shank and a smooth fiberglass surface. A nickel sheath covers the blade as protection against lightning strikes and erosion.

Blade 861398 was one of 490 that failed an ultrasonic inspection in the field. That inspection showed a possible flaw about fourteen inches from the hub. The blade was shipped to Connecticut and forwarded to Rock Hill, where, on June 7, 1994, fastened in a rubberized cart, it came into the hands of Chris Bender.

Bender had been working ten- and twelve-hour days, more than sixty hours a week during a two-week stretch, handling as many as five blades a day. Not that he minded. Anything over forty hours paid time-and-a-half.

Technicians inspecting the 490 returned blades looked into the blade's hollow core through a borescope. The long thin rod, a strawlike device, had an eyepiece at one end, a mirror at the other. A fiber optic cable passed down the rod's interior and provided an intense white light.

What Bender saw through the borescope was a one-to-one image, not enhanced, the picture as seen by the naked eye.

On this day, he moved the borescope up and back so he could see the length and breadth of the blade's interior walls. Up and back, up and back, he made six passes in all, slowly and methodically, each pass lasting several minutes, each overlapping the last to ensure complete coverage of the walls.

Bender searched for a white powdery residue that might indicate the presence of corrosion pits. He also looked for tool marks that might have been left by another technician. His job was to determine if any physical evidence suggested why the blade had failed its earlier ultrasonic inspection.

In a best-case scenario, the "flaw" registered in that earlier test would prove a false reading. That, or it would be a superficial irregularity on the taper-bore surface easily sanded away. *Blending* was the technician's term for that sanding. On second inspection in most cases, the "flaws" turned out to be harmless.

At its worst, a blade that had failed inspection carried a fatigue crack deep in its aluminum shank. Ultrasound examinations were designed to detect flaws ranging from the small to the potentially dangerous.

The Rock Hill bosses made certain that technicians knew lives were at stake. Every plane crash, whether the aircraft was a jet or propeller-driven, was discussed at the shop's seven-thirty A.M. meeting. For his part, Bender long ago had determined to work on every blade as if it would be attached to a plane carrying his family.

That June day in 1994, with blade 861398 at his borescope, Bender found no signs of corrosion pits, cracks, or tool marks. Neither did he see evidence of the rough taper-bore surface sometimes left by shotpeening, a process by which steel shot or glass beads are air-propelled against a blade's surface in hopes of improving its resistance to cracking. Early on, Hamilton Standard had determined that this process wasn't necessary and the FAA agreed; many blades, including 861398, were not shot-peened at all.

Yet something had caused 861398 to fail its ultrasonic inspection. That "something," as Bender had been trained to understand, likely was a surface blemish somewhere inside the blade's hollow core. So, as he had been trained to do, Bender used an air-powered gun and several grinding wheels with progressively finer grits to sand the spot—"blend it"—on the blade's taper bore where tests had indicated a possible flaw.

He set his drill rod to the depth of the area of the blade's inner-wall aluminum that needed sanding. Then he ground away about two-thousandths of an inch, a measurement roughly the width of a single strand of hair.

He blew air into the taper bore to remove the gray dustlike particles and then polished the surface to remove his own sanding marks. The goal was to return the surface area to its original finish; to leave behind sanding marks was to risk adversely affecting the next ultrasound test, possibly even keeping it from detecting a deeper flaw. Bender checked his polish against examples on a flat rectangular plate, four inches by six inches; it featured a series of annotated small squares, each with a different surface finish. The final test was done by feel: He rubbed a wood dowel over the blended surface and over the plate's squares to be certain he'd achieved the original finish.

It was tedious, time-consuming, and essential work, and he thought he'd gotten it just right. This polishing process was followed by another borescope inspection before the technician signed off on blade 861398. He wrote in small, tight letters, misspelling a word: "No visible falts found, blend rejected area." Then his initials with the date: "CSB 6/7/94."

He believed he had done his work well. He had done it the way he had been trained to do it, with the equipment he had been given.

Chris Bender had no way to know, nor any reason to think, that this blade yet contained a fatal flaw.

In August of that year, blade 861398 underwent another FAA ultrasonic inspection and was approved for flight. From Hamilton Standard the blade was returned to Atlantic Southeast Airlines, where it was installed on the left propeller assembly of an Embraer EMB-120, also known as a "Brasilia," a thirty-passenger commercial aircraft identified as N256AS.

In the next eleven months, that blade racked up 2,398 hours of flight while transporting perhaps thirty-five thousand passengers through the Southern skies. It had made an estimated 187 million revolutions without incident when it feathered to a stop at Macon, Georgia, on the night of Sunday, August 20, 1995.

Part II

Crew, Aircraft

2

O N THE MORNING OF MONDAY, August 21, 1995, ASA's 10:05 flight from Macon to Atlanta was delayed. Captain Ed Gannaway, First Officer Matt Warmerdam, and flight attendant Robin Fech dutied-in forty-five minutes early, only to learn that maintenance needed extra time in the hangar.

Their aircraft, N256AS, had been brought in to Macon at eleven-thirty the night before for the basic "C" check, required at thirty-three hundred flight hour intervals. Arriving ASA Captain Gerald Ash reported that the Brasilia had handled normally on the ride in, except for one of the air circulation units, which put out only hot air after takeoff. Apart from that minor glitch, N256AS had seemed no different to Ash than any other Brasilia. Overnight, mechanics had performed the mandatory checks, including a visual inspection of the propellers for evidence of leaks or damage. None was noted.

The crew was coming off a hard weekend of flying: heavy rains, interminable ground delays, surly passengers. On Saturday night, as midnight approached, Gannaway, Warmerdam, and Fech had struck a forlorn pose: standing at the curb in the lamp-lit rain at the Tri-Cities Airport in east Tennessee, the end of a grueling fifteen-hour day that began in one small Southern city and ended in another, standing together but feeling alone and waiting for a motel van that was, like everything else that day, late. When they arrived at the motel, Gannaway made a quick call home to his wife, Jackie. The captain had left his house at six A.M. and seventeen hours later his voice was heavy with fatigue. "Hard day," he said. "Bad weather." The motel's night manager unlocked the motel kitchen for Fech. She took a small box of cereal, a carton of milk, a Styrofoam bowl and plastic spoon to her room. Not exactly five-star dining, but it helped her sleep. The crew made it back to the Tri-Cities Airport by seven-thirty the next morning and returned home to Macon in time for Sunday dinner.

Now, up and ready on a Monday morning, they had six flights scheduled, with an overnight in Albany, Georgia.

More than a living, this was their life.

The 10:05 A.M. flight to Atlanta had a full load, thirty passengers, plus an ASA "deadhead"—Captain Tony Abeloe riding in the extra jump seat.

During the delay, Abeloe chatted with Gannaway.

Gannaway seemed at ease to him, well rested, and he had a fresh haircut.

Abeloe went outside for a smoke. There he found Warmerdam reading a paperback, cigarette in hand.

When N256AS finally pulled up to the gate, Warmerdam conducted his pre-flight walk-around inspection. Usually, this was a five-minute pro forma final check that harkened to aviation's pioneer days when pilots made structural inspections because no one else knew what to look for. Warmerdam went through the checklist from memory, as did virtually all pilots conducting six or seven walk-arounds in a single day.

He searched the tires for cuts, excessive wear, or perhaps a protruding screw. On each side of the plane's nose, he checked for clogs in the pitot-static ports, which provided information to cockpit gauges showing altitude, vertical speed, and airspeed. He checked the leading edge of both wings for damage from bird strikes. He assessed the overall condition of the Brasilia's exterior.

He also looked at all eight propeller blades, four on each of the two engines. He made certain the protective seal at the attached end of each blade wasn't leaking oil. He examined the blades for damage. Spinning blades produce not only thrust but a tornado of activity on taxi that can lift objects from the ground, such as rocks, which on rare occasion strike and damage blades.

In the eight blades on this Brasilia, including blade 861398 on the left assembly, Matt Warmerdam found nothing remarkable.

3

WITH JUST TEN PASSENGER ROWS, the Brasilia had room for only one flight attendant. Into this tight space Robin Fech (pronounced FECK) brought her Southern sensibilities: When you entered her plane, you entered her home, which meant she would treat you right unless, of course, you treated her wrong.

The sound of red-clay Georgia resonated in her voice. Businessmen from other parts of the country, hurriedly making connections through Atlanta, might have forgotten momentarily what region they had entered, but only until Fech greeted them—*"Hi, hon-eey!"*—and then they remembered. The South.

Fech had a sense of fun and Bette Davis eyes, big and hazel, filled with light. When her mood swung, though, it was as if darkness had fallen; the hazel turned gray.

On a flight several weeks earlier, an ASA passenger had come to know Fech and the strength of her personality. Fech was delivering her pre-flight instructions as the Brasilia taxied out to the runway. In the back row a passenger was sharing a good loud laugh with his colleagues.

Suddenly Fech's voice boomed through the plane: "You're not paying attention in seat 10D! This stuff could save your rear end someday!"

The scolded passenger fell silent.

A thousand flight attendants undoubtedly have wanted to say such a thing but in the name of good manners did not.

Robin Fech said it. This was her plane. This was her style.

* * *

At her ASA interview in February 1993, Fech had realized the flight attendant hiring process was designed to deglamorize the job.

ASA's information packet for flight attendants read like a Surgeon General's health warning: "long hours . . . walking, bending and lifting up to 70 pounds . . . changing locales, variable hours . . . dry air . . . dim lighting, confined spaces." It sounded like work in a coal mine.

But Fech was not easily deterred. She was thirty-four, single, without a college degree, and starting over. In 1987 she'd married a hometown boy, her godmother's son no less, with the reception in the grand ballroom of the Georgian Hotel in Athens, Georgia. Her parents had celebrated their wedding there thirty years earlier. Fech later realized *that alone* should have provided warning, given what became of her parents' marriage. "The best party I ever went to," Fech would say of her wedding. "I just went home with the wrong person." After the divorce in 1992, she'd considered becoming a paralegal or a respiratory therapist. Then a friend mentioned ASA.

ASA had emerged as the Southeast's dominant regional airline. It had started in 1979 flying DHC-6 Twin Otters five times a day between Atlanta and Columbus, Georgia. As Atlanta boomed in the eighties, ASA developed a shrewd and efficient spoke pattern across the region. ASA carried 12,000 passengers its first year, 350,000 in its fifth. Delta Air Lines took note and in 1984 made ASA its business partner, a regional "Delta Connection." By 1995, ASA was serving sixty-four markets with more than 4,100 flights per week from hubs in Atlanta and Dallas–Fort Worth.

For her job interview, Fech arrived at ASA's headquarters to a room full of would-be flight attendants. She introduced herself to each of them. Then she arranged for an exchange of telephone numbers so they could trade information learned in their interviews. The applicants were moved to a larger room where they stated their names, where they lived, and why they wanted to become a flight attendant. Then came one-on-one interviews, after which Fech was told, "We'd like you to come back for another interview, but please don't say anything after you leave the room." Too late for that—her phone line lit up that night, and through the Fech-orchestrated pipeline, applicants knew who was in and who wasn't.

Fech spent four weeks in ASA's intensive training program. "Barbie Boot Camp," she called it. She learned how to dress and how to carry herself. She studied the wording for all pre-flight and in-flight announcements ("Your seat cushion has been designed as a flotation device. Should you need it . . ."). She memorized the three-letter airport codes. Some were easy: Lexington, Kentucky, was LEX, Greenville/Spartanburg was GSP. For trickier ones, ASA assigned silly words to help flight attendants remember them: Waco was ACT ("A Cowboy Town") and Alexandria, Louisiana, was ESF ("Extra Swampy Forest"). She learned that "blueroom" meant lavatory and that "deadheading" referred to an ASA employee flying as a nonpaying passenger. She also learned never to reach without first looking into a seat-back pocket when cleaning the interior of a plane. One flight attendant had done that, only to be stuck by a hypodermic needle.

Above all, Fech understood that passenger safety was her primary responsibility. Her flight attendant class trained for an array of emergencies. In one scenario, a pregnant passenger went into labor while, at the same time, another passenger suffered a heart attack. In a second scenario, a cigarette caught on fire in the restroom up front while a passenger in back stepped into the aisle even as the FASTEN SEAT BELT sign was illuminated. Trainees had to respond quickly, definitively, by the book. In another test, an instructor, acting as captain, called from the cockpit to say an emergency landing was planned. The flight attendant was to respond by asking the captain a series of questions: What type of emergency is this? How much time do I have to prepare the passengers? Will there be a warning or bells to signal landing? What will be my signal for evacuation? Each trainee also had to make the formal emergency announcement— several minutes long—and they had to say it verbatim. Nerves overtook some trainees, but Fech held up.

In 1993, her first year at ASA, Fech earned $12,400 for work that was hard and could be demeaning; more than once, passengers addressed her as, "Oh, waitress." In time she made overnight trips below the "gnat line" of central Georgia, to the Mississippi coast, and to the Tri Cities of east Tennessee. For some sixteen-hour days, she was paid for eight hours; her pay clock didn't start, according to ASA rules, until the chocks were removed from behind the wheels of the plane. Time spent helping passengers on and off the plane didn't count, a sore subject for ASA flight attendants.

Still, Fech loved her job. She loved the camaraderie among flight crews. She especially loved takeoffs, sitting back in her jump seat and feeling the twin-engine turboprop lift smoothly into flight. She loved the feel of the Brasilia. The Silver Bullet, she called the small plane. She had mastered the walk down the Brasilia's narrow aisle. She swiveled her hips slightly as she walked so as not to bump passengers, sometimes raising her hands overhead and pressing them against the overhead compartments on each side for balance. She got used to the occasional complaints from arriving passengers: "I'm not flying on this little bitty thing!" or "Oh, my God, it's a prop plane!" Her standard reply: "Aw, c'mon, let's have some fun!" She liked being the sole flight attendant. It meant responsibility, for the passenger cabin was entirely hers.

As a flight attendant, she wore blue polyester slacks and a matching vest, gold earrings, an ID badge with wings, and a big navy blue bow in her brunette hair. She understood the theater of her profession. She projected her voice over the plane's roaring props. She had the gift of gab with passengers and an intuitive sense as to which ones wanted to laugh and which ones wanted to be left alone. Either way, she could deliver.

Through childhood and into her late twenties, Fech had danced, first ballet and then jazz, and later served as a dance instructor at her mother's ballet studio. In time her ankles could no longer take the punishment. In the years since she'd given up dancing, the straight lines in her facial features had turned smooth, and rounded out. But she retained a valuable lesson from those days. When the spotlight came on, she could perform.

Most ASA flights lasted an hour or less, too brief to serve meals. Over and over, Fech filled her serving tray with soft drinks and dry roasted peanuts. When she heard the inevitable "I thought we got a steak," Fech dropped peanuts on the smart aleck's tray table, said, "Here's your steak," and winked.

Fech was intrigued by her passengers; they were at once the greatest satisfaction and the greatest mystery. On each flight she never knew who, or what, she was getting. During idle moments in flight, Fech sometimes imagined what her passengers' lives must be like. She based her assumptions on their mood or appearance, never knowing if she was right, or even close.

At home, Robin Fech kept an old photograph of her father. The young Duane Fech had been a naval pilot, part of the elite Fleet Air Gunnery Unit. The photograph shows him as a dashing aviator in his hero suit, helmet in hand, climbing into an open cockpit. "Isn't he handsome? He was a glamour boy," she would say.

Her parents met because of a plane crash. In 1955, two months before she was to marry a navy pilot, Claudette Underwood's fiancé was killed when his jet slammed into a mountain. Her late fiancé's squadron sent a close friend to the funeral to present her with the U.S. flag. The friend's name was Duane Fech.

Claudette, who was a Delta "stewardess" during those white-glove days, married Duane a couple years later. They settled in Athens, Georgia, Claudette's hometown, where two daughters were born, Robin and Clemmie. The marriage got shaky, Duane moved to South Georgia to start a catfish business, and it wasn't clear to Robin, only a third grader, if they were to follow or if he had left them. In time they joined him.

Hearing their parents argue and exchange obscenities during the ensuing years, Robin and Clemmie clung to each other, sisters in the truest sense. The marriage finally broke up in 1973 and Claudette took the girls back to Athens, where she opened her ballet studio. Duane went his own way, later remarried, and if he became only an occasional presence in his daughters' lives, that was all right by Claudette. A steel magnolia, she wasn't much in the mood to share her daughters with Duane, anyway.

While Clemmie shrugged off the separation with her father, her older sister seethed. Robin had always wanted the thousand and more hugs that most little girls want from Daddy. She felt abandoned by her father. She always had hoped to make him proud of her, but never could.

In the summer of 1994, Duane learned he had cancer; doctors removed part of a lung. Clemmie visited him in Gainesville, Georgia. They talked about their lives and about heaven, and they made peace between them. Robin also visited him, but had no such conversation. The family always said that she and Duane were cut from the same stubborn cloth. Besides, Robin figured there was no circle to close in their relationship. "What we had was more like a spiral."

Duane fought the cancer into the spring of 1995. Two days before he died, his daughters came to his hospital room. They saw him drawn and ashen, soon to fall into a coma. Robin thought her father looked "like a person in a coffin."

Duane Fech was a man's man. He loved a round of golf and a good stiff drink. He was not a wordsmith. From his bed, he said to his daughters, "Girls, I recognize that y'all haven't had it that easy . . ."

And he could say no more.

Loving him and angry with him, Robin Fech stood in silence by her dying father and cried.

Back at her Macon apartment on Sunday night, August 20, 1995, after the long weekend of flying through the Tri Cities, Robin Fech was thinking of her boyfriend and missing him terribly. She'd met Chris Price on the job a year earlier. He was an ASA mechanic, as quiet as Fech was chatty. As she loved the give-and-take and cutting up with her frequent flyers, he loved the solitude and challenge of working with airplane engines.

She was thirty-seven, he twenty-three, though that didn't matter to them. He acted older than his age and she acted younger than hers. Both came with Delta pedigrees, Fech's mother once a stewardess, Price's father a career mechanic.

They were drawn to each other by the circumstances of their lives. She'd gotten divorced, his engagement had broken off, and now they shared positions at the low end of the ASA totem pole.

Fech had no illusions about her life: In August 1995, nearing middle age, she was earning barely $20,000 a year. Her "stage" was a passenger cabin thirty-one feet long twenty-four thousand feet in the sky. Hardly the stuff of dreams, but she was getting by, having some fun, and Chris Price played a large part in the equation.

Fech and Price were based in ASA's maintenance shop at Macon's airport, ninety miles south of Atlanta. The maintenance hangar was set alongside the runway, just down from the main terminal, so close that mechanics walked from one to the other. In Macon, ASA stationed eight flight crews—captains, first officers, and flight attendants—plus about forty mechanics. It was a tightly knit group with a fondness for cigarettes and a romance with flight. Most were in their twenties or thirties, some had military backgrounds, and virtually all hoped to move up to the larger airlines, "the majors." By consensus, ASA workers felt overworked and underpaid, a typical attitude in the regional airline industry.

Fech and Price lived in the same apartment complex near the Macon airport. A romance blossomed. She had no shortage of moxie and didn't ruffle easily, or, as she put it, "I don't let my panties get in a wad." At home she wore a nightshirt that read: "A Flight Attendant's Job Is to Save Your Ass, Not Kiss It!"

She was also a good listener. Price, solemn and inward, told Fech his most private thoughts. Together they often stayed up past three A.M., talking about everything and nothing, about love and life. They took trips to

Florida, spur of the moment, leaving at seven o'clock on a Monday morning, when Price got off work, or to Lake Sinclair, near Milledgeville, to sit by the water with their cigarettes and a twelve-pack of beer. They didn't have money, but they had spontaneity and they had each other.

ASA had just leased new aircraft—BAe-146s, British-made—and Price was among a group of mechanics sent to Manchester, England, for several weeks of specialized training.

He'd been gone only a couple days when Fech dashed off a short note, which she'd mail the next morning at the Macon airport. In the arcane codes and vernacular of the airline culture, she wrote:

1st thing Sat. morning AC#211 didn't get to the gate until 10:45 so we ferried to GNV. We sat on the ATL taxi for 2 hrs before TRI cities overnight because of weather so we ended up overblock after all. A long 15 hr day but we didn't lose $.

She signed with her nickname: "Miss Me—Rah."

Then she applied bright red lipstick and pressed her lips against the note.

4

DUBLIN WAS LIKE MANY OF Georgia's 159 county-seat towns: It staked its name on good living, good churches, and good people. It was 130 miles from Atlanta, which suited its residents just fine. The last thing Dubliners wanted was the big city.

The Gannaway place was set in a leafy enclave of suburban homes, without an ounce of pretense. Neat and spacious, it had a stone facade, a two-car garage, a yellow box at the curb for *The Macon Telegraph* (the nearest big-city newspaper), a swimming pool, and a stream-fed pond in the backyard. Ed, the outdoorsman, mounted a deer head above the fireplace. Jackie, his pacifist wife, tried not to look.

Tourists may have known Dublin best as a resting place along Interstate 16 between Atlanta and Savannah. To Ed Gannaway, it was a wonderful spot for a father to teach his three boys about hunting, fishing, and flying. The youngest, nine-year-old Rob, considered his father as mighty as the sky; in his bedroom, he kept a fleet of toy airplanes.

On a Friday in late summer or early autumn, when his flying schedule allowed, Ed Gannaway might lunch at the Dublin Rotary Club, work the afternoon away in his yard or at his garage workbench, take in dinner with Jackie at the Touchdown Club, watch the local high-school football team, and make it home in time for the eleven o'clock news. It was a nice life. He didn't socialize much with other ASA pilots. When he got back to Macon, he usually headed home, an hour's drive, to Jackie and the boys.

A few years earlier, he had delayed accepting a promotion from first officer to captain so he wouldn't be forced to move to Atlanta. Finally, in March 1993, he took the captain's job but commuted from Dublin for more than a year, driving the two hours to the big city. He spent three nights a week near the Atlanta airport with other ASA pilots in a "crash pad" so dingy Jackie called it "the dumpiest place." His transfer to the Macon base in 1994 allowed him to keep his home in Dublin, where Jackie had grown up.

Like Robin Fech, Gannaway had returned home Sunday night, August 20, exhausted by the weekend trip. Earlier that afternoon, a colleague had spotted him in ASA's operations lounge in Atlanta. His white captain's shirt was wrinkled, his shirttail hung loose. The colleague figured, correctly, that Gannaway had been flying all day.

Sunday night, his home was abuzz with activity. Monday was to be the first day of the school year, and Craig, sixteen, Russ, fourteen, and Rob were filled with excitement and dread. The boys tucked in, Ed Gannaway watched a *National Geographic* special on television and went to bed about eleven.

He awoke on Monday, August 21, at 7:15. Already the boys were running late. Over coffee in the kitchen, he offered to drive them to school. He was scheduled to duty-in at the Macon airport at 9:20, forty-five minutes before the 10:05 flight to Atlanta, the first of six flight segments on this day. He would spend the night in Albany, Georgia, then return home the following afternoon.

Since Jackie had flowers to deliver to school for an open house, she announced that she would drive the boys herself. That evening, they were planning to have a small party for her mother's birthday, balloons and all.

As she rushed for the door, Jackie Gannaway saw her husband standing in front of the bathroom mirror. Lean and boyishly handsome at forty-five, Ed Gannaway wore a T-shirt and running shorts. A compulsive exerciser who competed in triathlons and marathons, he was headed out to run a few miles before driving to Macon. During free moments at airports, he sometimes would disappear for twenty minutes. "Where you going?" a crewmate would ask. "For a walk," Gannaway would say. At the Atlanta airport, he walked the terminals, downstairs, alongside the internal subway. A couple times, flight attendants tried to walk with him, but they quickly gave up because they couldn't keep up with his brisk pace. Ed Gannaway's own father, Lawrence Craig Gannaway, a turkey farmer in Draper, Virginia, had died of a heart attack at forty-seven—a death that devastated Ed, then six years old. Though his mother later remarried, and he grew close to his stepfather, Ed Gannaway always felt cheated that he'd never really known his father. Ed named his first son Lawrence Craig.

Now that he was in his mid-forties, he vowed he would watch his sons grow old. He would be a central presence in their lives.

"You all have fun at the party tonight," he said to his boys.

Then he told his wife of nineteen years, "Have a good day." Jackie was nearly out the door when he added, "I'll call you."

The commuter industry is a post–World War II phenomenon, though its roots pre-date the first world war. In their history of American commuters, R. E. G. Davies and I. E. Quastler point to the 1914 St. Petersburg–Tampa Boat Air Line as a progenitor of today's commuters. That line, which lasted three months, used flying Benoist boats to carry one passenger at a time (typically a vacationing northerner) on an eighteen-mile air ferry service across the bay. A year earlier, Harold McCormick of Chicago and Alfred W. Lawson of New York flew daily between their homes and offices; Lawson even called himself "New York's First Airboat Commuter."

By the early 1960s, an expanding band of small independent airlines became known to the Civil Aeronautics Board as "air taxi operators" or "third-level airlines." In time they were acknowledged as "commuter airlines." In 1975 commuters carried 7 million passengers.

As small and midsized cities across the nation became economic engines during the 1980s, the commuter industry, largely through revenue-sharing agreements with the majors, reached out to those cities' hub-and-spoke operations and prospered as never before. Commuters, reinvented as "regional airlines," carried 26 million passengers in 1985. Ten years later, they carried 57 million. By the early 1990s, nearly 70 percent of U.S. communities offering scheduled air service depended exclusively on regional airlines. The projections for the twenty-first century were astonishing: 120 million regional airline passengers annually by 2010.

Regional airlines seek to match the appropriate aircraft to each market. For air routes of less than three hundred miles, the turboprop remained the best tool in terms of power-to-weight ratio, reliability, and cost effectiveness. The Brasilia met that need splendidly.

In the summer of 1995, ASA, with eighty-three planes in its fleet, including sixty Brasilias, was the largest single Embraer EMB-120 operator in the world.

That was just fine with Ed Gannaway, who was enamored of the Brasilia, and the way it reacted to controls with sports car agility. He once told Jackie, not as a boast, but as an article of faith, "I think I can get one down in a field somewhere if I have to."

He never worried about being involved in a plane crash. Ed Gannaway believed in the people who built and inspected airplanes. Beyond that, his love affair with flying would not allow such pessimism. Jackie figured it was a necessary denial common to all pilots.

Even so, anytime a commercial plane crashed—a United Airlines DC-10 in Sioux City, Iowa, a USAir DC-9 in Charlotte, an American Eagle

ATR in Roselawn, Indiana—Gannaway wanted to hear every news report. He felt a profound connection to the pilots and their families.

Gannaway had been an ASA first officer in April 1991 when an ASA Brasilia crashed on approach to the Brunswick airport on the Georgia coast, killing all twenty-three aboard. He hadn't known the ASA crew personally, and he'd heard about the crash only after returning from a family vacation. Still, the nature of the event gave him a chill. The crash of ASA Flight 2311 was well known because two famous men were among the passengers—former U.S. Senator John Tower of Texas and space shuttle astronaut Manley "Sonny" Carter. Their Brasilia fell straight out of the sky, in a nosedive, and crashed in a compacted mass in woods three miles from the Brunswick airport. An investigation revealed that the left propeller assembly had a worn part that allowed an uncorrectable movement of the blades. National Transportation Safety Board investigators placed blame not with Embraer or ASA but with Hamilton Standard for its deficient design of the propeller control unit and with the Federal Aviation Administration for having approved the design.

The Embraer EMB-120 had suffered one other devastating crash in the decade since its 1985 arrival in the United States. Five months after Brunswick, a Continental Express flight crashed in Eagle Lake, Texas. That plane's horizontal stabilizer, or top of the T-type tail, separated from the fuselage during flight. The plane disappeared from radar at nine thousand feet and spiraled into the ground. A farmer watched the fiery end in a cornfield from across the Colorado River and said, "It shook the ground, it blowed so hard." Fourteen died and investigators discovered why: Forty-seven screw fasteners had been removed the night before during a scheduled maintenance—and not replaced.

In November 1994, the National Transportation Safety Board (NTSB) concluded a nine-month safety study of the commuter industry. Overall commuters were said to have an accident rate 1.7 times that of the major carriers, but the board cautioned that this rate included helicopters and planes with ten seats or fewer. Excluding those, it said the accident rates were more comparable.

But the board also made several significant observations: (1) The rapid expansion of commuters had outpaced federal regulations; (2) the American public didn't realize that planes with thirty passenger seats or fewer typically operated under less strict safety guidelines; (3) the public didn't understand code-sharing agreements between commuters and major airlines (ofttimes, passengers wrongly believed a major carrier not only owned its revenue-sharing commuter affiliate but was responsible for its safety measures); and (4) commuter pilots flew longer hours and received less training than pilots at the major airlines (of commuter pilots surveyed by the NTSB, 87 percent said they had flown while fatigued due to inadequate rest periods).

As a result of this study, the NTSB called for the FAA to place most commuter operations under the same level of regulations as the majors, a recommendation that was adopted, though it wasn't put into effect until March 1997.

After dropping off the boys at school, Jackie Gannaway drove to her office. There, at about nine o'clock, she received a phone call from Ed's stepfather, Arthur "Lucky" McGrane. During World War II, Lucky, a B-25 pilot, had been shot down over the Pacific and had survived on a raft for several days.

Lucky was calling from South Carolina with terrible news: Ed's first cousin Jenny McLear had been killed Sunday in a small plane crash.

Lucky had phoned Ed at home to tell him about it, but no one answered.

Ed and Jenny were close. Jackie dreaded having to break this to him. She decided she would wait and tell him that night, once he arrived in Albany, Georgia.

* * *

Though Ed Gannaway had a family history of pilots (his uncle Bobby McLear was a P-51 flier during World War II), he took a circuitous route to flying. He graduated from Presbyterian College in Clinton, South Carolina, in 1972. He worked in construction, then at a car rental agency, and later as a salesman for an office equipment company. His midlife career crisis came early: He was thirty-five, married with three children, working for a pest-control company in Dublin, making $30,000 a year. He wanted a job that stirred his soul. Jackie had completed her master's degree in social work at the University of Georgia and was working at the Carl Vinson Veterans Administration Medical Center in Dublin. With her blessings, Ed began flying lessons in the mid-1980s.

A natural in the cockpit, thrilled by every aspect of flying, he pursued the craft eagerly. He became a flight instructor to build flight hours. "He is trying very hard [and] has excellent attitude," a flight trainer wrote in shorthand of Gannaway. "Will do well—if given enough time. Shows good judgment & does not quit."

Early in 1987, Gannaway stopped at the First United Methodist Church in Dublin. It was an official visit. On the job for a pest-control company, he carried a small tank filled with pesticide. He sprayed in and around the church, in corners and in the shrubbery, where roaches and water bugs sometimes gathered. At the church he saw "Brother Jack"— the Reverend Jack Key—and asked if he had a few moments to talk. To the minister, Ed Gannaway was just a good ol' boy, easy to know, not one to draw attention to himself in church. Now Gannaway told him he was thinking about quitting his job to chase a dream. "I've always wanted to be a commercial pilot," he said. The Reverend Key asked, "Is Jackie agreeable to that?" "She is," Gannaway replied. But he said he wouldn't make much money early on and worried about dropping the family's financial burden on Jackie. Brother Jack was encouraging. "You're young," he said. "Go for it." Then he quoted from the Book of Isaiah:

"'They who wait for the Lord shall renew their strength, they shall mount up with wings like eagles . . .'" Ed Gannaway broke into a smile.

Gannaway applied for pilot jobs at various airlines in the year that followed, frustrated by the long wait. In 1988 ASA hired him as a first officer.

He would emerge as a confident pilot. Over the years, he handled a few emergencies. As an ASA captain in 1994, he once lost an engine but landed his Brasilia on the second engine without further difficulty. Jackie had seen true fear in him only once. Returning home late one day, he looked frazzled, drained. On his run to Gulfport that day, he said, thunderstorms had forced him to divert from three airports. Each time he prepared to land, dark storms massed around him. With his fuel low and a full load of passengers, he told her he'd prayed for a safe landing. He made it, finally, in Alabama.

Now he hoped to fly for a major airline, the sooner the better. Regional airline pilots typically were younger and less experienced than those flying for the majors. In 1995 Gannaway was a seven-year commercial pilot, with nearly ten thousand flight hours, numbers that would bear strong consideration from the majors. But it was not simply a matter of wanting to fly bigger, faster planes. At forty-five, he wasn't getting younger, and he'd reminded colleagues he had "mouths to feed." A veteran ASA captain such as Ed Gannaway in 1995 topped out at about $60,000 a year, while a Delta captain made upward of $180,000, with a superior retirement package. The financial pinch was especially severe for ASA first officers. Their starting pay was about $15,000.

Only recently Gannaway had been paired in the rotation with a young first officer named Matt Warmerdam. He told Jackie this new pilot was good and that he wasn't lacking for self-confidence.

At twenty-eight, Matt Warmerdam was a man-child in the cockpit: six-foot-three and more than two hundred pounds with a boyish face, mischief written all over it. He was playful, at times sarcastic, a Californian living out his childhood dream of being a pilot. At the age of six, Warmerdam hung a model airplane from the ceiling in his bedroom. He'd watch the plane and let his imagination roam. A self-described "airplane freak," he earned his pilot's license while in college, flying Cessnas and later Piper Seminoles.

Now, twenty-two years after getting his first model airplane, Warmerdam was happy at work, happy in his marriage. If he earned only $15,000 a year and folded himself into cramped ASA cockpits (at the risk of suffering what he called "Brasilia butt"), these were small prices to pay for a dream.

Warmerdam had been hired by ASA in the spring of 1995 from Flight-Safety International in Vero Beach, Florida. FSI profiled and rated its graduates, who then entered a pool from which several regional airlines obtained their new hires.

Warmerdam was one of six FSI graduates hired by ASA. He spent six weeks in ground school in Atlanta and three weeks in the Brasilia simulator, known to pilots as simply "the Sim." Inside the simulator, pilots in training look out through a duplicate of the Brasilia's four large cockpit windows. They face nightmarish scenarios; even when they can't salvage their plane, they'll fight until the end, when the screens in the Sim either freeze or turn red. ("How'd it go today in the Sim?" one pilot trainee might ask another. The dejected response: "I crashed the Sim.") Inside the simulator, Warmerdam studied a video re-creation of Runway 9-Right at the Atlanta airport, a night landscape complete with images of car and truck headlights along the interstate. Next he performed his night-flying training in Dothan, Alabama, finishing on a Sunday night. The training process was intensive and exhausting. When it was done he expected a few days off. Upon phoning for his schedule Monday morning, however, Warmerdam was told to report to his new base in Macon at once. He made his first ASA flight the next morning at six o'clock, Macon to

Atlanta. He thought it no different from being in the simulator, except for hearing the muted voices of passengers beyond the closed cockpit door.

His new ASA colleagues were struck by Matt Warmerdam's loving words about his wife, Amy. They had met in 1990 in Warmerdam's hometown, Santa Rosa, California. He'd taken a job selling stereos and was trying to save money for flight school; she attended junior college. A mutual friend sent her into the store. Warmerdam not only sold her a stereo, he gave her the employees' "family discount." They soon became inseparable, and he began pretending to pull an engagement ring from his pocket. Finally he did it for real, on a knoll in the California wine country.

It was all still so new to Matt Warmerdam in the summer of 1995. Weeks earlier, Robin Fech and Chris Price had welcomed the Warmerdams to Macon, delivering homemade lasagna to their apartment.

5

THE WAITING ATLANTA-TO-GULFPORT passengers saw their plane pull up: a Brasilia, silver and sleek, its propeller blades thrumming, bright red, orange, and yellow stripes along the fuselage and tail, a black-tipped nose, and passenger windows seemingly as small as a ship's portholes.

Out on the ramp, a cluster of ASA Brasilias waited, mosquitos gathered across from Delta's big birds. In all, fifteen Brasilias were scheduled to leave from ASA's gates between 11:49 and 12:20, bound to points across the South, including Myrtle Beach, South Carolina; Meridian, Mississippi; and Fayetteville, North Carolina.

Dwarfed in size and glamour by L1011s and 737s, the Brasilia was an $8 million, high-performance aircraft capable of flying 345 miles per hour at twenty-five thousand feet. Sixty-five feet nose to tail, it had a wingspan of nearly equal length. With its Pratt & Whitney of Canada engines, it was a machine of power, speed, and extraordinary stamina. Each operated with a captain, first officer, and flight attendant, many of whom were young and ambitious and saw their work on the Brasilia as a necessary step toward the big leagues of commercial flight.

So cramped was the Brasilia's cockpit, regional pilots joked, "You don't get into a Brasilia. You *put it on.*" Some likened the cockpit to a pair of jeans, tight, though quickly familiar—same as the propellers' loud, insistent hum. To a veteran Brasilia pilot, a change in the propellers' hum might be the first indication—even before a change registers on the cockpit gauges—that something has gone wrong with the aircraft.

The Brasilia had been a mainstay of the American regional market since 1985, when the first one was sold to ASA. It vied in popularity with the Saab 340 and dominated the fleets of Comair and Skywest.

The 1984 revenue-sharing agreement with Delta had increased ASA's earnings by 84 percent in the first year. The growth possibilities in the burgeoning Southeast made it clear that ASA needed to develop a fleet superior to its existing five de Havilland Dash 7s and fifteen Embraer EMB-110 Bandeirantes.

In the Embraer family, the Brasilia followed the Bandit: It was bigger, faster, more sophisticated, and up from nineteen seats to thirty.

The Brasilia N256AS flown into Atlanta by Gannaway and Warmerdam had been in service for nearly six and a half years, hardly an old plane. Its exterior was beat up by rain and hail, dust and bird strikes, the wear and tear you'd expect in a commuter plane that had completed 18,171 flight segments.

ASA was getting its money's worth out of this plane: 18,171 flight segments was 235 per month, nearly eight takeoffs and landings each day. Up and down, up and down, eight times a day over six and a half years, the average flight lasting about fifty-six minutes. N256AS was a workhorse.

In one sense, flying in the Brasilia was reminiscent of aviation's earlier days. In the big jets, you felt as if your living room moved through the sky. But in a Brasilia, you felt the vibrations of flight. In Rows 2, 3, and 4, nearest the propellers, your body vibrated in tune with the plane.

Passengers boarded the big jets through an enclosed passageway, stepping from one air-conditioned compartment to the next. But to get to a Brasilia, ASA passengers walked down two flights of terminal stairs, then out of the building, onto the cement ramp, through the weather, and up the plane's lowered staircase.

Walking to the Brasilia, ASA passengers might look up and see their pilot and first officer through the cockpit windshield, close enough to observe them at work. A baggage handler waited beside the plane. Since the Brasilia's overhead compartments were small and narrow, the baggage handler put any oversized carry-on luggage in the rear cargo hold. The baggage handler also made certain that passengers didn't step behind the propellers.

The Brasilia's retractable staircase, barely the width of a thin man's body, led to a main passenger door that was little wider. The flight attendant backed away as passengers entered because there was not enough room for two people in the entry. Once inside, anyone taller than five-foot-six had to duck, or tilt their head to the side, to avoid banging it against the sloped ceiling.

The Brasilia's ten rows contained a single seat to the left of the aisle and two to the right (except for the first row, which contained only two seats, and the last row, Row 10, which contained four seats, but no aisle). Because its seats were smaller and thinner than those in the big jets, passengers were much closer to everyone and everything. If you sat in the single row, even moving your left arm could be difficult; the seat was nearly pinned against the fuselage wall. If you sat in one of the two seats across the aisle, your shoulder brushed your neighbor's. If you were overweight or tall, you hoped the passenger beside you was gentle and forgiving or, at the very least, hadn't had a bad day.

Conversations, especially those in the back of the plane, farthest from the props, sometimes drifted and could be heard several rows away. The Brasilia was a shared experience. From Atlanta to Gulfport, that experience was designed to last eighty-six minutes.

Part III

Passengers

6

MONDAY, AUGUST 21. Pre-dawn, in Bangor, Maine, Jennifer Grunbeck looked at her ticket and froze. Her 6:45 A.M. flight was, in fact, her 6:30 A.M. flight. The race was on: She grabbed her coffee and four-year-old son, Johnny, and dashed to the car, spilling the coffee along the way. With her husband, Bob, driving, they made it to the Bangor airport in time, only to discover she'd forgotten her purse. Her husband got money from an ATM and Jennifer ran off to the Business Express Saab 340, a propeller-driven plane, for the first of her day's three flights. The Grunbecks worked for a company that owned and managed hotels. They were young (Bob thirty-one, Jennifer twenty-eight) and mobile—more mobile than they'd wanted, having moved several times for the company, from Florida to New England, back to Florida, and just four weeks earlier, to Bangor. Bob served as general manager for several area properties, including a Fairfield Inn. Jennifer was an assistant purchasing manager, buying items for hotels, ranging from forks to beds. This was to be her sixth trip to Biloxi and the newly opened Isle of Capri, a casino and resort. There she would deliver two oversized books filled with purchase orders. She hated saying good-bye to her son. "When are you coming home, Mommy?" Johnny asked. "I'll be back on Friday," Jennifer Grunbeck replied.

She added, "And this will be the last trip for a while, okay?"

* * *

In the stillness of two A.M., at home in a Baltimore suburb, Dawn Dumm had pulled out two shirts—one cotton, the other synthetic. She chose the cotton shirt, even if it was more wrinkled. She would iron it. She also chose cotton pants.

If she was getting on an airplane in the morning, Dawn Dumm would wear cotton. That much was certain. She was simply looking out for things.

The iron was for neatness. She would look her best even as she prepared for the worst. Cotton, she'd heard, didn't adhere to your body in fire.

Dumm was a forty-year-old elementary-school teacher, attractive with soft features and a lovely smile. She also had a deep sense of foreboding, created by a series of personal hardships, including her father's cancer death and heart surgery for her infant child.

One bad thing after another victimized those closest to her. The common thread, Dumm decided, was that she'd had no control over any of it.

The silver lining was that she had endured. She was a survivor. The hardships had made her think about the frailty of life, and she leaned on her Catholic faith. Only recently she had become a Eucharistic minister in her church. On Sundays she handed out Communion wafers.

On this night, Dumm had returned home late with her husband, Larry, and their two young boys, Lucas and Zeke. They'd been camping in western Maryland.

Later in the morning she would fly to Atlanta and to Gulfport to visit her sister. Her sixty-four-year-old mother, Mary Jean Adair, would travel with her, and the last thing Dumm had asked her mother before she'd turned in was, "What are you wearing tomorrow?"

Adair hadn't decided. Make sure it's cotton, Dumm told her. If a fire broke out on the plane, Dumm explained, synthetic material would burn into your skin. Cotton would not. That's why women should never wear nylons on a plane, Dumm said. She also told her mother to wear long pants, even though it would be hot in Mississippi.

These were tips Dumm had heard from a travel expert on TV. She took the advice to heart and encouraged her husband to do the same on his business trips.

Some things in life you could control, others you could not.

Wear sturdy shoes, too, Dumm said. In case we need to make a quick escape.

Visiting from her home near Pittsburgh, Adair, who understood her daughter's careful nature, said she had brought only sandals and sneakers.

"Then wear the sneakers," Dumm said.

Their morning flight from Baltimore arrived to the usual bustle at Hartsfield Atlanta International Airport. Once Atlanta had been the center of the Confederacy's railroad system. After World War II, William B. Hartsfield, the city's wily opportunist mayor, saw Atlanta's future as the hub of air travel in the Southeast. By the end of the twentieth century, Hartsfield International Airport, less than fifteen minutes from Atlanta's city center, had become one of the world's biggest and busiest commercial airports. Its thirty-three thousand employees tended to more than two hundred thousand travelers daily through a hub that in the beginning served the Southeast and later came to connect the city with most of the United States, if not the world.

So big and important is the Atlanta airport, provincial Southerners say, "If you're going to heaven, you have to change planes in Atlanta."

ASA Flight 529 had a scheduled noon departure but already was running behind. The ASA gate area filled with waiting passengers, many departing on different flights, yet through the same gate. It made for a noisy, harried setting, the usual commuter frenzy.

Passing time, a few Gulfport passengers took note of one another.

David McCorkell, a thirty-seven-year-old divorced computer trainer, noticed a young woman in jeans and T-shirt, Renee Chapman. He thought her attractive in just his kind of way, informal, down to earth, no heels or makeup. He wondered, in passing, about her background. Maybe the last thing he would have guessed was that Chapman once had been a U.S. Army private.

Connecting from Dulles Airport near Washington, a young engineer named David Schneider spotted Jim Kennedy. He'd never met Kennedy, but knew him by face and reputation as a hard-driving financial consultant working with his company, Noell Inc., a German-based environmental engineering firm. Schneider and Kennedy were en route to Gulfport, where the company was overseeing the fabrication of metal gates for the Byrd Dam Project near Gallipolis; the gates would control the flow of the Ohio River.

Schneider and Kennedy made interesting counterpoints: Schneider was twenty-eight years old and stocky, his career on the rise, married four years, no children. Kennedy was sixty-two, tall and lean, a lifelong jock, married for nearly four decades, a proud paterfamilias with eight grown children, including seven daughters, and eight grandkids. Decades earlier he had given silly nicknames to his children. There was Katy, Genie Beanie, Be-So (as in, How can you *be so* cute?), Clare Maureen the Jelly Bean, Moopie, Haymouse, Maddy, and Handsome Harry Backstage. There was nothing he loved more than a Holy Day of Obligation, when he would parade his brood up the red-carpeted center aisle of the St. Rose of Lima Catholic Church in Newtown, Connecticut. His kids had worshiped his toughness and his humor. They'd grown up believing the Kennedy half-dollar was named in his honor, a notion he nurtured. For the past year Jim Kennedy had rented an apartment in Gulfport, flying home to his wife, Nancy, every two or three weeks. He didn't have a TV, just a radio. Because he told his kids, "My wants are many, my needs few," they playfully called him Gandhi. Like so many others raised during the Depression, Kennedy knew the value of a buck and drove himself each day to the brink of exhaustion.

Back in 1981, though, when darkness had consumed Jim Kennedy, his wife was left to wonder: Was it the alcohol or the pressures of job and home that got him first? Jim Kennedy was forty-eight then, married for half his life, his career stagnant, multiple college tuitions to pay for the next decade—a midlife crisis waiting to happen. A binge drinker, he came home from work later and later. At home, in bed, knowing he was driving back from some bar, Nancy would hear distant sirens on the roads of Newtown and worry that her husband might have been the cause. His daughters knew he was on edge and kept their distance. Nancy attended Al-Anon and, with the kids, set up an intervention to save him. He found out and wouldn't show up, saying, "Nobody is going to tell me what to do with my life." He lost his job from a downsizing company and no longer was the loving husband and father his family had known. Nancy filed for separation, citing "habitual intemperance," but withdrew the papers once he assured her he'd keep paying the bills. In 1981, Jim Kennedy had needed more than a job: He needed to run away. He went off to the desert, literally and figuratively, to Saudi Arabia, for a job as a financial manager. Nancy couldn't believe he was going to Saudi Arabia, even as she drove him to the airport. Six long years he was gone, returning only occasionally. Nancy and her children mourned him, cursed him, and cried over him. Nancy got a job and life went on. He returned in 1988, renting a house in New Jersey with two other men. Overqualified for most jobs—he had a master's degree and a lengthy career as a comptroller—he loaded bottles on trucks. Nancy heard about it and hurt for him. She'd never stopped loving him and she was stronger now, having endured without him. During one of his visits to Newtown, she said to him, "Why don't you come home and we can get back together?" The next morning, one Kennedy daughter whispered happily to another, "Dad's back!" And then days later, another whisper: "Dad slept upstairs last night!" It took time, but Jim Kennedy reclaimed his family and his career. He and Nancy would move to Maryland. He became a consultant earning six figures. He sent notes and letters (with checks) to the kids, paid their credit-card bills. He and Nancy became strong again, stronger than before. He did not explain his long absence to his children, saying only, "Your mother, God bless her, she's a beautiful woman." At church, Jim Kennedy rarely missed Confession.

Now, waiting at the gate in the Atlanta airport, David Schneider thought to introduce himself to Jim Kennedy. Then he decided to wait until Gulfport.

Sitting nearby, Tod Thompson, a blond Virginia deputy sheriff, felt the stares of others, especially those of the man across the way in the air force uniform, Major Chuck Lemay. The .38-caliber handgun in Thompson's black overnight bag made him self-conscious. Thompson was new to fugitive retrieval and he didn't want some lunatic to take the gun from him, least of all in an airport. He had placed the bag between his feet.

Sitting beside the young deputy, Charlie Barton had no such worries, even with a weapon concealed on his hip. Then again, Barton was the consummate pro at fugitive retrieval. A hulking, balding lawman for thirty-five years, the last eight with the Loudoun County (Virginia) Sheriff's Department near Washington, D.C., Barton had made many trips like this one: He and Thompson were to retrieve a teenager who had stolen checks from his father's checkbook to buy a 1995 Ford Mustang.

Barton was a law-enforcement lifer, all cop. His big strong hands produced a handshake that could cause pain to an unsuspecting well-wisher. He rarely talked with colleagues about his home life. His wife, Macil, was a Jehovah's Witness, a religion Barton didn't understand; since his wife didn't drive, he shuttled her on errands. They had a son, a hardware store clerk, and a toddler grandson. Charlie Barton sometimes called his daughter-in-law with tips that would keep his grandson safe from harm. Work was the center of Charlie Barton's life. It was what he knew and did best.

To him, this fugitive retrieval was ho-hum stuff, hardly worthy of Thompson's tension. Earlier Barton had made his traditional stop at the airport gift shop to look for knickknacks to bring back to his buddies at the sheriff's department. Sometimes he bought shot glasses or colorful pins, other times postcards featuring pretty girls. His colleagues loved him for it.

Flying into Atlanta from Hartford, Chuck Pfisterer arrived at the gate more than an hour early. Pfisterer was a nervous flier. He heard every noise a plane made, plus some he imagined. He did not like to fly in snow or rain. He did not like flying in clouds. He did not like going up in the air, not even on a ladder. Upon entering a plane, he always tried to establish contact with the pilot or copilot, if only to say through the open cockpit door, "How's it going?" or "Weather look good?" He needed to know other people were aboard and that he was not alone in the sky. He was a sensitive guy quick to embrace his wife and grown daughter. He had a booming voice, the kind you'd expect from a man with a fifty-four-inch waistline. The life of the party, friends called him, and for Chuck Pfisterer, there was only one way to fly—with a Jack Daniel's in hand.

At the gate now, the big man didn't look forward to sitting in the little plane. He fretted about the overcast skies and light rain. He considered canceling his reservation and waiting until morning. He worked for a Connecticut paper company and was bound for Wiggins, Mississippi, to visit a mill his company had bought. He'd turned fifty the previous fall and he accepted that flying was never going to be easy for him. "How's the weather in Gulfport?" he asked an ASA gate agent.

About the same as in Atlanta, he was told.

Fidgety, Pfisterer left the gate area to smoke a few cigarettes.

Sonya Fetterman traveled alone. Twenty years before, the beauty queen with the rhythmic, sweet-sounding Spanish name, *Sonya Marie Villarreal,* had been crowned Miss Teen San Antonio. Tiny, barely five feet tall and one hundred pounds, with cascading brunette hair and liquid green eyes, she still could turn heads. She wore shorts for the flight to Gulfport.

Thirty-seven years old, the mother of three, married for the third time, she could be carefree at one turn, dramatic and stormy at the next.

Fetterman had had dark visions lately. A few weeks before, on another flight, she had suddenly, hauntingly, felt someone's presence beside her. She believed that someone's fate, possibly hers, had been sealed. Frightened, she had turned to the window, staring into the clouds. She wept.

She stepped off the plane that day and phoned her younger brother, Nathan Villarreal. "Nathan, are you okay?" she asked. He was fine. Her voice was tense. "Are you sure you're not lying to me?" She was nearly in tears. Her brother said, "Sonya, what's wrong?" Instead of answering, she said, "Have you heard from Mom?" He said she was fine. "Nathan, do you *know* that Mom's okay?" He replied, "I think so. What's wrong?" and only then did she tell him about her flight, and the presence she'd felt.

She said the presence might have been their older brother, who had died tragically in Texas years before. She had never stopped grieving over his death, and now she thought he was warning her about something, but . . . *what?*

Shaken, Sonya Fetterman told her younger brother that she had made some decisions. "There are going to be some changes in my life," she said. He wasn't sure what she meant. She didn't elaborate and he figured, With Sonya, you just never know. They agreed to talk when she got back to Texas.

The Reverend Steve Wilkinson sensed big changes ahead. A day earlier, in a small Baptist church in Illinois, Wilkinson had preached two trial sermons about why bad things happen to good people. The chairman of the Gateway Baptist Church's pastor search committee, Robert Simmons, listened carefully. He thought the Mississippian was a good fundamentalist, a "teacher preacher," who, in his suit and tie, stood upright, both hands upon the lectern, and made his points systematically, with clarity. The Gateway church was in Millstadt, Illinois, a bedroom community to St. Louis, close enough so that, if you stood on a nearby hill, you could see the Gateway Arch in the distance. The search committee sought a pastor who, in time, would fill the pews on Sundays, a pastor who would relate well to youths. Wilkinson fit that role well: He even looked like a kid. He was only five-foot-five, with deep blue eyes and ash blond hair in an "evangelical cut," never a strand out of place. He spent the weekend in Simmons's home, even frolicked on the living-room floor with his host's grandkids. Wilkinson had a warm, common touch. The committee had heard several other ministers preach trial sermons, but their styles and messages weren't a good fit. Members listened to two tapes of Wilkinson's mailed-in sermons and liked what they heard. The only concern among some members was that, at thirty-five, Wilkinson was still single, though someone made the point, convincingly, that the prophet Paul was single, too, and so was Jesus Christ. Wilkinson wanted the job. Back home he was working the night shift, in the stockroom at a local Wal-Mart. At Gateway, he preached without notes. He spoke of how God puts people through trials to steel their character. Using precious metals as his analogy, Wilkinson explained how a refiner superheats metals into molten liquid and then skims away impurities that rise to the surface, until finally the impurities are gone and he sees his own reflection in the boiling liquid. God does the same with man, he told Gateway's members. Early Monday morning, Simmons drove him back to the St. Louis airport. They'd enjoyed each other's company, and as he drove off, Simmons saw the Reverend Steve Wilkinson, in his blue jeans and tennis shoes, and realized he was the perfect fit.

Arriving at the gate, Dawn Dumm was surprised, unpleasantly so. She and Adair had expected to fly to Mississippi on a jet, a Delta jet. Their tickets said "Delta Flight 7529." They'd never heard of ASA.

Only from the gate agent did Dumm learn that ASA was "the Delta Connection," and that the airlines had a revenue-sharing agreement. Delta Flight 7529 and ASA Flight 529 were one and the same.

Dumm wasn't happy. She liked neither surprises nor small planes. But she and her mother needed to get to Mississippi. This trip would be brief.

She asked for two seats in front of the wing, one by a window. She explained that her mother liked to look out at the view during flights. Dumm made certain Adair wouldn't be looking out onto the wing. She was given front-row seats: 1B and 1C.

When the flight was called, Dumm and Adair moved to the door and walked in line down the stairs. A ticket-taker at the bottom pointed to the line of Brasilias and said, "Your plane is over there." In a light rain, Dumm and Adair held newspapers over their heads. As Chuck Pfisterer walked with them, his glasses fogged over.

Dumm saw a flight attendant at the aircraft door. She asked if she was boarding the correct plane, and Robin Fech nodded yes. Dumm and Adair ducked their heads and stepped inside.

Pfisterer sat in 6C and struck up a conversation with the man beside him, Major Lemay, a meteorologist from Offutt Air Force Base in Omaha. Talking eased Pfisterer's nerves. But moments later, an arriving passenger holding a *USA Today* and a boarding pass stood before him. "I think I've got 6C," Alan Barrington said.

Pfisterer looked at his own seat assignment—6A, not 6C. He moved across the aisle and told Lemay, cheerfully, "I'm leaving, but I'm not going too far." Still, he felt more isolated in the single-seat row.

At the gate, standby passenger Angela Brumfield heard her name called by the gate agent. Brumfield was eager to get home to New Orleans to share her good news with the family.

She had finished her second interview with ASA. She'd applied for an opening as a flight attendant. She'd taken a written personality test first, then she'd gone through a formal interview. An ASA official had asked one question about the Brasilia's cramped quarters: "How do you feel about it?" Brumfield said it was no problem. She felt comfortable in the small plane.

She got the job and was asked how soon she could start training. They agreed on October, five weeks away. She even wrote the particulars in her *Flight Attendant New Hire Manual*: "Oct. 2, 1995. 5:00 p.m. Sheraton Hotel. 1325 Virginia Av. East Point, GA."

A twenty-seven-year-old African-American, Brumfield felt her life taking a wonderful turn. She wanted new adventures, preferably outside of Louisiana, where she'd grown up. She was ready for marriage, but her boyfriend wasn't. So now she took charge, moving to Atlanta without him. She knew the ASA job would be demanding. "You will be living out of a suitcase," the *Flight Attendant New Hire Manual* said. "Your day can, and often does, consist of 12 hours on duty. During this time you must continuously remain pleasant, well-groomed and sensitive to your passengers' needs."

Tough talk, but she liked it—a new beginning.

Brumfield rushed outside, entered the Brasilia, and sat in her assigned seat, 2C. But something seemed amiss.

"Is this plane going to Gulfport?" she asked.

The flight attendant shook her head. "Chattanooga," she replied.

She pointed Brumfield to the next Brasilia in line. As she hurried in a light rain over to Flight 529, Brumfield saw the pilot, Ed Gannaway, pointing at her through the cockpit window, as if to say, Here comes one more.

She placed the *New Hire Manual* in her garment bag to be stored in the rear cargo hold. Angela Brumfield, in the correct plane now, sat in 2C, behind Mary Jean Adair.

With all twenty-six passengers aboard and the pilots finishing their checklist, an overhead light panel fell from above the fifth row. It struck the head of passenger Lucille "Ludie" Burton. A retired teacher from

Asheville, North Carolina, she had the look of a refined woman, hair up, nicely appointed. She exuded civility, and when she talked, people listened. She sat with her husband, Lonnie, a former school principal and physically imposing man. His voice was a deep tenor. When the young deputy Thompson saw them at the gate, he noticed their kind faces and thought, They look like somebody's parents. The Burtons were leaders of the African-American community in Asheville and were bound now for Biloxi for Lonnie Burton's final meeting as a board member of a regional association of community action agencies. They loved playing the casinos and had made trips to Las Vegas and Atlantic City. In Gulfport, Ludie Burton intended to play the slot machines. Her luck with the slots had been uncommonly good.

An ASA mechanic with a screwdriver reattached the overhead light panel. As he did, Lonnie Burton moved to a vacant seat in the eighth row, an emergency exit area with more legroom. In 6A, Pfisterer watched Lonnie Burton and thought, These little planes aren't comfortable for big people like me or tall people like him.

As the mechanic departed, Fech asked, "Did you get it fixed?"

"I think so," the mechanic replied.

Hearing this, Mary Jean Adair looked to her daughter. "Don't you think we should get off?"

Dawn Dumm shook her head. They needed to get to Mississippi. "Just think of it as an adventure."

Part IV

9:20 to Impact

7

THEIR *ADVENTURE* **ONLY BEGINNING,** passengers sat three across in the narrow seats with thin backs. The red seat coverings were worn and frayed in spots.

To Dawn Dumm, turning back from her front-row seat, it had the look and feel of a city bus.

From the paneled cockpit door to Row 10 in back was thirty-one feet.

That tight space, claustrophobic to some, contained twenty-seven lives, full and varied: Catholic, Baptist, Methodist, Jewish, agnostic, white, black, Asian, Latino, never married, married, once divorced, twice divorced. Ages ranged from eighteen (Jason Aleshire in 3A) to sixty-nine (the Burtons). The passengers had eighteen spouses, forty-one children, and more than two dozen grandchildren.

Living in an age of flight, most passengers board planes without a second thought, never questioning how twenty-four thousand pounds remain aloft. For some, flying is an act of denial, a refusal to acknowledge that they have risen from the ground and ceded physical control of their lives. But for most, flying is more an act of faith, faith in the people who build, inspect, and fly planes. They accept the exactitude of flight, the overall safety and speed of it, and for good reason. Arnold Barnett, an applied probabilistic and statistical modeler at the Massachusetts Institute of Technology, calculated aviation accident rates in the United States for the 1990s, the last decade in the first century of manned flight. Barnett concluded that a person's chances of dying in a turboprop crash on a

U.S.-based regional airline were so small that, on average, he could fly once every day on such a plane, without dying in a crash, for nearly eight thousand years.

At 12:23 P.M., ASA Flight 529 rolled on Hartsfield's Runway 8 Right. The Brasilia's composite airfoil Hamilton Standard propeller blades created a loud hum that became white noise. In Rows 2, 3, and 4, the vibrations made a passenger's excessive girth jiggle. As the Brasilia rose from the runway, Chuck Pfisterer, in 6A, said, "Get up! Get up!"

Jean Brucato, a forty-year-old accountant from the Atlanta area making her weekly trip to Gulfport, reached for the armrest to her left and squeezed hard, only to realize she was squeezing the forearm of the woman in 4B, Jennifer Grunbeck.

"I'm sorry," Grunbeck heard Brucato say. "I just don't like to fly."

On the 352-mile trip to Gulfport, pilots follow a navigational beacon southwest toward Montgomery, Alabama, and then to Semmes, Mississippi, before turning south to the Mississippi coast. ASA 529 was to arrive at the Gulfport/Biloxi Regional Airport at about 12:50 P.M., Central Daylight Savings time, one hour and twenty-six minutes after leaving the gate in Atlanta.

Several passengers nodded off to sleep. In the seventh row, Kevin Bubier read a golf magazine. For Bubier, golf was more reverie than sport, its peaceful nature the antithesis of his pressurized job as assistant dockmaster in the Maine shipyards. He worked for the Bath Iron Works at its overhaul facility in Portland. He had responsibility for as many as two hundred workers, including welders, blasters, tin-knockers, and pipefitters. If a big gray navy leviathan tipped over or broke the dock in half, there would be hell to pay. The classic image of the shipyard worker—big neck, all swagger—didn't fit the thirty-seven-year-old Bubier. He was modest, both in personality and in stature, with a streak of diffidence that ran as deep as his Maine heritage, five generations and counting. You heard that heritage in the way he said "shipyahds."

Across the aisle in Row 8, the Reverend Steve Wilkinson, on his way back to the part-time job in the Wal-Mart stockroom, could only wonder about his future. Would the Illinois congregation hire him as its new pastor? Returning home to Mississippi, Wilkinson would await the call.

In Row 6, Alan Barrington, a middle manager aspiring to climb his corporate ladder, opened a newspaper sports section and learned that his beloved Kansas City Royals had lost to Toronto, 4–3, in the bottom of the ninth.

As the Brasilia passed through dense air at twelve thousand feet, Robin Fech heard two chimes: the cockpit calling. By intercom, Warmerdam told Fech the minor turbulence would smooth out soon.

Fech, strapped in her jump seat, said, "Couple more minutes and then I can get up?"

"Yes, ma'am," Warmerdam said, teasing Fech with his impression of a Southern gentleman's voice.

Moments later the passengers heard the real Matt Warmerdam. "Ladies and gentlemen, good afternoon. Welcome aboard Atlantic Southeast Airlines," he began in his young, fresh California sound. "We're passing through thirteen thousand feet. The captain has turned off the 'Fasten Seat Belt' sign.

"However, if you're in your seats, we ask you do so with your belts fastened loosely around you . . . just in case we encounter any turbulence en route."

Ed Gannaway sat in the captain's chair. Passing through fifteen thousand feet, he made his 7,375th hour of flight in an Embraer EMB-120. He was not wearing his headset or his blue ASA captain's hat. It was a casual moment for a casual man—except for a noise in the cockpit.

Like all Brasilia veterans, Gannaway had grown accustomed to cockpit noises. Some pilots wore earplugs to filter out the higher and lower frequency sounds. In the turboprop, they expected to hear their blades at work, and the airstream passing over the wings. But there were other smaller, peskier noises. Almost invariably, tiny leaks formed along the Brasilia's cockpit windows and, at 275 miles per hour, they produced snakelike hisses. The captain's altimeter also was famous for its chattering, a buzzing sound from inside the mechanism.

But this rattle of unknown origin irritated Gannaway. He'd heard it before, near his panel or seat.

"Something underneath," he said.

"It'll drive you nuts," Warmerdam said.

Gannaway: "It *will* drive you nuts."

Atlanta Center interrupted the pilots' cockpit dialogue: "ASe [pronounced A-See, for Atlantic Southeast] 529, climb and maintain flight level Two-zero-zero."

With his left hand, Warmerdam reached across the panel and spun the altitude alerter to twenty thousand feet. The alerter emitted a beep when the plane climbed within four hundred feet of the preselected altitude.

"Two-zero-zero, ASe 529," Warmerdam answered.

Then, following procedure, he said to Gannaway, "Twenty."

12:43 P.M.   The Brasilia, on autopilot, climbed at 184 miles per hour through 18,000 feet. Its propeller blades turned at 85 percent, 1,100 revolutions per minute.

Warmerdam spun the altitude alerter once again to the next approved destination: 24,000 feet.

"Twenty-four," he called out.

Gannaway: "Twenty-four."

Then it happened.

It happened almost simultaneously with the captain's echo of his first officer's words. It happened on an ordinary day in the sky on a flight so routine, the pilots all but let the Brasilia fly itself while they mused about a silly little airframe rattle.

An explosive sound—sudden, angry, and metallic—from outside the fuselage, from the left side.

The plane fell suddenly to the left, as if in a sharp, steep turn, and it shuddered in the sky, as if it were a toy shaken by a child.

From the window seat nearest the mangled engine, the young woman who had served in the army, Renee Chapman, looked once out there, her eyes drawn by a sound that reminded her of a small cannon exploding. She quickly slammed shut her window shade. She didn't want to know.

Robin Fech's iced cups, ready to be filled with soft drinks, trembled, slid across a galley surface, and fell to the floor. The flight attendant grabbed the galley to steady herself. For the next thirty-three seconds, the plane shuddered, at times so violently Fech thought maybe they'd hit another plane.

That noise, so quick and loud, what was it? That noise: thuds, a series of thuds, like hammer blows. What was it? Passengers, with the chill of fear, knew only that they'd heard sounds unlike anything they'd ever heard in the air.

When they looked toward the left wing, toward the sounds, the thuds, looking in the direction of the plane's sudden falling, they saw signs of what happened. About five feet out on the wing, they saw the engine destroyed.

Once sleek and streamlined, the left engine now seemed a junk pile. Its cowling was mangled, its aluminum curled back and twisted by the force of whatever had happened out there. The engine's innards were exposed. Wires and cables whipped in the airstream. Fluids from steel-braided hoses spewed past the fifth-row window of Jim Kennedy. The engineer in the eighth row, David Schneider, thought it looked like a bomb had exploded in the engine.

Frightened passengers, shaken in their seats by the plane's shudderings, grasping for handholds, looking outside, also noticed the propeller unit was not where it was supposed to be. They saw the blades at a standstill, splayed against the wing's leading edge. Instead of four blades, several passengers on the left side saw only three and a stub where the fourth had been. Two dead blades formed a V against the wing. In Row 6, the nervous flier Chuck Pfisterer thought, Am I crazy?

Seven rows back, shaken so severely he felt he was falling, veteran deputy Charlie Barton rocked against his young partner, Tod Thompson. To keep his balance, Barton put out a hand and held fast to the first thing he touched, Thompson's thigh. As Thompson straightened his wire-rim glasses, which had been knocked sideways, he thought, We've run into a mountainside!

In the cockpit, Gannaway and Warmerdam were surrounded by the chaos of flashing red and yellow lights competing for attention with warning chimes and a synthesized female voice calling out, "Autopilot, engine control, oil."

A propeller blade had snapped in two. Later investigation and examination made it possible to say what caused the blade to snap. Deep within the blade's metal shank, there had been a fatigue crack. As the vibrations of flight intensified, the crack grew at an accelerating rate, rotation by rotation, atoms tearing apart. The crack reached a length at which it rendered the blade so weak it could no longer withstand the forces applied to it. So the blade broke into two pieces, snapping like a twig at a spot a foot above its connection to the hub. The bigger part of the blade, four feet long, flew away from the assembly and fell through the day's clouds toward farmland in Alabama.

Now the propeller assembly had three whole blades and only a stub of the fourth; its necessary symmetry was suddenly, and catastrophically, gone. That is, while two blades remained in position to balance each other's forces, the third whole blade had lost its partner and in the process had lost the carefully calibrated balance that enabled the blades to turn smoothly and precisely at twenty revolutions a second. Instead, the propeller assembly began a high-speed, unbalanced wobble that, in essence, beat itself to death. The blades' hammerings against the wing and engine produced the thuds heard by passengers.

The explosive sound was no bomb, it was metal being ripped apart. The haywire propeller blades created such torque that the engine was ripped from its two inboard mountings nearest the fuselage.

The two outboard engine mounts buckled and bent, yet didn't let go. So the propeller assembly and metal gearbox attached to it lifted together and flopped away from the engine. They lodged a few feet away against the front edge of the wing.

Improbably, almost unimaginably, more than four hundred pounds of metal stuck to the wing's front edge: the more than two hundred-pound propeller assembly, the bulky gearbox, and assorted metal casings. With this metal mass distorting airflow, the plane in effect lost the lifting power of its left wing. ASA 529 would have been much better off had all that metal fallen away. But it was refusing to fall away, seemingly determined to bring down the entire aircraft with it.

From the moment the propeller snapped, the Brasilia would fly only another nine minutes, twenty seconds until it crashed.

The first twenty-five seconds, it fell at the rate of fifty-five hundred feet a minute. A nine-story drop each second. Even before the synthesized cockpit voice called out its reminders, Gannaway pressed the red button on the left side of his yoke to disconnect the autopilot, the crippled plane now his to fly.

Dawn Dumm, sitting with her mother, first thought they'd hit a bird. *But this high? Maybe a peregrine falcon.* Ed Gray, a hundred-thousand-miles-a-year frequent flier from Connecticut in the twilight of his career as a construction industry consultant, thought, After all these years of flying, now it happens!

In the fourth row, Jennifer Grunbeck, who'd left Maine in a coffee-spilling rush, noted a film of smoke filling the cabin. Thompson and Fech noticed it, too. The smoke reminded Grunbeck of wet exhaust.

Pfisterer saw the spewing fluids, the brown oil, red hydraulics, and clear fuel. *This can't be.*

Suddenly the passengers detected a new noise. Or thought it new, for in truth it had always been there, but now they heard the right-side engine only, its roar seeming louder with the left engine gone silent.

Their little world in the Brasilia's cabin had gone askew, everything tilting left, noise on the right, the plane shuddering. Curiously, the passengers' disorientation meant that they had no sensation of falling. The initial drop, though dramatic, did not pull them out of their seats. Its steep turn had altered gravity's force, the so-called G-load, from the normal 1.0 to 1.25 G's. But they were in clouds, with no visual reference points, which is a circumstance that can deceive the inner ear so completely, a person can fly upside down without knowing it.

The passengers responded only to what they saw: the engine, a junk pile.

Beyond that they saw only clouds in a sheet of flat gray.

8

8:19 TO IMPACT. At 14,200 feet and falling, the descent seemed more controlled—at least Robin Fech thought so. When the propeller shattered, she was preparing drinks by the galley up front.

Rocking back, Fech grabbed the galley to steady herself. She felt the Brasilia move oddly, suddenly, a blur of motion, down and to the left. Even before she achieved full recognition of what the jarring sensation meant, Fech, under her breath, cursed.

The shuddering went on for fifteen seconds, enough for her to know a crisis was at hand, and then for fifteen seconds more. Fech held the galley as she looked to her passengers. All were staring out the left-side windows, transfixed. In their faces she saw confusion and terror.

Then the passengers turned to the flight attendant.

She gathered herself first, turning away to inhale deeply. She was terrified.

She leaned over Renee Chapman in 2A. She slid open Chapman's window shade. Out on the left wing, Fech saw the source of her fear. She closed the shade against the sight of the mangled machinery.

She smelled an electrical burn, acrid and full of chemicals. Somewhere wires were melting. The smell dissipated quickly.

Then came the passengers' questions, first from up front: "What happened?" "Are we going to be okay?"

Robin Fech had no idea, but she knew she had to hide her anxiety and reassure the passengers. If ever she needed the performer's poise taught by her mother, now was the time. Under pressure, she did what made the most sense. She improvised.

She placed her hand on a passenger's shoulder and said, "These planes are designed to fly on one engine." Fech was right, in a sense. Planes are designed so that no single system failure will render them unflyable. Of course, not all failures can be anticipated, and it's true that an engine loss or intentional engine shutdown initiated by pilots is uncommon. Still, in addressing the possibility of an engine loss, a designer must take into account the four forces acting on a plane during flight: thrust, drag, lift, and weight. In steady, nonaccelerating flight, lift and weight are balanced, and so are thrust and drag. Air moving over the surface of the wings produces lift (the amount of lift is controlled by the angle and speed at which the wings move through the air); the engine/propeller system produces thrust. For any given weight, there is a corresponding amount of lift required to maintain flight. A plane is designed so that one engine can provide enough thrust to overcome drag and provide enough speed to produce the necessary lift.

Fech knew it was true a Brasilia could fly on one engine when the inoperable engine had been shut down, and she hoped it was true of this mess. She spoke with a confidence she didn't have.

She told passengers, "It's one of the first things flight crews practice— going in with one engine." She did not make eye contact with any passenger; she was working her way to that point. In trying to convince passengers, she first needed to convince herself.

Moving down the narrow aisle, Fech shut the window shades on the left side, one by one, up to the fifth row. She snapped them shut, quickly and definitively. "We don't need to be looking at that," she told a window-seat passenger. "Let's just close this," she told another.

Once the shuddering stopped, the relative smoothness, along with the cloud cover, enhanced Fech's credibility with passengers. They believed what she was saying in part because they *wanted* to believe the plane was designed to fly on one engine.

But violent tremors soon undid her work. "That's just what turbulence feels like with one engine," Fech said. She was selling hope.

When she reached the sixth row, Chuck Pfisterer, the nervous flier, blurted, "Do you think we're going to make it?" Fech said, "Of course we're going to make it." Pfisterer kept talking, an edge in his voice. "How can that fly like *that?*"

His seat was adjacent to the back edge of the left wing. He liked sitting next to a window. It allowed him to see what was happening outside. It gave him context and proportion and some sense of control. But now he looked out and saw the busted propeller on the outboard side of the engine, one blade pointing at 45 degrees toward the cabin, another blade at 45 degrees toward the wing tip. He saw that the outer metal casing of the engine had peeled back, as if somebody had used a can opener. He saw the guts of the engine and those fluids blowing into the airstream, a mist of clear fluid he figured was fuel. *Is the engine about to catch fire?* He waited for the engine to come apart in pieces.

Pfisterer had been in tight spots before. He'd lost his first job when the company folded. He'd been without a paycheck for eight months, collecting food stamps, seeing his stay-at-home wife return to work. He sold the family silver so he wouldn't lose the house. Years later, at the paper mill, he'd been threatened by hourly workers. They thought him some smart-ass Cornell grad and company man, and pounded their fists on his desk in disputes about mill policy. Once a drunken man came in for a job interview with Pfisterer and, before leaving, urinated against the front door of the mill. It was enough for Pfisterer that night to ask his wife: "Am I stupid or am I just an idiot for working here?" Now, as the plane shook, he had more important questions to ask. *Holy Jesus, how could those blades be sitting on the front of the wing?* He wondered about the pilot and why the plane wasn't slowing down. *Where is he headed? What is his game plan?*

He had seen Fech on the intercom to the cockpit. But the pilots had not come into the cabin and he wondered if they could see what he was seeing.

He did not, and would not, pull down his shade.

Fech tried again: "These planes are designed to fly on one engine." Pfisterer did not believe her. He did not believe this plane could land on one engine, not based on what he saw out on the wing, not based on what he saw in Fech's eyes. He thought the worst. "We're not going to make it," he told Fech. He said it not as a question. It was a statement: We're not going to make it. He was going to die on this plane.

Fech could not sway him. In fact, their conversation had the opposite effect. Pfisterer began to sway her. He made her feel her own fear, her own inadequacy. He was emotionally overwrought. His panic, Fech decided, could ignite panic throughout the cabin.

She gave up on him. She stepped past him, toward Alfred Arenas in the next row.

Just then Fech heard two chimes. On the wall panel in back, only slightly larger than a postage stamp, a red light flashed. The cockpit calling. Thank God that Ed Gannaway is flying this plane, she thought. They'd flown together often, and once handled smoothly a medical emergency on a flight out of Augusta, Georgia. His voice soothed. If ever Fech needed soothing, it was now.

9

WHEN THE PROPELLER SHATTERED, the plane abruptly rolled left and dropped. In the cockpit, red and yellow lights—warnings and cautions—flashed on the instrument panel. A chaotic clamor filled the pilots' ears. Chimes signaled a master warning: *Ding, ding, ding*. A synthesized woman's voice called out, "Autopilot, engine control, oil." The voice, designed to alarm, was known to some ASA pilots as "Bitching Betty," sometimes shortened to "the Bitch."

The engine gearbox had broken away, spilling oil into the left engine intake. It produced smoke that was distributed through the air-conditioning and pressurization pack into the cockpit. Immediately the pilots shut down the pack, and the smoke cleared.

"We got a left engine out," Ed Gannaway said to Matt Warmerdam.

For twenty-five seconds, Gannaway and Warmerdam were on the ragged edge of losing control of their aircraft. During that time, the plane fell 2,750 feet.

"Left condition lever, left condition lever," Gannaway said, altering the pitch of the left propeller blades. He assumed the blades were still intact. And then he said, "Feather." To feather is to put the blades at a flat pitch, which produces the least amount of drag. It stops the blades from spinning. These were the so-called "memory items," a captain's reflex responses to a catastrophic problem or failure. Once the memory items were completed, a captain moved on to the more formal emergency checklist. Gannaway's initial response was textbook precise.

Now a red light flashed on the panel: a left engine fire warning.

"Yeah, we're feathered. Left condition lever, fuel shut off," Gannaway said.

To counter the plane's left roll, the pilots moved the wheel position to 40 degrees right.

To offset its descent, they adjusted the control column from zero degrees to 4 degrees nose up.

The chaotic clamor continued: *Ding, ding, ding* . . . "Autopilot, engine control, oil."

"I need some help here," Gannaway said to Warmerdam.

Ding, ding, ding.

"I need some help on this," Gannaway repeated.

The Brasilia pulled hard left. It was trying to respond to the pilots' maneuvers, but the laws of aerodynamics tried to turn the plane, flip it, and make it spiral into the ground. Gannaway did not yet know the source of the problem. Had the propeller assembly and engine gearbox not lodged against the wing, but simply fallen to the ground, controlling the plane would have been easier. But the odd, misshapen metal, clinging to the left wing, created uncorrectable aerodynamic turmoil. If ASA 529 had experienced a simple engine failure, or even a complete loss of the propeller with no resulting structural damage, Gannaway would have simply secured the failed engine, run the appropriate checklists, returned to Atlanta, and executed a single-engine landing. But the damage reduced the amount of lift that could be produced by the left wing and dramatically increased the amount of thrust required due to the drag created by the destroyed engine and propeller assembly. The physics simply wouldn't allow the ASA pilots to continue under steady, controlled flight.

Gannaway hadn't looked over his left shoulder and seen his destroyed engine, not yet. He was responding to its immediate, horrific effects: distorted airflow, excessive drag, and loss of wing lift on his left side. His plane continued to pull and fall.

The Brasilia's response confused him. The drag was not decreasing. "[You said it's] feathered?" he asked.

"It did feather," Warmerdam said.

Without looking, the pilots could not know that the mangled propeller assembly and gearbox hung off the leading edge of the left wing. They trusted their instruments, and those instruments indicated that the blades had feathered.

They took on their machine, white-knuckling their side-by-side steering columns. They stared wide-eyed into instrument panels: screens, dials, levers, and lights. They concentrated on their heading, altitude, airspeed, and the power setting on the good engine. The aural warnings sounded again and again. So did the chimes. *Ding, ding, ding.*

"What the hell's going on with this thing?" Gannaway said.

Fifty-five seconds after the propeller shattered, Flight 529's descent rate was now 3,500 feet per minute, a six-story drop per second. The airspeed had increased to 224 miles per hour; the pitch now was 5 degrees nose down and the left bank 15 degrees.

"Let's put our headsets on," Gannaway said.

The vibrating steering column, or yoke, shook in Gannaway's grip.

He said, "I can't hold this thing . . . help me hold it."

His headset on, Warmerdam's call went out. "Atlanta Center, ASe 529 declaring an emergency. We've had an engine failure. We're out at fourteen-two at this time," he said, referring to the altitude.

Atlanta Center responded: "ASe 529, roger, left turn direct Atlanta."

Flight 529 turned at once to the left, toward Atlanta.

The airport was nearly fifty miles away.

Still high in the sky, the pilots' fears and tension revealed themselves: heavy breathing, a squeal. One minute, twenty-five seconds after the propeller separated, their airspeed topped out at 230 miles per hour, their descent rate again surpassed five thousand feet per minute. They canceled the master caution warning; the red lights remained illuminated but no longer flashed.

Suddenly in the cockpit there was . . . silence.

Only labored breathing.

Gannaway pulled back power on the good engine, his hand wound tightly around the lever by his right thigh. He continued to experiment with the variables. The Brasilia's nose lifted, its speed decreased to 189 miles per hour.

Atlanta Center: "ASe 529, say altitude descending to."

Warmerdam replied that they were at 11,600 feet.

To his first officer now, Gannaway said, "It's getting more controllable here . . . the engine . . . let's watch our speed."

For the first time since the crisis began, the pilots thought not only of their aircraft, but of the people inside.

"I'll tell Robin what's going on," Warmerdam said.

The first officer hit the call button: Two chimes sounded and in the back of the passenger cabin a red light flashed.

Robin Fech picked up the intercom on the other side of the closed cockpit door, her back to the passengers. Hoping for a soothing call, she didn't get it. Hoping to hear Gannaway's voice, she heard Warmerdam's instead. This troubled her because she knew Gannaway liked to be in contact with the cabin and to be in total control of his plane. This was not a good sign.

"Okay, we had an engine failure, Robin," Warmerdam said. "We declared an emergency. We're diverting back into Atlanta. Go ahead and, uh, brief the passengers. This will be an emergency landing back in."

His tone was purely professional, no frisky "Yes, ma'am" Southern mushmouth now.

In such a moment, Fech had been trained to ask questions: *How much time do I have to prepare the passengers? Will there be a warning or bells to signal landing? What will be my signal for evacuation?* But now she asked nothing. She said only, "All right. Thank you."

* * *

At 10,000 feet, still falling at a rate of between one thousand and three thousand feet per minute, Gannaway realized he could not reach Atlanta. "We're going to need to keep . . . descending," he said. "We need an airport quick."

According to cockpit protocol, the captain always is in charge of the flight and always has the final say. In calm circumstances the captain will swap stick and rudder duties with the first officer, alternating from one leg to the next: As one flies the plane, the other speaks to air traffic control and runs checklists. The roles here were clear: Gannaway, already flying this leg, would speak to Warmerdam and the first officer would communicate with air traffic control.

Warmerdam radioed Atlanta Center: "We're going to need to keep descending. We need an airport quick and, uh, roll the trucks and everything for us."

Atlanta Center reported that the West Georgia Regional Airport near Carrollton, Georgia, was at their ten o'clock position. It was about ten miles away.

Flight 529 made a wide left turn over west Georgia, bound for Carrollton.

Gannaway thought procedurally now. He told his first officer, "Engine failure checklist, please."

Warmerdam could have pulled up the checklist on his panel display screen. Instead he chose a quicker route. He told Gannaway: "I'll do it manually here." He reached behind his seat for the *QRH*—the *Quick Reference Handbook*—and found the appropriate page, marked by color-coded tabs: "Okay," he said, " 'Engine Failure in Flight.' "

Together they went through the list, interrupted only by Atlanta Center asking first for the plane's heading, and then giving them a modified path to West Georgia Regional.

Flight 529 attempted to enter a right turn. "We're having, uh, difficulty controlling right now," Warmerdam told Atlanta Center.

He returned immediately to the checklist.

Warmerdam: "Condition levers, feather."

Gannaway: "All right."

Warmerdam: "It did feather." He noted the cockpit panel reading on the propeller speed and then moved to the next item on the list.

Warmerdam: "Okay, electric." The first officer looked to the overhead cockpit panel for the electric feather switch, used when the manual feather fails to work. "Okay, it did feather. There's no [engine] fire."

Gannaway: "All right."

Warmerdam: "'Main auxiliary generators of the failed engine'—off."

Gannaway: "Okay. I got that."

Warmerdam read the next item, the auxiliary power unit: "Okay, APU. 'If available, start.' Want me to start it?"

For a moment at least, Ed Gannaway was no longer thinking procedurally. He was thinking survival. He said, "We've got to bring this down."

6:45 to Impact. Robin Fech pushed the PA button, turned to face her twenty-six passengers, and said, "The cockpit crew has confirmed we have an emergency. We have an engine failure." She announced that the plane was headed back to Atlanta. She sounded firm even if frightened.

Chuck Pfisterer, in 6A, thought, Yeah you've got an engine problem all right!

Fech reiterated that the plane could fly on one engine. She also told passengers they needed to prepare, just in case. She did not deliver the lengthy formal emergency announcement she'd learned in training. She'd always thought it too long, slow, and boring. But she delivered the essence of that announcement, in her own way.

Make certain your seat belt is low and tight, she said.

Place your feet flat on the floor and review your emergency card.

She explained the brace positions. For all but a few passengers sitting by the bulkheads, that meant crossed wrists against the seat back in front of them, forehead pressed against the wrists. Fech insisted that each passenger demonstrate the brace position.

"You'll have to prove this to me," she said.

She asked if there were any questions. No one had any. She cleared off the kitchen galley and then moved up the aisle, saying, "Let me see it." As passengers assumed brace positions, Fech lifted an elbow here, pushed down a head there. She had been trained to do it. She just couldn't believe she now had to do it.

She had convinced most passengers that a safe landing was possible. In the fourth row, Ed Gray, on his way to Muscle Shoals to schmooze DuPont with his colleague across the aisle in 3C, Barney Gaskill, imagined a foam-covered landing strip and a bouncy ride in.

In Row 9, the young deputy, Tod Thompson, thought back to childhood fears. He wrestled with rationalizations. A roller-coaster ride once scared him as a boy. But he'd held on then, things had turned out okay, and he'd thought at the time, That wasn't so bad, was it? *It will be the same thing now.*

Thompson craned his neck to see the left engine. A few of the left-side window shades in the middle rows hadn't been shut. Thompson saw the twisted metal. His partner, Charlie Barton, looked out to the left wing, too. He saw what Thompson saw, and spoke not a word.

Charlie Barton went quiet, totally quiet.

Thompson didn't want others in the plane to know his fear, least of all Charlie Barton.

The plane shook in the clouds, side to side. Thompson reminded himself to think like a lawman: *Stay clear-headed! Do what you're told!* He tightened his seat belt, listened for the flight attendant's next words. Then he closed his right-side window shade, as if the sky would no longer exist if he couldn't see it.

* * *

In the seventh row, David McCorkell believed the plane would land just as the flight attendant said it would. Once, McCorkell had been a passenger on a plane that landed in a blizzard as fire trucks lined the runway. When that plane landed safely, every passenger applauded.

Air travel was a way of life for McCorkell. He left home in Minnesota each week on Sunday or Monday and flew to another city to train grocery chains how to use software programs. Then he flew home on Friday, washed his clothes, paid his bills, and started the cycle all over again.

This was David McCorkell, vice president of training, his life and his livelihood one and the same. At thirty-seven and twice divorced, he had the worn appearance of a man who no longer had the time, or inclination, to dream big dreams: a thick Teddy Roosevelt–type mustache, big enough to hide behind, eyeglasses that sometimes slid down the bridge of his nose, and shoulders that slouched.

The plane's shuddering tested McCorkell's nerves. He wanted to see the left engine. He leaned into the aisle, looked past Chuck Pfisterer in Row 6 out at the left wing. He saw the propeller blades. They were dislodged and bent and he noticed that they weren't turning.

The passengers' silence made him tense.

He looked at his watch: 11:45 A.M. Central time. In Gulfport he had planned to rent a car and drive to Mobile, Alabama. But now that this plane was going back to Atlanta, he worried that he would lose a half-day's billing. At eight thousand feet and dropping, his plane attempting to enter a right turn now, David McCorkell thought, I'm going to be out a couple hundred dollars.

The right engine, that's the first noise Alan Barrington had noticed after the propeller shattered. Barrington sat on the right side, in 6C, behind the good engine. He figured the pilots must have turned it up a few notches to compensate for the dead left engine.

The right engine revved louder than before, and lonelier.

Barrington looked at his emergency card as he awaited his chance to demonstrate the brace position for the flight attendant. He read about flotation devices and exit rows. He looked at the little drawings on the card and thought, If we crash, this card won't do me any good.

Barrington noticed that the man across the aisle, Chuck Pfisterer, could see out on the left wing. This was the same man who had sounded so distressed with the flight attendant moments ago, the man who had mistakenly sat in Barrington's seat before the plane took off, about thirty minutes ago. Barrington thought he saw tears in this man's eyes.

And that prompted a scary thought: He's got a better view than I do, and he's got tears in his eyes. . . .

10

4:46 TO IMPACT. The Brasilia continued to fall, though at a slower rate, about fifteen hundred feet per minute.

"Let me see it," Robin Fech told the man in 5A, Jim Kennedy. He leaned forward to demonstrate his brace position.

Jim Kennedy, for the moment self-contained, focused, and silent, was not at all like the nervous flier behind him. Chuck Pfisterer's fear was plain to see and hear. Kennedy was tougher.

He was a complex personality, living every moment to the fullest. He could be the sweet, affectionate patriarch who used to call to his eight children at bedtime, "Kisses through the bars!" They would lean through the banister, one by one, to give him good-night pecks on his cheek. He'd carried that spirit to his grandkids. Only recently, he'd told them, "I'm almost sixty-three years old, I'm six-foot-three . . . and I've got sixty-three teeth!" But, at another turn, Kennedy could be tougher, darker. He was Spartan, old-school, and fueled by a hair-trigger temper. The scar on his cheek was a remnant of a barroom fight from his college days at Niagara, which he once explained thusly: "John Barleycorn and I *don't get along*." Even now, in his early sixties, his punish-the-body asceticism played out many mornings with more than an hour on his exercise bike, leaving him sweat-soaked and muttering, "Jesus, Mary, and Joseph . . ." He proudly wore a Catholic medal, held a special regard for St. Jude as the patron saint of hopeless causes, and at home kept a picture of prize-fighter Rubin "Hurricane" Carter—imprisoned nineteen years for a murder he said he did not commit—as a reminder that no matter how hard life seemed, some people had it harder.

He maintained a fatalistic view of life. As he shoveled snow once from his driveway, one of his daughters had pleaded for him to stop his back-breaking work: "Dad, Lenny's uncle died from a heart attack shoveling snow!" To which Jim Kennedy replied, "If the good Lord wants me now, He can take me. I'm ready."

But Jim Kennedy was not ready, not even close to ready. He attended Mass daily, usually at seven-thirty in the morning, and was quick to pray, especially at stressful moments, even once from the couch, in front of the living-room television, as the Notre Dame basketball team played UCLA in overtime. His wife, Nancy, had said, "Tell me you are not praying!" Sheepishly, he admitted he was.

Jim Kennedy always had been a survivor. Now, as Flight 529 fell at 1,500 feet per minute, through 7,000 feet, this much was clear: If the plane crashed and fitness and determination alone determined which passengers survived, Jim Kennedy would live through it.

Robin Fech asked passengers sitting by emergency exits—Kennedy and Ludie Burton in Row 5, and David Schneider in Row 8—if they would accept responsibility for opening the doors once the plane came to a stop.

Softly, and with fright in her voice, Ludie Burton said, "No, no, no . . ." She said she wanted to move from 5C to sit with her husband, Lonnie, who earlier had moved to the back for more legroom.

Fech called for a volunteer. Someone had to sit at the emergency exit, she said, and that person would need to swap seats with Ludie Burton to keep the weight and balance of the plane roughly as it was.

There was a moment of silence.

Then, from the back row, a man said, "I'll do it."

Department of Justice attorney Bond Rhue stood. He was tall and graying, with a mustache and the confident air of an executive, even though he wore a comic tie with little pigs on it. (He thought the tie apt for a trip to the South: "I *am* going to the country, after all," he'd told his live-in companion, Kay Beckman.) Rhue worked in the DOJ's Organized Crime and Racketeering Section. The most experienced litigator on staff, the son of a Washington, D.C., cop, Rhue cherished cases with intrigue, and now he had a dandy. Organized crime had infiltrated the President Casino gambling boat in Biloxi. Using cards marked with invisible dye that were read at the blackjack tables by players wearing special glasses, the mob's cheating scheme had netted more than a half million dollars. A grand jury had been assembled, and arrests had been made in June, the fruit of a two-and-a-half-year investigation. Rhue served as cocounsel, working with the U.S. attorney's office in Mississippi.

In the spring, Rhue had been shooting the breeze with Frank Marine, his boss in Washington. They'd been daydreaming about retirement and Marine had said, "When I retire I'm going to open an Italian restaurant and become bartender and cook." A few weeks later, Marine received a certificate in the mail: a $500,000 life insurance policy listing him as beneficiary. Bond Rhue, for a small price, had taken out the policy at the Atlanta airport before a flight to Gulfport. A joke, Rhue explained later: "Hey, boss, something happens to me, I want you to go out and buy that Italian restaurant." A few weeks later Rhue made the same trip, Atlanta to Gulfport. Frank Marine opened his mail and found another certificate, another $500,000 policy. Marine shook his head and smiled at Bond Rhue's sense of humor. On this Atlanta-to-Gulfport flight, though, Rhue had taken out no such policy.

Rhue loved nothing more than standing before juries, and now he stood in the aisle, by 10B, the emergency card in his hand. He seemed to be speaking to other passengers when he said, "Don't worry. I've read this." There was even a smile on his face.

He took 5C. The Burtons resettled together in the back row.

* * *

Except for Fech, hardly anyone spoke.

Most passengers sat next to strangers. Many stared at the left wing, then at Fech, and then at the left wing some more.

The right engine whined on. Jennifer Grunbeck, in Row 4, realized she was not carrying any identification. In a hurry, she'd left her purse at home in Bangor. If something went wrong with the plane and it crashed, she wondered if anyone would know who she was.

In the ninth row, Charles Barton asked his deputy partner to open his window shade. Barton wanted to see the good engine. "No way," Tod Thompson said. "If that propeller isn't turning, I don't want to know." Barton didn't force the issue.

Fech told passengers to remove pens and other sharp objects from their pockets. Take off your eyeglasses, she instructed, and pour your drinks into the seat-back pockets.

Two rows forward, a Diet Coke in hand, Jennifer Grunbeck reached for the seat-back pocket. "Don't you think this will make a mess?" she heard Jean Brucato ask. "I think," Grunbeck said, "they are more concerned with what's going on outside the plane."

Alan Barrington, in Row 6, heard Fech's every word. Barrington was clearheaded and rational—then again, Alan Barrington, middle manager, always was clearheaded and rational. At thirty-five, he was a district human resources manager for a retail chain, working hard, even on some Saturday mornings. He was getting his 3.3 percent annual raises and playing the corporate game. He accepted mild criticism on his 1993 annual job appraisal with aplomb, writing, "I believe that this appraisal is very accurate. . . . You can expect significant improvement." In a corporate culture filled with regulations and acronyms, Alan Barrington aspired one day to become VP of HR.

Now Alan Barrington, too, thought: Did she say pour the drinks out?

He'd never before heard such an instruction. He thought he understood what the curious order signified. He closed his eyes and prayed in silence: "Heavenly Father, when this plane crashes and I die, I'm ready to go Home. But please, Lord, let me ask for just a few favors."

He asked first to die quickly.

Then he asked for his wife to have the strength to raise their four young children, and that his children would always remember their father's love. His boys were ten and seven—yes, old enough so that they might remember his love—but what about the twins, just three? Could his little girls possibly recall his love and, decades from now, feel it, really feel it? Alan Barrington prayed hard for that to be so.

Then his thoughts returned to the moment: *What does it feel like to have your head and limbs ripped off?* He imagined the plane breaking apart, jagged metal pieces flying at him. *Will I even feel it? Will I go to heaven immediately?*

Two rows ahead, Ed Gray wasn't thinking of God. For one thing, he didn't believe in God. Gray was a humanist. Spiritual, yes, but not religious.

To him, this was not about God. This was about mechanical failure.

When Fech told passengers to pour out their drinks, Gray looked at his orange juice and thought, It isn't polite to pour your orange juice into a seat-back pocket. But he put aside etiquette and did it.

He was, at sixty-three, a company man. A self-employed executive consultant, he presently worked for Morrison Knudsen, the Cleveland-based engineering giant. Gray had traveled so often during his career that his children, now grown, used to call him Uncle Daddy. At home, a business phone call always came before family. If a company said, "Be there," then Ed Gray was there: Chicago, Tokyo, London, wherever. He'd been married forty years, though his wife, Barbara, an artist, joked that she'd only been married for twenty—the other half, Ed was gone. The Grays lived in Westport, Connecticut, in a small house in a lush wooded area, not far from the actor Paul Newman. When Ed and Barbara went on their walks, they had two routes, playfully known as "the Full Newman walk" and "the Modified Newman walk" (half the distance). Not that

Ed had placed a high priority on leisurely strolls over the years. He hadn't missed a month's salary in forty-three years. He'd already decided he would work another seven years. Uncle Daddy would keep the paychecks coming.

Whatever had happened out on the left wing, Ed Gray had diagnosed the problem in his own way: Not God's doing, this was an abnormal part of life's natural circumstances and rhythms.

Five rows back, in 9A, Mike Hendrix knew he might die in a plane crash. He'd known that for some time. He'd even said as much recently to his wife, Linda. Hendrix, a thirty-five-year-old network engineer, knew planes and trusted them. If not for his eyesight, he might have become a commercial pilot years ago, like his father, a United Airlines captain. Instead, in the early eighties, Mike Hendrix did the next best thing and earned an FAA airframe and power plant license authorizing him to work on planes.

He later changed careers, becoming an engineer for Bechtel. He flew often to job sites. Six days before the Atlanta-to-Gulfport flight, he'd started a new job at Science Applications International Corp. He would fly often for this job, too.

Hendrix, pragmatist and fatalist, recently told his wife: Since I fly a lot, and because I fly on commuter airlines and different types of planes, my chances of being in a plane crash are statistically higher.

He also told her that if his plane crashed and the jet fuel ignited, his chance for survival was nil. He didn't expect it, but, he said, it could happen.

In Row 2, the young woman from New Orleans who had just accepted a job as an ASA flight attendant thought of death. Until that moment, Angela Brumfield had watched Robin Fech's every move. But now she was afraid. She didn't want to panic. When tears came, she stared at the ceiling, hoping to keep them from running down her face.

The deputy Tod Thompson, still refusing to open his shade, thought about the window at his side. *If this glass breaks, am I going to be sucked outside?*

In the cockpit now, Matt Warmerdam had two masters: his captain and the Atlanta Center air traffic controller. Both sought his undivided attention.

"Say your altitude now, sir," Atlanta Center called.

"Out of seven thousand, ASe 529," Warmerdam said.

The Brasilia's auxiliary power kicked on.

"Good start," Gannaway said.

"ASe 529, I missed that. I'm sorry," Atlanta Center said.

"We're out of six-point-nine right now, ASe 529," Warmerdam replied.

Warmerdam noted the auxiliary power: "Okay, it's up and running, Ed."

Gannaway said, "All right, go ahead." He had always been a by-the-books captain. Ed Gannaway wanted this checklist finished.

Another interruption by Atlanta Center: The Anniston airport in Alabama was also in the vicinity, though it was thirty miles to the west, much farther than West Georgia Regional. Gannaway asked his first officer, "What kind of runway they got?" and Warmerdam, on cue, put that question about West Georgia Regional to air traffic control.

Awaiting the answer, Gannaway told his first officer, "Go ahead and finish the checklist."

Warmerdam continued moving through the list, arriving finally at the still-functioning right engine. "You want max on this?" he asked.

"Go ahead, please," Gannaway replied.

The propeller speed on the right engine turned upward, stronger, louder, to thirteen hundred revolutions per minute.

Atlanta Center now had Gannaway's answer about the five-thousand-foot runway at West Georgia. The air traffic controller said, "It's asphalt, sir."

11

2:57 TO IMPACT. Atlanta Center called out, "ASe 529, I've lost your transponder, say altitude."

Falling, still falling, beneath radar now, Matt Warmerdam replied, "We're out at four-point-five."

Just then Flight 529 reappeared on the traffic controller's screen: "I've got you now."

West Georgia Regional Airport was beneath the clouds, eight miles away.

"We can get in on a visual," Ed Gannaway said.

An unknown voice from another aircraft visited the drama: "Good luck, guys."

Matt Warmerdam said, "'Preciate it."

In Row 3, Barney Gaskill, traveling for Morrison-Knudsen with Ed Gray, thought about his family. The fifty-seven-year-old Ohioan with a cherubic face imagined his wife, daughter and son, his grandkids and his elderly mother. They lived in different states, and in a dire moment such as this, that bothered him. Gaskill felt the need to address them, collectively.

David McCorkell shared not a sentence with the man beside him in the seventh row, Kevin Bubier. Their eyes never met, only their shoulders, touching in tight space.

McCorkell no longer bemoaned the loss of a half-day's billing. The looks of despair all around him deepened and darkened his thoughts. *What if we do crash?* And then: *I don't want to die.* McCorkell began to examine his life, to see it in context. He didn't like what he saw. He thought of his two sons.

He traveled so often they didn't know where he was right now. They were like most eighteen- and nineteen-year-olds, into their own lives, not his. McCorkell loved them unconditionally. He'd sacrificed so much for his boys, raising them as a single father. But now that they didn't want to continue their educations and get their college degrees, as he'd hoped they would, he felt almost deceived.

He thought of Lila.

Thirteen months ago, their marriage had ended. It was amicable: After seven years, they had even shared the same divorce attorney. His travel had wrecked the marriage. Too many nights away, too many airplanes.

The Brasilia trembled.

McCorkell didn't believe he should die alone. He became furious now with God. *Why me?* Had he not always met his obligations? At sixteen, he got a classmate pregnant. Young and afraid, they brought together their parents in the McCorkells' dining room and told them about it. They decided to marry and drove to South Dakota for the ceremony. Months later their first son was born, and then a year later another son. The marriage soon ended, David McCorkell assumed custody and he raised two boys—two boys who right now had no idea where their father was.

He felt alone, as never before. Deep within, he heard his own primal shout: *How could this happen to me?*

He was in a falling airplane surrounded by strangers.

He wanted a hand to hold.

He was angry, bitter. If he was going to die, at least he wanted to see someone familiar in his last living moment.

* * *

In Seat 1B, Dawn Dumm saw and heard everything. Her trouble was figuring out what it all meant. She not only saw the sheet metal peeled back on the left wing, she also heard the flight attendant's words with the cockpit.

The exchange baffled and concerned her. Dumm saw Robin Fech pick up the wall intercom a few feet away and heard her say, tensely, "Yes, sir?" and then, moments later, "All right. Thank you." Even though Fech had already told passengers the plane could fly on one engine, Dumm wondered if the pilots knew the condition of the left engine. Could they see the spraying fluids and the cables and hoses flapping in the air? Do they have rearview mirrors? *Why didn't the flight attendant tell them about it?*

Dumm also had to look after her mother. When the blade shattered and the plane fell, Mary Jean Adair, in the window seat next to her daughter, asked, "What was that?" They looked out the left-side window and then at each other. Adair shook her head. "I had a bad feeling about this flight," she told her daughter.

Even before Fech told passengers in the front rows to pour out their drinks, Dumm said, "Mom, you better drink your orange juice. If we have a rough landing, it'll go all over your white pants." Adair shook her head. She was worked up, tense. Her mind was on the left engine, not orange juice. Dumm took her mother's cup and drank the juice.

"What should we do now?" Adair asked moments later as Fech advised passengers to review their emergency cards. "Let's listen," Dumm whispered.

When they demonstrated their brace positions, Fech saw the shock in their faces. It was so stark she stopped making eye contact with mother and daughter. As Fech moved on to help other passengers, Dumm prepared Adair for the worst.

Dumm asked her mother to take her seat belt on and off, on and off. "If the door in front of us is blocked," Dumm said, motioning to the main passenger door to their left, "you'll have to get down on your hands and knees and crawl. Count the rows because the fifth row is where we have to get out." Adair grew quiet. Dumm knew her mother was frightened.

Dawn Dumm thought about death. She also thought of another possibility. *You can survive this*. She decided her life was in the hands of the pilot. She wondered again if the pilot could see what she had seen, on the left wing. She believed in the pilot, whoever he was, and told herself, If the pilot can take me that far, I can do the rest.

She thought about her husband, Larry, and their boys, Lucas and Zeke. *If only I could speak to them right now.*

She decided to write a note, just in case. If she died, they would know they were in her final thoughts. Dumm took out a pen from a fanny pack around her waist. Outside the cabin she saw only clouds, gray and cottony. Inside, she heard only Fech's voice, from somewhere behind. Dumm did not want her mother to see what she was about to do. She did not want to frighten her mother any further.

She used her right shoulder as a shield so Adair would not see her carefully tearing the cover from her paperback book, Thomas Flanagan's novel, *The Year of the French*. Dumm's hands trembled. *What can I say that will hold them for the rest of their lives?* She was a teacher, yes, intelligent, thoughtful—and now she also was a mother who might never again see her two sons. She rubbed the pen through her fingertips. Nerves scrambled her thoughts. She glanced over her right shoulder: Her mother was quiet.

Finally she wrote: "You are the Lights of My Life. Always, Mommy."

And: "Lucas and Zeke: Be Good Always."

And then one word more: "Prayers."

There, she'd done it. A message from Mommy. It gave her a sense of completion. She folded the note neatly, in fourths, and put it inside her fanny pack. She knew that if her body was found, her note would be found with it.

She heard her mother again: "What should we do now?"

"I think we should pray," Dumm said.

They wore cotton in case of fire. They wore sturdy shoes in case they had to make an escape. Now mother and daughter joined hands in one last preparation for disaster. Together they recited the Lord's Prayer. ". . . Thy kingdom come, Thy will be done, on earth as it is in heaven . . ."

12

2:09 TO IMPACT. The Brasilia was at thirty-four hundred feet, falling thirty feet per second, too fast.

For seven minutes, Gannaway had been focused on cockpit settings, numbers, levers, lights, and screens. He'd been responding to chimes and synthesized warnings, his eyes fixed on airspeed, pitch, and altitude.

Now, for the first time, he peered over his left shoulder.

Out on his left wing, he saw the mad jumble of metal parts that once was an engine and four propeller blades.

"Engine's exploded," he told his first officer.

Gannaway had never seen anything like it. "It's just hanging out there."

He did not describe it beyond that. Gannaway's instruments had not told him the full story. His eyes did. The Brasilia had not experienced simple engine failure. This was structural damage so extensive that a pilot of his experience—nearly ten thousand hours in the cockpit—would know the bad news: Questions that begged for answers had no answers. He saw junk wrapped around his wing's leading edge. The smooth stream of air necessary for flight had become a jumble of turbulence. His Brasilia was a wounded bird struggling to stay aloft and failing in the struggle. Of all the emergency checklists, there was none on how to fly with one wing. He had trained for emergencies, had practiced responses to a myriad of simulated disasters. Yet all of that preparation, and all his skill and courage, meant nothing now. There is no way to fly with one wing.

Turning back in his seat, silent, the captain heard an air traffic controller give Warmerdam a heading to West Georgia Regional: "ASe 529, roger. Expect localizer runway three-four approach and, uh, could you fly heading one-eight-zero—uh, no, sorry, one-six-zero?"

"Yeah, we can do that," Warmerdam confirmed.

In the first officer's right-side seat, Warmerdam could not see the structural damage and assess for himself its significance. He knew only what the captain told him, and Gannaway told him only the bare facts: *an exploded engine, just hanging out there.* For thirty seconds after describing the damage, Gannaway said nothing. Could he now, as he had once told his wife, bring the Brasilia down safely in a field? Now, in an emergency descent through clouds, could he even see an open space with time enough to get to it? With a field beneath him, could he then put down a 24,000-pound plane at 150 miles per hour on that land with its inevitable imperfections? Would anyone survive such a thing?

Pilots wouldn't be pilots if they answered such questions with anything but affirmatives. Gannaway had inherited a family legacy of World War II pilots. At the top of a ziggurat pyramid of fighter pilots, Tom Wolfe wrote, stood those with the moxie, reflexes, experience, and cool to land a brick on a skillet, "one of the elected and anointed ones who had *the right stuff.*" For Gannaway, this moment was not about his manhood. It was about his machinery. Would moxie, reflexes, and experience be enough with this dying plane?

Now, hearing Warmerdam confirm a route that would take them several miles south prior to a turn toward the West Georgia runway, the captain spoke for the first time since seeing the engine splayed against the wing's edge. On one engine, yes, they could fly that route; but not on one wing. They needed a runway and they needed it quickly. So Gannaway told his first officer, "We can get in on a visual. Just give us the vectors."

He was asking for directions that would put him within sight of that country airport. He would go straight in. He would try to land that brick on that skillet.

Voices filled the west Georgia skies, from LaGrange north to Rome, voices speaking in the aviator's clipped vernacular.

Radar controllers had protected the surrounding airspace for Flight 529 to make an emergency retreat to Atlanta.

Atlanta Center governs much of the airspace across the Southeast from its headquarters in Hampton, Georgia, twenty miles south of Atlanta's airport. Typically eleven thousand feet is the base of its airspace, and the point at which it turns over communications, but its air traffic controller had continued to direct Flight 529 for seven minutes more.

Only when Flight 529 fell to forty-five hundred feet did communications change over to Atlanta Approach, which monitors planes within a much narrower space: a forty-mile arc around the Atlanta Hartsfield International Airport, an area that includes West Georgia Regional.

A radar controller at Atlanta Approach had been closely tracking Flight 529. At one moment, the altitude indicator on his display screen read "100," which meant the Brasilia, circling about fifty miles southwest of Atlanta, was at ten thousand feet and descending.

About four minutes later the plane's altitude registered "045" (forty-five hundred feet) and then "XXX." His computer couldn't keep up with the Brasilia's rapid descent.

Even so, the controller wasn't alarmed enough to activate on his screen Map 1, the emergency map. The map depicts roads, lakes, and hospitals near the West Georgia Regional Airport, including Highway 316, which was in the northeast flight path of Flight 529. With that map, the air traffic controller could have advised Gannaway and Warmerdam of the emergency-landing possibilities, in case they couldn't make it to the small airfield. But the controller figured that, even with one engine out, the

Brasilia ought to be controllable for at least twenty miles. Besides, he never sensed distress or panic in Warmerdam's voice. Of course, the air traffic controller had not received a key piece of information from the pilots—an explicit description of the damage on the left wing.

More than five minutes had passed since the first officer had declared an emergency with Atlanta Center and called for fire trucks and emergency crews.

But with the changeover of air traffic controllers, from Atlanta Center to Atlanta Approach, there had been a slip-up. No one had notified members of the Carroll County Fire Department that a plane was falling through the sky toward them.

As soon as the flight attendant made it to Row 8, the young engineer David Schneider blurted, "I know how to do it!" He meant the emergency door beside his seat, the only one in the back half of the plane. It would be his job to open it.

Schneider had been concentrating on his responsibility, a massive one as he saw it. He looked at the handle a dozen times. *What if it gets stuck and I can't open it?* He read the emergency card a dozen times. *If there are any women behind me, I'll let them out first.* He saw two women near him, both in Row 10: Sonya Fetterman and Ludie Burton.

Now Robin Fech stood before him. "I know I'm supposed to pull this handle right here," he said, pointing to the emergency exit. Schneider said it with such confidence, such total command, Fech felt appreciative.

She had someone to count on.

But then her eyes met David Schneider's and she sensed that Schneider knew: She was afraid.

On the left side of the cabin, Fech saw passengers inching up their window shades.

* * *

David Schneider had already decided that, on this day, he was immune to death. What he felt approached invincibility: It was the arrogance of youth. *You know when you are going to die, and I am not going to die.* The twenty-eight-year-old Schneider believed it. *This is not going to happen to me today.*

It was that simple. Schneider felt the plane dropping, but it wasn't as if the descent was so severe that his stomach rose into his throat. The plane was flying well enough, he thought, and they still had their landing gear.

He'd also heard the flight attendant say several times that they could fly on one engine. He had no reason to think he would die.

Besides, Schneider had other plans. He had a good job, a good marriage. He liked his life. He was an engineer, and each time he changed jobs his new boss told him, or at least implied, that he was a rising star. His salary was proof of that, growing handsomely, and every year 16 percent of it went toward his 401(k). He was charging hard into the future, planning to get his MBA, with every expectation of becoming a vice president of operations by the age of forty. By fifty, who knew? Maybe he'd already be retired, traveling the world, doing volunteer work.

From 8C, Schneider looked several rows ahead to 5A, the man in the blue knit shirt and blue-jean shorts: Jim Kennedy. They'd never met, yet Schneider felt a connection to Kennedy. They were en route to Gulfport as colleagues. Schneider felt a need to keep track of Kennedy. It made him feel less alone.

He also reached out to his faith. Schneider prayed a form of the rosary: an Our Father, a Hail Mary, and a Glory Be, ending with: ". . . as it was in the beginning, is now and ever shall be, world without end. Amen."

13

1:28 TO IMPACT. Stepping past David Schneider to the U-shape formed by Rows 8, 9, and 10, Robin Fech noticed Ludie Burton standing beside her husband, Lonnie, in the aisle by her back-row seat.

"What are you *doo-ing?*" Fech asked, sharply, stretching out the syllables. "You've got to sit down now." Lonnie Burton reached to help his wife. When Ludie Burton was introduced at his retirement dinner eleven months earlier, he had sat with her at the head table, clasping his hands and shaking them back and forth in a silent cheer for her. Then he'd pushed together his palms, prayerfully, to give thanks not only for the years they'd spent together, but also for their shared years ahead. Now Lonnie Burton helped fasten the seat belt around his wife of forty-three years.

Just then Fech noticed that something had changed. She couldn't pinpoint what it was, but she felt the need to hurry to the front of the cabin.

She turned and headed back up the aisle, arms raised, hands against the overhead compartments on both sides of the aisle. As she went, Fech looked left, then right, left and then right, checking on passengers. She made it to the first row in twelve strides. She turned once more to look back at her twenty-six passengers.

Something had changed.

The light inside the cabin.

It was brighter now, as if a window curtain had been opened.

Passengers were looking outside. Fech looked, too, over Mary Jean Adair's shoulder in 1C.

The plane had descended beneath the clouds. Fech saw a rural mosaic: fields, pines, and scattered houses.

She'd landed in Atlanta a thousand times. This was not Atlanta.

In flight, everything is done by checklist, and in emergencies, sometimes more than one checklist. The procedure is to be followed strictly. So when his Brasilia came through the clouds, Gannaway thought to move on to his next list even as his voice betrayed the emotion of the moment.

Never a stutterer, he said, "Sing . . . single . . . single-engine checklist, please."

"Where . . . is it?" Warmerdam said. In the *Quick Reference Handbook* the single-engine checklist was among the hardest to find.

Atlanta Approach interrupted again: "ASe 529, say altitude leaving."

Warmerdam: "We're out at nineteen hundred at this time."

The thick treelines of Carroll County were beneath them now, stands of Georgia pines separated by open fields.

"We're below the clouds," Gannaway told his first officer. "Tell 'em."

Warmerdam didn't have a chance.

"You're out at nineteen hundred now?" came the reply. The altitude surprised the air traffic controller. Flight 529 had been at thirty-four hundred feet only one minute earlier: nineteen hundred didn't seem right. The descent was too much, too fast.

Warmerdam reported that they were coming in on a visual: "Give us a vector to the airport."

"ASe, 529," the controller said. "Turn left, uh, fly heading zero-four-zero. Bear—the, uh, airport's at your about ten o'clock and six miles, sir. Radar contact lost at this time."

Now Flight 529 was gone from the radar screen, not unusual at such a low altitude. The controller at Atlanta Approach might have been alarmed by the rapid descent, but when he heard Warmerdam confirm, "Zero four zero, ASe 529" without elaborating, he thought the plane was under control. He thought Flight 529 was about to land and that all was right. He would not hear from 529 again.

14

0:38 TO IMPACT. The Brasilia trembled in descent, pulling hard left. Under routine conditions, one pilot flies the aircraft with a gentle, almost casual, touch. But now two men fought to fly the Brasilia, manhandling its controls. Gannaway and Warmerdam were half-standing now. They wore seat belts across their laps and harnesses over their shoulders. Each harness was attached to an inertia reel that allowed for some movement but would, by design, lock on impact to keep them off the instrument panel. The two pilots straightened their legs against the rudder pedals, forcing themselves back against the seats. They pulled their yokes back and into their bodies, as hard as they could, the muscles of their forearms straining. It was as if they were not flying an airplane, but restraining a team of frightened oxen.

Gannaway and Warmerdam now saw a landscape of rolling hills, thick stands of trees, houses here and there.

They spotted an opening, a field to their left, a tiny plot between pines. Houses and electric power lines stood along one side of the field.

The aircraft trembled. An air traffic controller said the West Georgia Regional Airport was now about four miles away. No matter: The Brasilia fell toward the open field. The pilots would attempt to land wheels-up, on their plane's belly, by the books. In a coarse field, with its natural imperfections, lowered landing gear might break off or dig into the ground and cartwheel the plane.

A clutter of noises filled the cockpit: synthesized voices, rapid beeps, and then a warning: The plane's altitude was five hundred feet.

Air traffic control, again: "ASe 529, if able change to my frequency, one, one, eight-point-seven . . ."

The left wing tilted downward, airspeed decreased to 138 miles per hour.

"Too low gear," the Bitch called out, a reminder that the landing gear remained retracted.

The field drew closer.

Robin Fech, nearly shouting, addressed her passengers all at once now: "Remember, stay down, and after we get to where we are going, we have to be at a complete stop before we can get out."

She didn't have their attention and she knew it. On the right side, and in the back few rows on the left side, passengers were looking out the windows.

Fech looked out once more on the right side, again over the shoulder of Mary Jean Adair. She saw . . . treetops! *Where's my signal for landing from the cockpit?* There came no signal, no warning, no bells. Only treetops.

Had she done everything? She had not: *Oh, my God, I'm not in my jump seat!*

Fech backed up one, two, three steps, facing the passengers as she went, and commanding, "Stay down! Brace position! Brace position! Stay down!" Straight out of the flight attendant's manual, chapter 1, page 23: "Prior to impact, give the following commands: 'Brace position! Stay down. Stay down.'"

Veteran deputy Charles Barton and aspiring flight attendant Angela Brumfield raised their heads to look out at the trees once more.

Fech's voice rose: "Heads down! Heads down!"

15

FORTY MILES WEST OF ATLANTA, the metropolitan area gives way to farmland. There the Burwell Road community is typical. Two-lane asphalt roads bisect pastures and wooded land surrounding small towns.

Now, near Burwell, a man stepped from his screened-in back porch. He saw an airplane coming from the west, in a left bank and flying so low he could read the candy-colored *ASA* on its tail.

Something was wrong with its left engine, but what? The engine looked black, as if metal were missing. The plane passed over before the man noticed anything else.

A moment later, the Reverend Gus Koch was chatting with a neighbor about the wrath of Hurricane Erin, which had struck a few weeks before, and about trees that needed to be felled, when he heard, from above, the sound of an engine in distress. From the parking lot of the Shiloh United Methodist Church, the Reverend Koch looked for the source of the sound.

He saw an airplane only a few hundred feet above him, banked in a left turn, bearing down on the tree line of the Burwell Road community.

The air filled with vibration. "That plane is going to crash!" his friend Dennis Crews told him. The men did not see the damaged left wing, but Koch sensed the pilot struggling to keep the little plane aloft. It was heading for the trees. For an instant, to Koch, the plane was soundless, like a glider, without power. It passed so low he heard the *whooooooosh.*

16

0:08 TO IMPACT. Through the closed cockpit door, Fech heard the Bitch.

Terrified, she tightened the strap on her jump seat. Holding her head upright and rigid—separated only by a thin wall from Ed Gannaway's head—Fech placed both hands beneath her thighs in her own brace position.

She shouted to passengers, "Hold on, y'all! This is going to be rough!" She closed her eyes.

Matt Warmerdam fought on. Seeing the trees, feeling the plane's vibrations, hearing the instrument warnings and the Bitch and an air traffic controller's voice and then Ed Gannaway pleading in his headset, "Help me, help me hold it, help me hold, help me hold it," Warmerdam, on sensory overload, held on to the yoke.

Just then he imagined his wife. A pretty final image. As Dawn Dumm had inscribed words of good-bye on paper, Warmerdam spoke to be heard later on the cockpit voice recorder. The last words were his. He said, "Amy, I love you!"

17

IMPACT. In the brace position, Chuck Pfisterer shut his shade for the first time and told himself, You're dead! He had not removed his eyeglasses as Fech had instructed. Unaided, his vision was 20–400. A person about to die has rights, he figured, and he intended to see what death looked like.

Kevin Bubier wore an odd grin. He turned to the stranger beside him in Row 7, David McCorkell, and said, "Good luck." Staring back, saying nothing, McCorkell buried his face into the seat back ahead.

In the third row, engineer Barney Gaskill saw the trees and an open field, the same landscape he'd seen beside many airports. He pressed his forehead to his wrists and figured the runway would be next. Gaskill told himself: "Cakewalk."

In the front row, beside her daughter, Mary Jean Adair made the sign of the cross.

The Brasilia ripped through the trees, losing none of its momentum. As the left wing gouged the hay field, from the front of the plane came a woman's scream. Angela Brumfield, no longer wanting to become a flight attendant, heard the scream and whispered, "Oh, God, oh God, oh God . . ."

18

THE REVEREND GUS KOCH, from his church parking lot, heard the trees breaking—it was like a sudden harvest in the local timber season. Then, on the other side of the tree line, about nine hundred yards away, he heard the plane crashing, a horrific sound, like thousands of garbage cans and rocks being smashed together, a noise that went on and on, rocks and cans, cans and rocks. And then, finally, silence.

The Reverend Koch ran to his 1981 Dodge pickup truck, as fast as a middle-aged Methodist minister in old leather boots can run. He knew about death and dying. He'd been an army medic in Vietnam in 1969, a New Jersey teenager in a jungle with the 25th Infantry. There he'd seen young soldiers with their lower halves blown off. The young soldiers, afraid to look down, between their legs, had looked up at Koch with fright, asking only if their manhood was *still there.* He'd learned how much damage the human body could sustain and still survive and also how little it took—a pinhole in just the right place—to kill a man. He'd become a nineteen-year-old philosopher of death.

Gus Koch had found his adult calling as a philosopher of life. He'd been in the Burwell Road community only two years, but he understood the place and its people. "Burwell is a small parish in the middle of nearly nowhere," he later wrote, "with widely spaced houses and closely spaced hearts. . . . Philosophers live here, and craftsmen. Great cooks and corn-shuckers walk side by side with school teachers and hay farmers. Naturalists thrive here, and go to church with chicken farmers and cattlemen. In Burwell you are loved in spite of your sins, and tolerated in spite of your successes."

Now the Reverend Gus Koch pulled onto Burwell Road, nine hundred yards to drive, tires screeching as he went, certain that when he got to the other side of the little forest he would see a smoldering hole in blackened earth.

Paul Butler heard trees breaking, too. Butler sat in his living room, reading a book, his back door open on a cloudy summer day, as ASA Flight 529 crashed into his hay field. Butler looked up from the page. Half turning, he saw through his open door something big and metallic passing behind his shed and across his pasture. Then he heard—what was it? Metal banging on the ground? He thought, What the hell?

Butler first thought someone had turned over a hay baler. The brick mason had bought the old Robinson place three decades before, not to farm it, but to live on it. Carroll County farming was dominated by hay, livestock, and timber. As far as Butler knew, nothing other than hay had ever been farmed in his back pasture, unless it was cattle, and that was before his time. His pasture ran uphill and had been terraced decades earlier for erosion purposes. Over time the terraces had worn down into small rounded humps. The pasture was a peaceful place that filled on summer nights with the sounds of crickets, tree frogs, and owls.

Butler rushed outside. About a hundred and fifty yards across his field he saw an enormous dust cloud. It took a moment for the dust to clear. Butler stood there, not sure what to make of it. Finally he saw a shattered airplane, its cockpit pointed right at him. It might as well have been a spaceship.

He ran inside to a ringing phone. His mother-in-law, Connie Jackson, was on the line. Jackson lived across the street. She had been placing a bottle of hair spray in her bathroom vanity when she heard the crash. She thought it was thunder—until she looked across the pasture and saw the tail of a broken airplane. She called Butler and asked, "Is that a plane in the field?"

Yes, Butler replied. "Now hang up so I can call 911." And that's what he did.

Next door, Butler's sister-in-law, Polona Jeter, was at her dining-room table when she heard trees breaking. She looked out her back window and saw Flight 529 about to hit the field. Before her husband, Billy, had even made it across the living room to her side, she said, "Bill, a plane's crashing!" The Jeters watched the Brasilia hit the field, bounce off the first terrace, and lift into the air. They saw it hit the field a second time and break apart, its tail section spinning a slow 180. It looked like two planes now, and both were sliding toward the Jeters' little corn patch: 200 yards away, then 150 yards, and then 125 yards.

Polona Jeter said, "Bill, we've got to get out of here. It's coming this way!"

Part V

Fire in the Field

19

THE BRASILIA CARVED OUT a V in the tree line; pieces broke off the left wing tip and fell into the pines. The plane then rolled left toward the hay field, where new grass and clover grew for the fall cut.

Then began a macabre dance of physics, the plane striking the ground at 138 miles per hour, and bouncing, spinning, twisting, and sliding until, its motion defeated by contact with the earth, it would settle finally to a stop.

The left wing dug into the earth first. The wing ripped away from the fuselage as dirt clods, dust, and rocks flew. Fuel spilled from ruptured tanks in the torn wing.

The plane's nose struck ground next, on its left underside, near the captain's rudder pedals.

Now the one-winged airplane, airborne again, bounced up a ridge about a hundred feet and skidded through the field, its belly gouging a narrow groove, four inches deep and a hundred and fifty feet long.

Ed Gannaway's head slammed against the heavy framing of the cockpit windshield. Robin Fech's head hit the thin wall behind her jump seat. The prayerful Jim Kennedy was catapulted from his seat in 5A. Bond Rhue, the federal attorney who had moved next to the emergency exit at 5C, fell on top of the woman a row ahead, accountant Jean Brucato.

As the plane made in Brazil and bound for the Mississippi coast skidded through the field in west Georgia, the fuselage shattered into two sections. Twisted by torque, the front section carrying the flight crew and passengers in the front four rows spun to its right, with its nose finally stopping at a right angle to the plowed groove.

The back section slid tail-first around the nose and rolled onto its right side, so curiously situated that its underbelly nearly faced the pilot's window.

Sitting in the front row with her mother, Dawn Dumm screamed but couldn't hear herself over the sound of ripping metal.

Across the aisle, Renee Chapman, the young army veteran in 2A, felt the plane's belly sliding across the ground. Then she felt dirt thrown into her face.

In the back section, during the final moments of the descent, David McCorkell had been transfixed by the movement of the plane's wings. The left wing tilted dramatically downward in a way McCorkell had never experienced at landing. The angle seemed to him beyond recovery. He heard loud noises he could not decipher—the plane striking trees. He leaned forward in the brace position, holding the back of seat 6B. McCorkell felt the ground scraping hard against the plane's underbelly. Fearing his feet would be ripped from his legs, he lifted them.

In the adjacent seat, Kevin Bubier heard metal breaking—no, it was more like metal *screaming,* louder than anything he'd heard in the Maine shipyards. He felt debris falling against him. Eyes closed, he felt the plane tumbling and then rolling onto its right side. His right shoulder was forced against the plane's wall, hard enough to make the shoulder hurt. He did not know he was sliding across a hay field, until he opened his eyes. His face was pinned against the window, right cheek flush against the glass, and he watched in terror as grass and dirt were plowed up inches from his face. *Will the window break? Will I get sucked outside?* He heard himself pleading with the window. *Please don't break! Please don't break! Please don't break!*

One row forward, Alan Barrington opened his eyes, for only an instant. He saw objects flying at him: small luggage, broken pieces of the ceiling, flying bits he could not identify.

The nervous flier across the aisle, Chuck Pfisterer, his body tossed like a ragdoll's, only waited for blackness to come.

The plane came to rest in pieces.

Passengers and crew had sixty seconds to get out. Then would come fire.

The first fire truck took five minutes to reach Paul Butler's hay field. The nine minutes and twenty seconds of falling to Earth seemed little more than a heartbeat in time. The next five minutes in the hay field would seem without end.

20

DUST ROILED OVER THE AIRCRAFT, which lay in pieces in a pasture filled with crickets spooked to silence by the alien object in their midst. The front section of the fuselage, still upright and with the right wing yet attached to it, seemed connected only by a common fate to the back section, which had rolled over onto its right side. A wind tunnel had roared through the interior of the passenger cabin, coherence becoming chaos, a shrieking hellstorm ripping at overhead cabins and insulated interior walls, tearing seats from the floor, pulling down from the ceiling slinky emergency oxygen masks, whipping up eyeglasses, purses, newspapers, and bags of peanuts, and breaking open the plane's metal skin beside Jean Brucato in 4C. All twenty-nine people aboard survived impact, though a few were severely incapacitated. Inside the cabin, passengers were confused, dazed, semiconscious, frightened, and bleeding. Some, in back, hung upside down; others, beneath fallen objects, had vanished from sight. From the cockpit . . . silence. Humidity and light stormed in, and so did heaps of dirt; the whole plane quivered until finally all movement ceased—except for the plane's fluids.

From a hole in the right wing poured fuel and hydraulics, a fire waiting to break out. The Brasilia has four fuel tanks, two in each wing, one inboard and one outboard, separated by the landing gear wheel well but interconnected by tubes for fuel transfer. The left wing, and its two tanks, had been torn off by impact and left behind in the debris field, 125 feet from the fuselage. But the intact right wing contained about 175 gallons of fuel, much of which poured out of the inboard tank and formed puddles beside the back section of the fuselage. (For forced landings, big jets have a mechanism to dump fuel to reduce weight and, secondarily, to reduce the chance for postcrash fire; a Brasilia has no such mechanism.)

Almost immediately after the fuselage came to a stop, passengers heard crackling sounds: shredded cables and wires sparking. It took a minute or so for the vapors rising from the pools of fuel to reach those sparks. A fire was born, first in patches, on the ground, just beyond the threshold of the fuselage. But the fuel vapors traveled, in search of ignition, and found a willing source, behind the cockpit, in an oxygen cylinder. The fire spread quickly there, engulfing the area and moving into the cockpit, a steady flame shooting out from the roaring oxygen cylinder. Soon flames rose high above the fuselage and burned outward in a grass fire with a radius that would reach fifteen feet.

Some passengers got out quickly, before the fire. But most passengers in the back section of the fuselage—rolled half over onto its right side— needed more time. They would face a moving, raging, fuel-fed inferno, its 1,800-degree blue-orange flames snake-licking inside a black fog, leaping from fuel to panty hose, from alloy metal to human flesh.

The British psychologist Helen Muir has studied such scenarios. In test-fuselage simulations of emergency evacuations, Muir saw volunteers climb over seats, push past one another, and become so entangled as to block exit doors—all for a five-pound bonus ($7.80) awarded to the first people out.

"Basically," Muir said, "they were all greedy."

Muir's tests at Cranfield University's College of Aeronautics suggested that young men have the greatest statistical chance for survival. Children and the elderly fare poorly. Men survive more often than women.

About 8 percent of people, Muir said, are "life survivors," who, given the slightest opportunity, will find a way to safety. About 12 percent won't escape under almost any circumstances; their "behavioral inaction" is based on their feeling that "in an emergency they will die, and so they stay there and die."

As different as people may be, given varied backgrounds and experiences, Muir believes they have one thing in common. For the May 1996 issue of *The Aeronautical Journal* of the Royal Aeronautical Society, the psychologist/professor wrote: "In a situation where an immediate threat to life is perceived, rather than all passengers being motivated to help each other, the main objective which will govern their behavior will be survival for themselves, and in some instances, members of their family. . . . The evacuation can become very disorganized, with some individuals competing to get through the exits."

To get out of the fuselage, ASA 529 passengers in the plane's rear section would have to face the hellish fire and dare to run through it. They would have only a fraction of a second to do it. To fall at the plane's threshold would be to die.

So intense was the heat radiating from the fire in the field, it burned down through the human layers—through skin, muscles, and nerves.

The latter was the body's great gift because once the nerves died, the victims in the hay field no longer felt the pain.

In the front section of the fuselage, behind the cockpit, Robin Fech, unconscious momentarily, awoke to an eerie darkness. Still sitting in her jump seat, as in flight, though slumped on her left side, facing the lavatory and closet, she looked to the floor. *Damn, I've lost a shoe!* She knew the Brasilia intimately. But the area around her was no longer recognizable. Wires, cables, and broken pieces of the plane hung from the ceiling, poking at her at odd angles. The metal kitchen galley had fallen across the aisle. With debris piled on top, it became a wall to Fech, hemming her in. She turned to her right to check the main passenger door: It had buckled in and could not be opened. Her thoughts cleared. *My God, we've crashed!* She heard a few moans, then more. She was in darkness except for a solitary orange light. She recognized the light as fire. "Get out!" she screamed to passengers on the other side of the debris. "Get out of the plane now!"

As the Brasilia's underbelly slid across the earth, David McCorkell knew death was only a moment away and that he would die alone, accompanied only by his anger with God.

But then the scraping and sliding and the roaring of lions stopped and McCorkell smelled smoke and he saw . . . light.

He thought not of the man beside him in 7C, Kevin Bubier, who had wished him, "Good luck." Nor did he think of the man one row forward, Alan Barrington, still stuck in his seat, both arms pinned over his head. For that matter, McCorkell thought not of the man dangling from a seat belt above him, Chuck Pfisterer.

David McCorkell thought only of one thing—the light. He reacted to the most basic human instinct of all, self-preservation. He undid his seat belt and stood on the right-side wall. Moving forward, he stepped on debris that concealed Jim Kennedy.

McCorkell took five steps, his eyes fixed on the light.

He saw sparking wires. *This plane's gonna blow!* The hole beside Jean Brucato's seat in 4C extended into the fifth row; it was jagged-edged and wide enough for two people to pass through together.

As McCorkell stepped out of the broken plane, a fluid splashed across his shoes. He was in a field now as wide and spacious as the fuselage was narrow and confining.

He moved quickly, certain that every second mattered. McCorkell was only a recreational jogger. But now the traveling businessman in long-sleeved cotton shirt and tie, slacks and loafers, ran like an athlete; he knew that if he did not, the stampede of passengers coming from behind would trample him. He listened as he ran for the sound of the airplane exploding.

McCorkell ran toward pine trees. Another man ran ten yards in front of him. McCorkell tried to catch him. This man, thin and in good shape, captured his attention. Who was he? McCorkell did not recognize him as Air Force Major Chuck Lemay, who had been sitting in 6B, the very seat McCorkell had leaned toward in his brace position.

But McCorkell wasn't thinking clearly now as he raced thirty yards, and then fifty yards from the plane, running slightly uphill in Paul Butler's field. He thought this uniformed man barreling toward the distant trees must be the pilot. *And he's running away!* This confused McCorkell; it just didn't seem right. *How can the pilot run from his passengers?*

A safe distance away now, McCorkell slid to a stop in the grass, unaware that his loafers were soaked with fuel. He turned to look back.

He saw no stampede. No one was emerging from the plane. *Where is everyone?* Just then he saw a flame.

In the front of the cabin, the scramble began. In 2A, Renee Chapman blacked out just as dirt hit her face. Unconscious for only seconds, she awoke to find her seat had dislodged. She was lying atop passengers in 2B and 2C.

Chapman saw blood on her T-shirt but it wasn't hers. It came from Angela Brumfield, below her in 2C. Brumfield had a gash above her eye.

Suddenly the man in 2B, engineer John Tweedy, pushed Chapman's seat off his chest. The plane's right wall had peeled back like aluminum foil between the second and fourth rows. Tweedy hurried through the hole that would provide the primary escape route for those in the plane's first few rows.

In a panic, Tweedy fell to the ground, then stood, only to fall again. He thought to run away. But seeing the dazed and bleeding Brumfield behind him, he offered his hand to her. She took his hand and followed him out.

Renee Chapman stepped through the opening and walked away in a daze. Upon seeing the grass and pines, she wondered, Where am I? The answer, the Mississippian decided: In the middle of nowhere.

Barney Gaskill extricated colleague Ed Gray from beneath debris in 4A. "Don't worry, buddy, I'll get you out of this," Gaskill said. He pulled Gray across the aisle and through the right-side opening that Tweedy and Brumfield had used.

As Gray emerged from the fuselage, he smelled smoke, and then his pant leg caught flames. He heard someone yell, "Roll on the ground, Ed!" In his confusion, Ed Gray looked around for someone named Ed. Gaskill pushed him down. Gray rolled and the fire on his pant leg went out. He winced and suddenly grabbed at his chest.

Gaskill pulled Gray away from the plane, all the while fearing that his buddy was having a heart attack.

Instead of looking for her lost shoe, Robin Fech kicked off the other. Inside the front of the fuselage, she crawled through a fire-lit hole of debris and over the metal kitchen galley that, unknown to Fech, trapped and concealed Dawn Dumm and her mother in the front row.

On the other side of the galley, Fech expected to find passengers. Instead she saw no one, only destruction. On the right side of the cabin's aisle, at Rows 4 and 5, the plane's interior was in ruins. The walls and ceiling had tumbled and rained down in heavy pieces. An opening in the right wall revealed daylight, and Fech instinctively rushed to it. She saw John Tweedy trying to get a foothold in the field, all but running in place and falling in debris. "Move!" Fech shouted.

She left the plane in stockinged feet. Now, bleeding profusely from the left temple, her right wrist and collarbone broken, she ran out on the right wing, shouting again, "Move it! Let's go!" She jumped several feet to the ground, unaware that on her way out, beneath debris piled inside the cabin, lay an unconscious Jennifer Grunbeck.

* * *

On that right side of Rows 4 and 5, Grunbeck had been sitting near Jean Brucato and Bond Rhue.

Shaking, disoriented, and tilted slightly to the right in her seat, Brucato pushed Rhue's large frame from her and stepped through the opening in the right wall out into the field. She smelled fuel, realized she was soaked in it, and then heard screams behind her. It was the man who had been on top of her—Bond Rhue. He was on fire and trapped in the plane's opening. Brucato, in her flowered dress, came back to the flames in an attempt to rescue a man she didn't know. She saw terror in his eyes. She rolled him in the grass and put out his flames. She told him she would not leave him.

Grunbeck had been on Brucato's left, inches away. Unlike Brucato, she had been pulverized by the crash forces: her back broken in two places, liver lacerated, collarbone fractured, a lung collapsed. Unconscious and unseen inside the plane, Grunbeck's body leaned forward, still in the brace position.

She might have died in that position, but she felt someone's weight— perhaps Robin Fech's—on the debris covering her. Grunbeck awoke and coughed, as smoke and fire closed in. She struggled with her seat belt and coughed again, harder. With her leather boots, she kicked at what was left of the plane's right-side wall. She broke free but stumbled into flames.

Hard as she tried, Dawn Dumm could not budge the weight atop her. The large metal kitchen galley storing drinks and snacks had fallen across her chest, pinning her in 1B. Her mother, Mary Jean Adair, quickly got out of her seat in 1C, went to her knees, and tried to lift the galley from underneath. Adair couldn't move it, either. When hot hydraulic fluid scalded Dumm's head, shoulders, and back, she tucked her chin and screamed.

Adair shouted, "Please help my daughter! She's being burned!" But no one was left to help in their section of the plane; in time, though, the spraying and the scalding stopped.

Somehow, with mother and daughter pushing at the metal galley, it moved off her. Still, Dumm's legs were trapped by fallen objects. She pulled out her right leg first. Her right shoe had fallen off. She couldn't understand why. These were sturdy shoes, after all, and she'd worn them for that reason. The shoe was supposed to come off only when unbuckled.

Then Dumm pulled hard on her left leg. It, too, came free, but her left foot was . . . gone. She pulled harder on the leg and suddenly the left foot flopped out. It was nearly severed. Dumm shrieked. She thought, *My God, I've lost my foot!*

She pushed herself back on her seat and sat on the headrest. She examined the front section of the cabin. Over piles of metal and fiberglass, shattered overhead bins and the broken kitchen galley, she saw the flight attendant's jump seat. It was vacant. *Where is the flight attendant?*

Then she looked to the back. Thick smoke made it seem as if someone had hung a black sheet across Row 4. All around her, the seats were empty. *Where is everybody?*

Just then Adair said she couldn't find her glasses or purse. "What should I do?"

"Leave them," Dumm said.

Dumm pulled herself into the second row, stepping on the bones of her left leg. She made it to 2B, John Tweedy's vacated space, and then slid over to 2C. To maintain her balance, she held the jagged remains of the plane's right wall. With her mother in tow, Dumm stared out a hole in that wall that extended into the front row, beside Adair's seat, where it became smaller and triangular. From here, Dumm looked out and saw on the other side of the wing, perhaps twenty feet away, a peculiar image—the flight attendant standing in the field with a man wearing only his underwear and another man holding what appeared to be a briefcase.

Black smoke billowed. "We're still here!" Dumm shouted. "We need help!"

She saw the flight attendant's head turn, but no one responded.

She would have to do it alone.

Dumm had done her best to prepare for such a crisis. She had worn cotton clothing and sturdy shoes. Falling through the sky, she had prayed the rosary and written a last note to her husband and two boys. Now, blocking out the pain in her foot, she inched out the hole, onto the wing, and sat there for a moment. Then she moved toward the wing's front edge, several feet above the ground. She heard her mother scream: "Help me, I'm being burned!"

Behind her Adair stretched out across the wing, on her back, where flames from underneath shot up and scorched her, burning her shoes and her white cotton slacks. Dumm would not leave without her mother. Splaying her legs, she inched back up the wing, grabbed Adair and pulled her closer.

Together, mother and daughter made it to the ground, near the cockpit window, out of the plane at last.

Dumm crawled a few feet from the plane, then looked back to her mother. Adair wasn't moving. Dumm said, "Mom, we have to get away from the plane."

Matt Warmerdam found himself in a pilot's hell: stuck in his cockpit seat, unable to move, inhaling smoke. Melted plastic, from panels in the ceiling, dripped on his shoulders. Flames he could not see flashed against his back, legs, and left arm. He did not see his flesh burning, but he felt the flames scorching down through the layers of his skin. Once his burns reached the nerve endings, the pain died.

Burns are seldom uniform. Whether they are superficial (first-degree), partial thickness (second-degree), or full thickness (third-degree) depends in part on the temperature of the attacking heat and the duration of exposure to that heat. Skin, on average, covers more than two square meters in total surface area, though in most places is less than two millimeters thick. As flames attack skin, the epidermis, or outer layer, has little strength and dies off quickly. The under-layer, or dermis, is thicker and stronger, and gives skin flexibility. The dermis often discolors from burns, turning dark yellow, gray, or a charred brownish-black, unless the burns extend deeper, down into the muscle or even to the bone.

A victim may suffer burns across 100 percent of his body yet move about easily and talk coherently, at least briefly. Skin, after all, does not keep a person alive. It regulates body temperature, serves as a water barrier, and also, as part of the immune system, protects the body against infection. As long as oxygen continues to reach the brain, a burn victim can talk and even walk. Stories are legion of burn victims unaware of their predicament, so completely have they blocked out the pain. In a relatively short time, though, acute pain sets in, along with other complications. The chest swells. The lungs and heart are overtaxed. Breathing becomes difficult.

Warmerdam made the mistake of looking once at his burned left arm. It had turned an ugly white. It reminded him of a nasty cut, in which the skin splits open and exposes white fatty tissue inside. His arm looked so gruesome he held it behind him so he wouldn't see it again.

Beside him, Ed Gannaway lay dead, curled in nearly the fetal position. Gannaway no longer wore his shoulder harness—it had burned away—and his body had rotated in his seat. His head faced away from Warmerdam, toward the side windshield, and his lower half was contorted so the captain sat on his left foot. On impact Gannaway had been knocked unconscious, though apparently his body had reacted to the flames, moving as far as possible from them, but with barely any room to maneuver.

The young first officer, in only his fifth month on the job, tried to focus. He reminded himself of procedure: "The captain is dead, the chain of command comes to the first officer. We are in the middle of nowhere. . . ."

The smoke was getting to him. He needed air.

He reached behind his seat for the emergency crash hatchet, FAA required. He swatted it at the glass side panel to his right. He swatted again and again. It was like chipping at a thick block of ice. His right shoulder hurt, so he swung with his left hand in a short, choppy motion, woodpecker-like, until he was panting from exhaustion. Then he yelled, "I need some help!"

On impact, Jim Kennedy was thrown from 5A across the aisle and into the maelstrom. His six-foot-four frame lay across the right-side windows, between seats and overhead compartments, his head near an opening. He was on the fringe of consciousness.

That opening was the only escape point for the fourteen passengers in the back half of the cabin. Already traumatized by the descent and impact, these passengers now experienced the spatial disorientation produced by the fuselage's position. Their portion of the fuselage had rolled half over onto its right side; passengers walked on windows and bins that once had been overhead. In about sixty seconds that opening behind Kennedy's body would become a wall of flames, and so anyone moving through that space, or through the flames, would first pass over Kennedy.

Two passengers in the sixth row, McCorkell and Lemay, had quickly bolted from the plane, before the flames set in, almost certainly stepping on Kennedy on the way out, without knowing it. But the others needed more time. To these disoriented passengers, the blue-orange glow of the rising flames initially brought a sense of awe and wonder. The flames created, oddly, civility. Passengers in back formed a line.

But that civility passed as the plane's metal skin burned at 1,800 degrees, throwing off an apocalyptic heat. In their adrenaline-driven rush to get out, five passengers would be confronted by Kennedy's unmoving body. Would they stop to help him? Would they run?

When the sliding stopped, Kevin Bubier, in 7C, pushed away clutter, his hands working slowly at first, then furiously. He freed himself in a few moments and then tried to stand, but . . . how? And on what?

Only then did Bubier realize that what once had been the plane's right-side wall had become its floor.

All around him, passengers in the back rows stirred. They, too, began to dig themselves out. In the plane's middle section a few seats had broken loose from their floor bolts.

Several rows forward, on the plane's right side, Bubier saw light where a hole had been ripped in the fuselage. Through that hole, Bubier could see grass and trees, a field.

He heard a voice call out, "Somebody help me!" The voice came from above him. It was Chuck Pfisterer. Pfisterer had opened his eyes, unsure if he was still in this life or in an afterlife, only to discover that he was stuck, dangling in the air, his girth hanging over his seat belt. He punched at his seat belt but it wouldn't unfasten. He looked down at the two seats on the right side of Row 5, crushed against the ground. Pfisterer didn't see Jim Kennedy beneath that debris. He saw and heard no one.

"Somebody get me down!" Pfisterer shouted again.

Bubier stood on the right wall, wobbly in the knees. He saw his escape route and knew he should break for it. Instead he placed his right hand against overhead compartments, beside his shins, and then reached up to help Pfisterer.

In 6C, Alan Barrington had separated both shoulders, broken two ribs, and the pile of weight atop him kept him from lowering his arms. For a moment, his neighbor in 6B was on top of him, too, but then Chuck Lemay was gone.

Now Barrington pushed his feet against the plane's floor. He attempted to force open his seat belt. No use.

Through small crevices in the debris, he, too, saw the opening in the fuselage. Only about seven feet away, it seemed much farther. What he saw in that opening brought him to panic: dark smoke.

Barrington struggled, alone, furiously, against the weight above him. Bit by bit, he pushed pieces here, pieces there. He freed his arms, unlatched his seat belt, and stood against the right-side wall.

Already a line of passengers was forming in the plane's back five rows.

Flames covered only the lower left edge of the opening and black smoke blew across the rest of it. The radiated heat pushed passengers back into the safety of the cabin.

Barrington, not yet first in line, stepped forward and nearly tripped on someone. At his feet, he saw a man lying faceup against the right-side wall, between seats and overhead compartments—Jim Kennedy. He'd seen others walk on Kennedy on their way out.

Barrington reached down to him. Kennedy did not reach back. Barrington cleared a few objects from Kennedy's chest. He saw that his eyes were closed. Just then Barrington became aware of a voice above him, calling for help, though he concentrated still on this unresponsive man at his feet. Heat, intense and expansive, began to move inside the cabin.

Again Barrington heard the voice from above: "Somebody help me!" The cry came from the man across the aisle in 6A, Pfisterer. Barrington had heard him calling out earlier, though he hadn't responded. Pfisterer's pleas became, like a ringing alarm clock, a distracting part of Barrington's dream. He looked up and saw the big metal buckle of Pfisterer's seat belt. "Somebody get me down!" Pfisterer cried out again.

From the back of the fuselage, Barrington heard another man shout, "For God's sake, will somebody help that man!" At the same moment, Barrington and Bubier reached to help Pfisterer.

As his seat belt unfastened, Pfisterer fell—onto Barrington. Pfisterer rose and walked through the opening, untouched by fire.

Barrington needed a few moments to gather himself.

Every second mattered now.

Eleven passengers remained in the back section, nine men and two women. With Bubier and Barrington were the two Virginia deputies, Tod Thompson and Charles Barton, and Lonnie and Ludie Burton. There was the young minister, the Reverend Steve Wilkinson, and the diminutive Texan, Sonya Fetterman, still dangling from her seat belt in 10A. There were also three young engineers from different companies: Mike Hendrix, in only his second week of a new job; Alfred Arenas, a native of the Philippines; and David Schneider, whose only personal connection on the trip (even if they'd never met) was the consultant to his engineering firm, Jim Kennedy.

The eleven stood in the chaos and clutter. Their panic and anxiety mixed with incredulity. Their perceptions became narrowly focused. It was as if they wore blinders, so intent were they on escaping. Later some passengers would have no memory of others who stood beside them, yet vividly remember the image of flames in the opening more than fifteen feet away. Memory is a collection of images that have passed through our eyes and moved through the nervous system to the back of the brain where they are recorded. In moments of intense anxiety, a number of images might be seen but not acknowledged. Only those that are acknowledged—the fire in the opening, for instance—are likely to be recorded in memory.

Psychologists say people have different coping skills. In emotional turmoil, few have the resources to go beyond taking care of themselves. The overriding motive of each of the eleven passengers in the back section was self-preservation, with the exception of the Burtons. They looked out for each other.

Now the flames intensified, filling the opening. But then, in an instant, they lowered. Standing in line, Barrington thought fire trucks must have arrived. He imagined the plane had barely missed a runway lined with rescuers. He imagined firefighters spraying foam. "They got it!" he said excitedly, from his place in line. "They got it!" But then a gust of wind brought the flames back across the lower portion of the opening. Barrington's hopes caved in. *There's got to be another way out!*

He looked to the back of the cabin. There he saw a surreal image: the plane on its side, the sole emergency exit in back, by 8C, pinned against the ground. Darkness had settled over the back rows. The faces of people trapped inside were stone-faced, without emotion. Barrington heard no screaming, no crying. The people in back looked to him almost like figures in a painting. It was as if they were alive but not real. *They look like zombies!*

Time was passing: more than a minute since the plane had come to a rest. As he turned forward, Barrington's own voice rose: "You have to go through the fire! Just go! Go! *Go!*"

Distracted now from the man at his feet, Barrington saw two men in front of him disappear into the flames. Now he was first in line. He stood before the widening blue-orange veil. He watched the flames lick up and down, up and down. He timed the flames' movement. Finally he leaped through them and into the field, landing with a somersault.

Standing behind Barrington, Kevin Bubier concentrated not on the flames but on the feet he'd spotted sticking out from beneath seat cushions inside the opening.

Someone was under those cushions, someone who'd been trampled by others. Bubier fell to his knees and pushed aside the seat cushions, picking up where Barrington had just left off.

Each object he pushed away revealed another piece of Jim Kennedy: white sports socks, a single red stripe near the elastic bands, blue-jean shorts.

Bubier worked fast, against time. He felt alone in this task until he called out, "Somebody give me a hand!" and then, almost miraculously, a helping hand appeared. Who it was, Bubier did not know, but he said, "Help me get this guy up!" Together, Bubier and the helping hand pulled on Kennedy's arms and then grabbed him from his shirt collar. They had half-lifted Kennedy, pulling his upper torso off the right-side wall, no small feat, for he was a big man. In a narrow space framed by fire, Jim Kennedy seemed massive.

For only an instant Bubier looked into Kennedy's chiseled face. In the center of Kennedy's forehead, Bubier saw a dab of blood, as if he had taken a blow. Barrington had seen Kennedy's eyes closed. But now Bubier saw that Kennedy's eyes were open, almost *too open*. He wasn't looking at Bubier. He was looking through him. Bubier thought it was a frightening, faraway look, a dead man's stare.

Now the fire caught Bubier's attention in a way it hadn't before. When he'd first seen the flames, Bubier could make out a blurred image of what was beyond: a field and gray sky. But now the fire had grown into a raging holocaust, hotter than anything he'd ever experienced.

Suddenly Bubier heard crackling, popping sounds, the fire moving, growing. From the other side of the veil he heard primal screams from passengers in the field. Bubier held one of Kennedy's hands—a large hand, limp in his own palm.

Bubier saw his own life in jeopardy. He let go of Kennedy's hand. First in line now, staring into the flames and fearing his face would melt, Bubier broke through the fire with raised hands covering his face. Against his right leg, he felt an intense blast of heat.

The helping hand had belonged to David Schneider. The young engineer's faith in his own invincibility had been tested during the crash. As the back section of the fuselage had turned onto its right side, Schneider, in 8C, held his right arm against the plane's inner wall. He felt the ridges of the ground and had feared a rock or stick might break through his eighth-row window. His left arm fended off flying luggage and metal fragments. Once the sliding stopped, he knew he was liberated from his responsibility, opening the only emergency exit door in back. It could not be opened.

Climbing from a thicket of broken objects, Schneider saw the flames. He shifted into an adrenal mode of self-preservation. The line of passengers in the rear section had formed by the time he freed himself. In the rush to the opening he heard the powerful voice of a man behind him, probably Barton, calling, "It's going to be okay! Everybody help each other!"

The man's sharp command shook Schneider from his self-survival trance. He refocused and sensed others refocusing as well. For a brief moment, their movements slowed and a modicum of civility appeared.

With every second precious, Schneider saw the bottom half of the trampled man's body near the fiery opening. He reached down to help and became aware of another man's helping presence. Together, Schneider and Bubier tugged at the man and lifted him from the debris that had covered his upper body.

Schneider looked into the man's face. What he saw—rather, *who* he saw—brought him to his knees.

"Jim!" he said, kneeling and shaking the man from his shirt collar. *"Jim Kennedy!"* Schneider had watched Kennedy throughout the plane's descent. Kennedy had hardly moved, never turning to look at passengers in the rows behind him. Still, Kennedy had been Schneider's reference point and even a source of comfort throughout the crisis.

"C'mon, we've got to get out of here!" Schneider shouted, his face inches from Kennedy's. His colleague did not respond.

"You've got to get up!" Schneider shouted.

Schneider eyed Kennedy carefully, searching his body for signs of injury. He saw none. Kennedy's eyes were open, but Schneider sensed no light in them, no recognition.

Still on his knees, inside the shattered plane, Schneider heard the crackling and popping of an inferno.

He realized Bubier was no longer there. Neither was civility.

The fire's angry sounds had frightened everyone. A few hurried past Schneider; one brushed his side, knocking him fully onto his right knee.

Schneider's universe was reduced to Jim Kennedy and fire. He looked into the flames: This fiery opening was his exit point. It was his portal, and Kennedy's, too. It was their only way out.

"You've got to get up!" Schneider said.

Eyes open, but . . . nothing.

Schneider heard metal sizzling, a small explosion, a mini-burst, several mini-bursts, the fuel reaching a new source.

He left Jim Kennedy.

David Schneider no longer felt the arrogant immortality of youth. He'd already prayed his Our Father, his Hail Mary, and his Glory Be. Now he would time his jump. He would wait for that instant when he saw the fire's tendrils lower.

And just then he leaped. Embraced by the fires, Schneider heard a splash—his sneakers and blue jeans sponging fuel—and as he reached out for balance, he felt the plane's jagged metal edges rip into the flesh of his right palm.

The Virginia deputies, last in line, came next. When the back section had rolled to a stop, Tod Thompson felt Charles Barton's body draped over him. Thompson's face pressed against his ninth-row window. He pushed Barton up and in a moment both rose to their feet.

Thompson immediately noticed the two women in the back row. He saw Ludie Burton, dazed though seemingly unhurt. A half hour earlier he'd seen her enter the plane with her husband, and made note of her kind face. But now the retired teacher stood on the right-side wall, near her husband, and Thompson heard her asking softly for God's help. Thompson had watched Sonya Fetterman read a newspaper during the flight; now Fetterman hung horizontally from her seat, unable to unfasten her seat belt. Thompson moved beneath her, undid her seat belt, and let her down on his sloping shoulders. He and Barton moved Fetterman and the Burtons in front of them.

Now Thompson spied the opening near Rows 4 and 5, with daylight bursting through. In seconds that daylight became fire. He watched passengers in a line pushing back toward him, away from the flames.

Then Thompson heard a voice—it was Barton, and he was taking charge, Charlie being Charlie, Charlie calling out to the others in front, "There's no other way out! We'll have to go through the fire!"

Even before the propeller broke, Thompson had looked to the fifty-seven-year-old deputy as his role model. Barton had done fugitive retrieval seemingly a thousand times. He knew the ropes and was worthy of respect. And now, especially now, Charlie remained his role model. Thompson watched Charlie's every move.

As passengers disappeared into the fire, the line grew shorter.

Thompson remembered his Smith & Wesson gun. He'd worried in the Atlanta airport that someone might try to take it. It remained in the black overnight bag at his feet, along with a change of clothes. As the line moved forward, Thompson retrieved his bag.

Watching passengers lunge into the flames, without the benefit of a running start, gave the young deputy strength. *If they can do it, I can do it!* Charlie Barton stood in front of him, and in front of Charlie he saw a younger man, likely David Schneider, leap into the flames.

As Barton approached the opening, Thompson heard Charlie say something—not to him, but to a man lying inside the fuselage. He couldn't hear the words, but whatever Charlie said was brief and definitive, the same as everything he'd ever heard Charlie say.

And then Thompson watched the old deputy enter the fire. As Charlie Barton passed through the flames, he dropped his wallet, a deputy's silver badge inside.

Thompson felt a blast furnace's heat. He imagined his face melting. Then he saw the man near the fuselage opening, the one to whom Charlie had spoken: a big man in blue-jean shorts.

That man said to Thompson, "You've got to help me out!" Already moving into the flames, following his role model, Thompson replied in a rising voice, "You've got to get out!" Then, in a sweeping motion, Thompson protectively moved his black bag—with the Smith & Wesson handgun inside—in front of his face and entered the fire.

Flames licked at Thompson's triceps, held out wide, almost as an offering to the fire in the name of shielding his face.

Thompson hopped over a small wall in the fuselage, and now the hay field reached up to him. The young deputy broke into a full run, bound for the distant tree line.

Three people remained in the plane: the pilots and Jim Kennedy.

21

WHEN THE FIRE TRUCKS AND RESCUE teams pulled up, Paul Butler's hay field resembled a Civil War battlefield. Passengers were scattered—some walking, some badly burned, others badly burned *and* walking.

In a false comfort, some burned passengers moved through the hay field, talking rationally, even as they were dying.

In his old truck, the Reverend Gus Koch had sped down Paul Butler's driveway, then past the house and shed in back. Instead of the expected smoldering hole in blackened earth, he found a burning, broken plane with people emerging from it on fire.

As Deputy Sheriff Charles Barton stepped out of the fuselage, Koch ran to him. In Koch's mind, it was as if he was running back to 1969. He was no longer a minister but a medic, running through a field in Vietnam. He saw flames shoot upward from Barton's head.

Koch shouted, "Get on the ground!" Barton didn't hear him. Barton walked on, thirty feet from the plane, and staggered slightly, his entire body engulfed in fire. Finally he fell. Koch used his hands to swat at the flames. He unsnapped his red suspenders next and pulled off his shirt that read, "J Team—Working for Jesus." With the shirt, Koch beat out Barton's flames. He heard the deputy say, "Where am I?"

* * *

In the field, directly in front of Robin Fech, Alfred Arenas was engulfed in flames from the waist down. He wasn't sure what to do, which fire to put out first. His feet? His legs? His arms? Arenas begged for help.

"Roll on the ground!" Fech screamed. Rolling, Arenas felt his sneakers and jeans melting into his skin. His shirt burst into flames. Arenas was small, five-foot-seven, and boyish-looking; a few passengers mistook him for a teenager. Chuck Pfisterer reached down to Arenas, but an intense heat caused him to draw back.

Fech thought, If I take off his sneakers, I can pull off his pants, but when she looked at Arenas's sneakers again . . . there were no sneakers. They were gone. In seconds they'd melted into the soles of his feet. Fech screamed, "Roll! Roll! Roll!" Then, not knowing what to do, she turned away.

Alan Barrington, Kevin Bubier, and David Schneider had delayed their escapes with individual and shared attempts to rouse Jim Kennedy. They had no way to know if he was dead or alive. They had a choice to make: Do I wait to see if he responds or do I save myself? Kennedy's unresponsiveness frightened them. The primal sounds they heard outside the fuselage and the possibility of death, framed by fire, made their own deaths seem seconds away. So they'd left Kennedy behind to save themselves. What they could not have known was that after they left, Kennedy, still on his back, spoke to the young deputy, Thompson, saying, "You've got to help me out." So Kennedy was alert enough to know he was in mortal danger. He may have seen Barton and Thompson disappear into the flames even as he called for help.

The last passenger inside the burning plane, all Jim Kennedy had then was an astonishing will to live.

Kennedy stood. He faced the fire. He moved toward the heat, toward the light.

Jim Kennedy felt the heat of 1,800-degree flames.

What moved him to face the fire? His family, his life's work, St. Jude—they were in his head, certainly. But he had risen from the floor in answer to man's fundamental instinct for survival. He moved to the fire because it was the only way out.

But he moved too late. The fire had spread into the field. Grass burned outward from the fuselage in a semicircle pattern, five yards deep and advancing. Kennedy moved into that fire, stepping from the plane into fuel puddles. Slathered in fuel, he heard a cacophony of screaming voices.

Tod Thompson had made it about fifteen feet into the field, away from the fuel, away from fires burning the grass. He dropped to the ground and rolled. Virtually untouched by fire, Thompson stood and looked back to where he'd been. There, through the fiery opening, he saw a man emerge, the man to whom he'd just spoken, Jim Kennedy. The man moved slowly, too slowly, swatting his hands at the flames, and then falling in an area that defied rescue. Thompson saw the man and the fire become one—a burst of light.

The sounds filling Thompson's ears were horrific: other passengers in the field crying for help. All about him, people ran, rolled, and thrashed against fire. He heard a woman's plea. It came from the grass, nearer the tree line, closer to him. It was the woman he'd just seen in the back row softly asking for God's help. Thompson ran to Ludie Burton and put out her flames. She moaned in the grass. Then she asked for her husband.

Behind Robin Fech, on the ground near the right wing, flames shot from Jim Kennedy's chest. Since falling, Kennedy had crawled fifteen feet outside the fuselage.

It is rare for a man to burn to death in a field. Typically a burning death occurs in confined space where fatal gases are trapped and inhaled. In a wide-open field, death by fire would likely be from asphyxiation (unless heart failure strikes first) as the flame consumes its victim and eats away all available oxygen. The burn victim is left to struggle for air, falls quickly into unawareness, and then dies.

Fech rushed to Kennedy, removed her vest, and slammed it against flames at his midsection. On Fech's order, Pfisterer removed his pants and slapped them against the burning man. Pfisterer also took off his shirt and used it, though Kennedy no longer moved. He had rolled on the wallet dropped by Charles Barton. Kennedy lay on his back, body swollen and discolored, arms locked at the elbow, legs locked at the hips and knees.

Fech reached down to him, but someone, she didn't know who, touched her elbow lightly. Only by that signal did she realize that her passenger was dead.

Shaken, bleeding, in pain, Fech saw confused passengers walking back to the burning plane. "Get away!" Fech yelled. In her left hand, she held her broken right wrist. "Everyone get away from the plane now!" Seeing death and fire, she heard voices crying out now from all directions.

Behind the Butler home, Kevin Bubier approached a woman in a flowered dress sitting in the grass. "You okay?" he asked. It was Jean Brucato, the accountant making her weekly trip to Gulfport. Trembling with fear, Brucato said her back hurt. Bubier calmed her, and in a moment they hugged. Sitting beside her in the grass, Bubier felt pain in his right leg and pulled up his pant leg. The Maine shipyard worker saw his own burned flesh. "Aw, man."

Brucato flinched. "I don't want to see it," he heard her say.

Bubier suddenly grew faint. The woman in the flowered dress now soothed him. He noticed her hair. It was lovely, light brown, permed with thick curls. She was kind and generous. As he drifted in and out of consciousness, Bubier thought of this woman in the flowered dress, not knowing her but clinging to her as a symbol. *Who was she?* He wondered if she might be his guardian angel. Whoever she was, Bubier knew he would love her always.

Twenty-five seconds after he'd run from the plane, David McCorkell watched black smoke rising from twisted aluminum. The plane's T-tail had turned on its side; its nose cone had crumpled, like a soda can. Fire began to fill the hole in the plane McCorkell had just stepped through.

Where is everyone? McCorkell did not understand it. He'd had time to get fifty yards away. From this vantage point, he couldn't see the other side of the plane. He thought passengers had to be emerging on that side.

It was all so odd. Less than a minute before he had angrily accepted his own death. Now it was as if he was no longer even a participant in this plane crash. He was a spectator, standing in a field, near pine trees, watching a plane burn.

He thought to run away, to save what he could, himself. *The hell with everything! Just run. RUN!!!* But where were the other passengers? This question consumed him. *Why are they taking so long to get out?*

Finally he saw movement on the other side of the plane: a younger man in flames, perhaps the Reverend Steve Wilkinson, his clothes peeled away, running naked into the woods.

Other passengers appeared. They, too, were on fire. They screamed and tore at their clothes. Their pleas drifted across the field: *"Help me! Hellllp meeee!"*

McCorkell had a moment of indecision. *What do I do?* He didn't even know these passengers. They were perfect strangers. Here he was at midday, in midsummer, in the middle of a field, hearing their cries, looking for them through black smoke. *What do I do?* He had convincing reasons to stay where he was. Here, at a distance, his survival was assured. Among the first passengers out, and now among the farthest away, he'd run from a danger he only imagined. Yet now, when his fears were realized, McCorkell, rather than run away, decided to return to the danger. As others came out, he went back.

* * *

Her left side burned, her hair singed, Mary Jean Adair sat in the grass, still near the cockpit, exhausted and in excruciating pain. Her daughter, Dawn Dumm, crawled back to her. "Mom, we have to move. It could blow up." Adair only shook her head.

Several passengers and Robin Fech came to them. Fech pleaded with Adair to keep moving, but the grandmother was unwilling. Besides her burns, Adair had suffered multiple fractures in her right foot.

As Dumm again crawled from the plane, she called back, "Mom, we have to get away from the plane!" No response. Dumm called back to her again: "Mom, we have to move!"

Fech continued to yell to other passengers across the field: "Move away from the plane! Get as far away as you can!" Fech didn't understand why some passengers were walking back to the burning fuselage. Shock, maybe.

She called to Dumm, "Your mother won't move unless you call her!" Again Dumm urged Adair to move.

Chuck Lemay, who had been among the first passengers to get out, reappeared. He dragged Dumm to a safer distance. She clutched her foot as he pulled. She said, "Please go help my mother. Pull her away from the plane."

Tod Thompson went to Adair. The young deputy tried his best to convince her to move: "Do you have any grandkids?"

Adair nodded.

"Then why don't we get you up and move so they can see you again?" Thompson said.

Crawling alone now through the field, Dumm noticed the lovely maypop blossoms growing on vines. She watched a butterfly and reached out to grab it. It flew from one maypop to another and she crawled after it. It became like a game of tag: The butterfly was *it,* and as the butterfly flew farther from the plane, maypop to maypop, Dumm crawled in slow pursuit, trying to touch it. It was a return to childhood. The butterfly's wings quivered en route to another maypop and Dumm followed, blood flowing steadily from her foot.

As her pain brought a growing darkness, Dumm knelt and recited the Lord's Prayer: ". . . Thy kingdom come, Thy will be done, on earth as it is in heaven . . ."

She saw three people on a knoll, residents of nearby houses. Frantically, she waved to them. Elbert Eason, a retired power company foreman, came and reached out to her. Eason had an easy manner, a kind face full of creases and warmth. He embraced Dumm, assured her that he would stay by her side.

Dumm reached into her fanny pack and pulled out the good-bye note to her husband and two sons written on the inside cover of her paperback novel. She gave it to him.

Dumm's face and voice were full of fear. Eason elevated her leg to stop the blood from gushing. He retrieved a wet towel and used it to wash Dumm's face. Dumm asked him to call her husband, Larry, back in Maryland. She recited her home number. Eason promised to call.

Dumm watched the field grow darker, darker. She was about to lose consciousness.

Check on my mother, she pleaded.

Thirsty, so thirsty, Dawn Dumm held the towel in her mouth, biting it to fend off pain and also to drain water from it. Then the field went black and she lost consciousness. Elbert Eason saw her stop breathing. He reacted instantly, heroically: He gave her mouth-to-mouth resuscitation.

Circling back to the burning plane, David McCorkell heard a voice from inside the smoky cockpit.

"I need some help!"

Through a hole in the blackening glass he saw the first officer pinned in his seat. Matt Warmerdam held a small hatchet he'd used to break a hole in the side windshield.

McCorkell talked to the pilot through the glass. He saw Warmerdam's young face, frightened and red from the heat. He saw, too, the plane's torn and pockmarked aluminum skin, and the underside of its nose canted in and crumpled.

Warmerdam pressed his face to the hole and told McCorkell he didn't have enough room to swing effectively at the glass. He passed the hatchet through the hole to McCorkell, asking for help from a man he did not know.

McCorkell banged away at the thick windshield. He closed his eyes as glass shards flew toward his face and stuck in his mustache.

When McCorkell's left hand tired, he switched the hatchet to his right. Black smoke filled the cockpit. Warmerdam pressed his face to the hole, gasping for air. McCorkell thought, oddly, of a garden hose; he wished he had one at this moment. He noticed the youngest passenger, eighteen-year-old Basic Airman Jason Aleshire, standing beside him, in his jeans, T-shirt, and crewcut, wanting to help. He'd already seen Aleshire body-block several burning passengers and roll them on the ground. Small and compact, Aleshire acted as if engaged in combat, with aggression and a sense of purpose. Whoever he is, this guy's a he-man, McCorkell thought.

Bit by bit McCorkell widened the hole from six inches to eight, and then to ten inches, a misshapen triangle. Then McCorkell said, "C'mon, let's get you out of there." He reached inside the glass to tug on the broad-shouldered, six-foot-three Warmerdam. But the hole was only big enough for the first officer to stick out his head and an arm. "Stop pulling me," Warmerdam said. "It's too small."

A loud pop beneath the cockpit sent a blast of heat at McCorkell's legs, pushing him back eight steps.

Fire raged on one side of the plane, and more smoke filled the cockpit. Behind Warmerdam, McCorkell heard a roaring sound. He could not see, on the other side of the cockpit, the emergency oxygen cylinder, with a blown valve and a long steady flame blowing from it.

Frightened, McCorkell wondered what to do.

In Warmerdam's view, nothing could cause the plane to blow up now; that happened only in movies. Any popping sound, he figured, had to be a lead-acid battery overheating and discharging. (He hadn't considered the oxygen cylinder, though. According to Carroll County Fire Chief Gary Thomas, the release of oxygen could have prompted a flash fire outside the cockpit; if the valve on the oxygen cylinder hadn't opened, Thomas said, the pressure buildup might have transformed the cylinder into a projectile and launched it several hundred yards.)

Warmerdam cried out: "You aren't going to let me die, are you?"

Passengers nearby flinched at the first officer's terror. Tod Thompson thought of the handgun in his bag and wondered: Should I shoot out the cockpit glass?

Behind him, McCorkell saw Fech bleeding profusely from a head wound. She held her right arm, bent at the elbow. Fech had assumed her pilots had gotten out. She said nothing to McCorkell. In her stern look, though, McCorkell saw a message: He returned to the glass.

McCorkell banged harder even as more glass shards flew into his face and gritted teeth. His eyes were open now, squinted, and he took short, rapid whacks at the glass. He felt certain the plane would blow up any second. He wanted to help the pilot, but he did not want to die doing it.

On a back swing, the hatchet head flew off. McCorkell cursed, and reattached it. In a few moments Carroll County Sheriff's Deputy Guy Pope appeared, the first of the rescue workers. McCorkell handed the hatchet to Pope, pointed at Warmerdam, and said, "The pilot's still in there."

Now it was Pope's turn. He banged at the glass. "It's getting hot in here," Warmerdam told him. "Get me out!"

The hatchet head flew off again. McCorkell heard an approaching siren, and then he saw a fire truck appear. Pope had sent someone to get an axe from Paul Butler's house. Seeing the hatchet break, Warmerdam shouted loud enough for everyone in the field to hear, "Tell my wife I love her!"

He disappeared back into the cockpit darkness.

* * *

Jason Aleshire jumped on the first arriving fire truck. He commandeered a hose and pulled it toward the cockpit. Two more borrowed axes had broken against the glass side panel. Together, Pope and Aleshire guided the hose to the hole in the windshield. Pope feared the first officer was dead by now. Still, he called to him, "Put your head up here and keep breathing!" To his surprise Warmerdam returned to view, sucking hard for air.

The water pressure was too strong for Aleshire to handle the hose. So Pope took it and made certain not to aim the water directly at Warmerdam. He directed the surging water first at the burning oxygen cylinder and then, changing the register to a fog-spray, on the first officer.

There was a moment of quiet. Those watching feared the worst. But then they heard Matt Warmerdam's voice, quieter now, saying, "Put more water on me."

Warmerdam soon heard other men and their axes at work. All the while, he meditated: *I've got work to do. I've got to make sure passengers get away from the plane.* He even considered that he had four off-days coming up. He told himself he'd still be able to make that planned trip with Amy. The fire truck's cool water sprayed across his body, the most glorious gift he had ever received.

The county's co-fire chief, Steve Chadwick, rushed in and his crew doused the entire cockpit. More cool water sprayed over the first officer.

Extricating him took time. Chadwick realized the first officer couldn't be pulled through the glass side panel. His crew finally broke through the back of the cockpit, tearing away metal and pulling back burned-out wires. Stepping inside, Chadwick saw a motionless Warmerdam from the back: third-degree burns, almost to a charcoal state, from the crown of his head and down his back. In nineteen years of fire fighting, he'd never seen anyone survive burns like this. A fatality, Chadwick thought.

But then the fatality turned and said, "Get me out of here!"

Startled, Chadwick caught his breath, then replied, "That's exactly what we're fixin' to do!"

Chadwick climbed on the back of the first officer's seat and, using the force of his own 220 pounds, stomped on the seat.

Warmerdam was removed on a backboard. He looked up at the fire chief and said once more, "Tell my wife I love her!"

Chadwick, more optimistic now, said, "No, you tell her!"

Another firefighter stepped inside the burned-out cockpit moments later. There he found Ed Gannaway. He reported to Chadwick, "The pilot's a Signal 48," the code for deceased. An autopsy would indicate that Gannaway had died of burns and smoke inhalation.

David McCorkell watched Warmerdam carried away by paramedics, his burned arm held rigid in the air. He won't survive, McCorkell thought.

Walking to a triage area hastily arranged across the field, behind Paul Butler's house, McCorkell heard the moans and screams of burned passengers. He felt the eyes of a rescue worker upon him. McCorkell's shirt was ripped open across his chest and he'd suffered small burns on several fingers. Now he translated the rescue worker's look: *You son of a bitch, you ran, didn't you? How dare you survive when women and old people were not taken care of!* The rescue worker never said a word, but a sense of guilt settled on McCorkell.

As neighbors and rescue workers filled the field, a shirtless Alan Barrington walked along the tree line toward the tail of the plane. He'd barely had time to wipe away his tears. Barrington had seen passengers on fire, done what he could to help, scorching his fingers against one man's burning socks, though who this man was, Barrington wasn't sure. He'd flapped his shirt and then grabbed fistfuls of dirt and grass and thrown them at the attacking flames, to no avail. Then, and only then, had Barrington turned his back. He knew the man was beyond help. He couldn't bear to watch someone burn.

Now Barrington came upon another passenger, in his thirties, burned across most of his body. The man wore only underwear; his other clothes apparently had burned away. He was walking toward a house at the edge of the field. "Why didn't you get burned?" the man asked Barrington. He asked calmly, nearly matter-of-factly.

Barrington didn't know what to say. What could he say? At this moment he thought he was the only person on the plane who had not been burned.

He answered honestly. "I don't know."

Barrington did not make eye contact.

The burned man was Michael Hendrix, an engineer beginning the second week of a new job. Hendrix walked away from Barrington, past the Butlers to the house next door, on the other side of the corn patch. On the porch he met Polona Jeter. She had watched the broken plane sliding toward her home. Her husband, Billy, had gone out to the field to help.

She and Hendrix stood before each other. A silent moment passed.

"I was on the plane," Hendrix began.

"Yes," Jeter said, "I saw."

Hendrix said he needed to call his wife in Maryland. Jeter watched as Hendrix stooped slightly, in pain. "Why don't you sit down right there," she said. She brought her phone to the porch. He recited the number and Jeter dialed for him, though in her nervousness, she misdialed one digit. Hendrix dialed himself and got an answering machine. He had inhaled fire and so he spoke softly. Polona Jeter heard him say, "Linda, my plane crashed. . . ."

The middle of nowhere, is how Renee Chapman had assessed the crash site. She walked in a daze from the fuselage into the field, where she encountered a middle-aged man, burned, in the grass. He wore a white shirt, sleeves rolled up to the elbows, and a tie. But his pants were gone, his shoes melted, and his legs burned nearly to the bone.

He told her his name was Bond Rhue. He identified himself to Chapman as the man who had changed seats with the woman who didn't want to sit by the emergency exit.

Rhue asked Chapman if she thought he was going to die. "No, you're not that bad," she said. His face and arms appeared sunburned, his hair singed. "You just look like you've been laying out in the sun," she told him.

Rhue asked, "Is my tie crooked?" His tie, which featured playful pigs, had mostly melted.

Chapman nodded.

"Would you straighten it?" Rhue asked.

Chapman took a deep breath. Then she said, "Why don't we just take it off. . . ."

In his hay field, Paul Butler passed out blankets to injured passengers. He came upon an anxious and agitated Rhue. "I'm going to die," Rhue said.

Butler lied. "Nah, you just look red. It ain't that bad."

But Rhue persisted. "No, I've got third-degree burns. I'm going to die."

Putting a blanket over him, Butler said, "Just be calm, man."

In her jeans and T-shirt, Chapman moved across the field. She sat in the grass and fumbled with her cigarettes. David McCorkell approached and asked, "Can I have one of those?" Chapman's pack of Winston Lights had crumbled in her pocket during impact. Only one cigarette in the entire pack didn't snap—as it turned out, Chapman's good-luck cigarette, the one she had pulled from the new pack and turned upside down for good luck. Watching black smoke rise from the fuselage, Chapman and McCorkell bummed a light from a neighbor and sat together in the field. A spot of blood by his nose, McCorkell stuck out his hand. "My name's Dave," he said. Chapman took a long drag. "I'm Renee. . . ."

* * *

Chuck Pfisterer's throat was parched. He turned from the field and walked to the Butler house. He yelled inside but no one answered. He stared across the street. Staring back at him were three women, including Connie Jackson, Paul Butler's eighty-two-year-old mother-in-law.

Pfisterer approached. He wore his underwear and bloodied T-shirt, brown loafers and socks. In his hand he held his belt and wallet, which he'd retrieved from the field.

Only moments before, Connie Jackson had received a call from her daughter across the street, Polona Jeter. Her voice shook as she said, "Mama, are you all right?" Connie Jackson said she was fine, hung up, and went out on her porch. Not knowing what else to do, she cried. In between sobs and the arrival of two neighbors, she said, "Lord, help them."

Now Pfisterer arrived at her porch and said, "I hate to bother you, but could I have a glass of water?" She went to get him water. He asked for a phone. She led him inside. He phoned Connecticut, but his wife didn't answer, so he called an office colleague, who agreed to get word to her.

Chuck Pfisterer asked Connie Jackson, "Where are we?" She mentioned Burwell, Bowdon, and Carrollton, names he'd never heard. They spoke for a few minutes, until a paramedic arrived and escorted Pfisterer to an ambulance. Pfisterer thanked Jackson, then left.

It wasn't until much later that Connie Jackson realized she'd never asked the man his name.

The Reverend Gus Koch comforted Deputy Charles Barton, who lay in a smoky heap. Tod Thompson rushed to his partner's side. Charlie's hair, eyebrows, and clothes were gone.

"This is my friend," Thompson told Koch. "He's a good man." Thompson looked ashen. "He's a *really* good man."

The young deputy said to Barton, "We're going to get you out of here. Hang on."

"This hurts," Barton replied, his voice barely audible. "Man, this hurts."

Thompson wanted to reassure his friend. He searched for a soft spot on Barton's body to place his hand. He saw only charred skin. Finally he gently touched Barton's stomach.

"Don't push so hard there," Barton said, wincing.

Thompson, shirtless and in jeans, shook his head, at a loss for what to do or say. "He's a good man," he told Koch again.

Koch, the medic, heard gurgling in Barton's voice and knew he'd inhaled fire. He knew Barton was in trouble.

Koch saw a crowd in front of the cockpit, someone trying to break open the windshield. Behind him he saw passengers gathered beside his truck. He saw bodies dispersed about the field, and it reminded him of triage drills. He saw the fuselage burning furiously, black smoke rising into a gray sky. He saw the flight attendant, bleeding, disheveled, nearly hysterical. "I've got to go back," he heard Robin Fech say.

"No," Koch told her, "the plane will explode."

He saw a tall black man stumble past. "I'm looking for my wife," the man said. Lonnie Burton's condition was worse than anything Gus Koch had ever seen in Vietnam. Skin sloughed off Burton's face and torso; his pants had all but burned off.

"You need to sit down," Koch said. Burton complied, but only for a few seconds. He seemed rational but fidgety. "I've got to find my wife," he insisted. He got up and walked away.

Behind the tail of the plane, Koch saw a young woman. No longer on fire, she wore blue jeans and was naked from the waist up. Her bra had burned in to her. Skin had melted away from her face. Smoke rose from her body as she stumbled about twenty-five feet from the fuselage. Wandering, she was alone. She fell, not far from burning grass.

Koch leaned beside Charles Barton and said, "Somebody else needs me. I need to go now." Nodding at Tod Thompson, he told Barton, "Your friend is here."

* * *

Gus Koch knelt beside the fallen woman. Her breathing was labored. From her nose and mouth, Koch pulled away loose flesh. "You should be able to breath better now," he said. Her jeans were burned, her hiking boots half-melted into her feet. She was virtually unrecognizable. He asked her name.

Jennifer, she said.

"Hi, I'm Gus."

She told him her husband's name was Bob and he worked at the Fairfield Inn in Bangor, Maine. She gave him the phone number. "Please call him. Tell him to get down here right away." And then she repeated the phone number.

Jennifer Grunbeck could not see Gus Koch as well as she could hear him. His voice was soft, soothing. She told him her feet hurt and asked if he would remove her boots.

Koch felt the fire's intense heat against his back. As a medic, he had carried bandages, scissors, and water; he wished he had those supplies now. He told her he couldn't remove the boots, at least not yet. Shifting winds blew flames across the grass, closer to them. "Jennifer, I'm going to leave you for a second. I'll be right back." Koch got up, moved several feet away, and stomped his old leather work boots into the ground, putting out flames in a circle, roughly ten feet in diameter. He went back to Grunbeck. She repeated her husband's phone number: "Tell him to get down here right away."

Koch knew he needed to keep Grunbeck talking and focused on something meaningful to her. He needed a hook, at least until rescue workers arrived. He asked if she had any kids. Yes, a son, she said. What's his name? he asked. Johnny, she said. How old is he? he asked. Four, she said.

Grunbeck had thought of Johnny from the moment fire burned into her jeans and rayon shirt, and she heard someone shouting: "Stop! Drop and roll!" This was the very lesson Johnny had just learned from firefighters visiting his preschool: If you are on fire, you must stop, drop to the ground, and roll to suffocate the flames. *Always remember that, Mommy,* Johnny had said. *Stop, drop, and roll!* Johnny even made her demonstrate the moves at home. Remembering her little boy's advice, she'd dropped to the ground and tried to roll but, with her back broken, couldn't. She watched her flesh burn, though quickly what Jennifer Grunbeck felt was nothing. Nothing at all.

Now Gus Koch had his hook. He asked: What kind of little guy is Johnny?

Is Johnny messy?

He mentioned his own daughter, now twenty-three.

What does Johnny like to eat?

Jennifer Grunbeck said, Hot dogs and macaroni and cheese.

The flames drew close again. Gus Koch looked back toward the plane. Black smoke made it seem like nighttime. He heard a man scream from inside the billowing darkness: "Help me! Help me!" The wind shifted in a few moments, restoring daylight. Suddenly a loud hissing emanated from the plane. Koch thought it must be a fuel tank about to explode. He instinctively covered Grunbeck, placing his body between her and the plane. The hissing sound, from the oxygen cylinder, stopped in a few seconds. Koch wanted to move Grunbeck from the spreading fire, but feared she might have already suffered a spinal injury. Moving her could make her injury more severe. They talked some more.

"My feet hurt, and my back hurts," she said.

He replied, "If you start hurting, that's a good sign."

Then he asked, "How did you get off the plane?"

She replied, "I kicked my way off."

"You're something else," he said.

He got up and stomped out the grass again. He returned to her and said, "You made it off the plane, Jennifer. There's no reason you can't go all the way."

Then he saw the arriving rescue workers. "We've got one over here!" Koch shouted.

The arriving EMT said, "I'm Bud," and moved beside Grunbeck. "This is Jennifer," Koch told him, "and she's got a four-year-old boy named Johnny."

Bud Benefield looked at Grunbeck. She had third-degree burns across most of her body. Her blouse had shrink-wrapped onto her skin. He noticed that she had inhaled fire. "Jennifer, can you talk to me?" Benefield didn't expect an answer.

"Yes, I can," she said.

Benefield did not believe she could survive. He figured her airways would swell, she'd go into shock, and her organs would fail. He put her on high-flow oxygen. Knowing Koch was a minister, Benefield told him, "I don't want you—or the man you work for—to leave me."

Other rescue workers arrived with a gurney, and Grunbeck was carried to an ambulance. Only the soles of her feet seemed to have been spared from the flames. How could any human being survive a burn like this? Benefield wondered.

Benefield told the paramedic in the ambulance, "This is one of the worst burns I've ever seen."

The paramedic said, "Have you seen my patient?" Benefield looked inside the ambulance and saw Ludie Burton, her hand curled into a claw, pleading, "Please, God, let me die!"

The professionals had arrived. Jennifer was en route to the hospital; helicopters appeared in the sky. Gus Koch noticed people walking through the trees. Already souvenir hunters were scavenging for plane pieces. It disgusted him.

He climbed into his truck and drove back to his nearby parsonage. He closed the parsonage door and balled up on the couch. Thoughts and images of Jennifer filled his head.

Inside an ambulance, Matt Warmerdam listened to the agonized screams of a woman beside him. It was Dawn Dumm, alternately crying out and biting a towel. Warmerdam asked the paramedic, "Why is she screaming so much?" "She's hurt her foot pretty bad," the paramedic replied. Panicked and frustrated, the paramedic was trying to rip open an IV bag filled with fluid, which Warmerdam assumed was for the screaming woman until the paramedic finally opened the bag and poured its contents on the first officer. Warmerdam tried to tell the paramedic, "You're doing good here, it's okay," but he couldn't get the words through his oxygen mask.

He heard Dumm, in an anguished voice, saying a Hail Mary. Just then, though, Dumm's prayers fell silent. Warmerdam, a Catholic, motioned to another paramedic, Joan Crawford.

Crawford had helped remove him from the cockpit while her husband, a firefighter, sprayed water. In the field Warmerdam asked Crawford about his chances for survival. Her answer was optimistic even though she thought he would die. Crawford removed some of Warmerdam's clothes and slipped his ASA name tag inside his underwear so the hospital would know who he was. Looking into the first officer's face, Crawford saw her own son, about the same age. Emotion overcame her. Inside the ambulance, she wept for Warmerdam. She leaned close to the first officer, and as she did, Warmerdam reached up with his burned hand and wiped a tear from her face. His humanity astounded her.

Then Warmerdam mumbled something Crawford couldn't make out. She leaned closer. He said it again, this time a little louder. Crawford nodded. She leaned toward Dawn Dumm and said, "He wants you to keep praying out loud."

So Dumm resumed her prayers aloud.

In a sporadic awareness, Jennifer Grunbeck experienced a blur of passing sounds and images: hearing the shrieking pleadings of Ludie Burton in an ambulance, floating through a hospital clinic in nearby Bowdon, people bustling all about, nurses cutting off remnants of her clothing, nurses cutting off her wedding ring even as she warned, "Don't lose it."

Feeling no pain, no pain at all, seeing a helicopter and being placed inside, thinking, Oh my God, they're putting me on something else that flies. "My name is Glen," said the man in the helicopter, and then someone else—or was it still Glen?—said, "Jennifer, we are putting you to sleep now." The mask coming down over her nose, coming down over her mouth, and then she was rolling on a metal bed in a hospital, a different hospital than before, lights overhead whipping past, a strobe-light effect, people talking about Jennifer, people talking to Jennifer, and then hearing a priest—a priest, what is he doing? He's doing the sacrament of last rites, da-da-da-da-da-da. "The Father, the Son, the Holy Spirit," da-da-da-da-da-da, and then, suddenly, feeling pain. Not pain from the burns. Rather, pain for this priest. "My God, this priest is in the wrong room. He's giving last rites to the wrong person." Beneath burn sheets, beneath bandages, beneath skin scorched across almost her entire body, deep in her thoughts, Jennifer Grunbeck already knew what neither the priest nor her burn unit doctors knew. "I'm not going anywhere."

Part VI

"You're the Hero"

22

J ACKIE GANNAWAY HEARD WORDS that no pilot's wife wants to hear. Just before two o'clock, she excused herself from a meeting at the Carl Vinson Veterans Administration Medical Center in Dublin, Georgia, to answer an urgent page. It was her mother calling. Because they lived in the same small east Georgia town, the mother and daughter were close and talked often.

"Jackie, do you know about the ASA crash?"

The pilot's wife said she did not. "A plane to Gulfport has gone down. And I don't think it would've been Ed's, but, you know, he flies to Gulfport so much. . . ."

"Gulfport?" Jackie Gannaway said. "Oh, it's not Ed's. He was going to Albany."

She wasn't sure of that; she didn't have her husband's itinerary. She told her mother she would call ASA's flight operations center.

Forty-two years old, a wife and mother, a college graduate with a restless curiosity and a master's degree in social work, Jackie Gannaway lived a Southern idyll. In the twentieth year of marriage to an Atlantic Southeast Airlines pilot, still in the town where she'd grown up, she and Ed Gannaway were raising their three sons.

Disturbed by her mother's call, Jackie Gannaway walked to her office. She tried to remember the morning scramble. She and Ed had talked hurriedly, the way working parents do when they have three children to get off on the first day of the new school year. She replayed the morning sequence in her head, searching for confirmation that this could not have been Ed's plane: *Why, Ed even said, just before I took the boys to school, that he was headed for Albany. He never mentioned Gulfport.*

Of course, to call flight-op was to admit the possibility that the plane down was Captain Ed Gannaway's. She knew flight-op didn't like calls from anyone, not even a pilot's wife. Call flight-op, Ed told her during his eight years with the regional airline, only if it's a real emergency.

She got right through to flight-op. "This is Mrs. Gannaway. I hate to bother you, and I'm sure this is a ridiculous call, but I heard there's been a crash of an ASA flight to Gulfport. And I just need to be sure that it's not my husband's flight." She spoke with a gentle pleading in her voice, as if by her tone alone she could draw from the flight-op people a confirmation that her worry was, in fact, ridiculous.

She heard no confirmation. No one told her to quit worrying, or to quit bothering flight operations every time she became anxious over a news report. There was only silence, and then: "Could you hold just a minute, please, Mrs. Gannaway?"

She knew. Ed was down.

She slumped against a wall in her office and heard the flight operations supervisor come on next. "I'm sorry to tell you," he said, "but it was your husband's plane. . . ."

The rest of his message came to her in fragments: ". . . everything we're hearing is good . . . a lot of survivors, we're told . . . We don't know the situation yet . . . The plane still looks pretty intact . . ."

Even as the flight-op supervisor spoke, helicopters carried print and television photographers toward the crash site.

It was all too real now, no need to be delicate, so Jackie Gannaway spoke more directly, firmly. "Keep in touch with me," she told the supervisor. "Call me and let me know what's going on."

She left the hospital to pick up the two oldest boys, Craig and Russ. A school bus would bring home the youngest, Rob. Jackie Gannaway wanted the boys with her because she would need them as much as they would need her. Driving home with Craig and Russ, she told them, "I'm sure everything will be okay. We just need to go home and pray."

There, in the home the family had made together, the boys sat with their mother and saw on television the smoking, charred, broken fuselage of an Embraer EMB-120 flown by their father. Jackie wanted more information than the television gave. She phoned hospitals near the crash site and asked each if it had admitted a patient named Gannaway.

No, came the answer each time. But call back. More crash victims are coming in.

With no news of her husband's condition, she told her boys, "Dad's okay." She believed it. She'd never experienced the death of a loved one. She couldn't allow herself to feel that pain now. She certainly couldn't allow the boys to feel it.

Soon the Gannaway house became a gathering place for those who heard about the crash and cared about the family, which seemed to be most of Dublin. Jackie's parents, Jake and Margaret New, arrived, as did colleagues from the VA and her family ministers. Almost everyone in town knew Ed Gannaway; he was a joiner, with memberships in the Rotary Club, Touchdown Club, bicycle club, country club, running club, and Boy Scouts. Friends, two dozen and then more, came to stand watch with the Gannaways. They turned on the televisions in the den and in the living room.

Three o'clock became four o'clock. No word from any hospital. No word from flight-op. More friends stopped by. They stood outside, talking quietly. Jackie and the boys moved from the crowded den to the solitude of the master bedroom. Together, they needed to be alone.

A television set atop a dresser brought into Ed Gannaway's bedroom images of his burned-out plane 180 miles away. The captain's wife and three sons now saw burned grass and charred metal. On the Brasilia's turned-up side they saw identification letters in red paint, N256AS.

They saw people: firefighters, rescue workers. Jackie Gannaway wanted confirmation that the captain was alive. She kept looking into the field on the TV screen, expecting to see Ed walking with his passengers, or perhaps helping them. *That would be Ed's style. Yes, he would help his passengers.*

Four o'clock became four-thirty became five. No phone calls, not enough news.

On the bedroom television, Jackie saw the front of the plane, where her husband worked. One of the boys said the cockpit looked pretty good. "Maybe Dad's safe." Jackie studied the burned-out cockpit more closely. She saw the right-side cockpit window with an odd hole in its center. She remembered Ed mentioning his new first officer, a young and eager pilot, Matt Warmerdam. She thought, That's not Ed's side, it's Matt's.

She looked for Ed in the field. She hadn't seen him since that morning when she rushed out of the house to get the boys to school. Now it was almost five-thirty, no word yet. She could see his plane, but she couldn't see the man she'd met on a girls' night out twenty-one years earlier.

A girlfriend had offered to arrange a blind date for her with a good-looking guy she'd known at college, Ed Gannaway. Jackie had said no, no thanks, no more blind dates for me. Out with a different girlfriend in Atlanta one night, Jackie heard a good-looking guy ask her to dance. No thanks, she told him, but this guy kept talking, and she rather liked him. He was nice, friendly, a gentleman.

So they danced and she asked his name and it was Ed Gannaway, and they always thought of their meeting as serendipitous. They were married a year and a half later, and now, with her husband and his plane in that field so far away, Jackie Gannaway thought once more about the last time she'd seen him, that morning when she'd rushed out the door to take the boys to school, and to deliver flowers at the school's open house and . . .

Oh, no. They'd always kissed each other good-bye. If some might think them old-fashioned, so be it. They were old-fashioned if that meant you loved someone so much you showed them that love. At every leaving, for an airport, for the veterans' hospital, for the boys' schools, Jackie and Ed Gannaway shared a kiss.

Jackie sat with their boys in the bedroom, waiting for word that her husband, and their father, was alive. She owed him that morning's kiss.

Two fatalities, **Craig Gannaway** heard the man on the news say. Staring at the thirteen-inch television in his parents' bedroom, trying to feel his father's presence, he told himself, The cockpit looks too intact. It has to be those people in the back of the plane who died. Then a newscaster said one of the pilots was dead.

It's fifty-fifty, Craig told himself.

He felt the room grow more tense. Jackie sat on the bed, with Russ and Rob.

The Gannaways' stream whispered out back. Friends, colleagues, and ministers watched televisions in the family's den and living room, or gathered in the driveway, talking quietly and waiting for news about Ed.

Past 5:30 P.M., more than four and a half hours after the crash, the captain's wife and three boys saw a TV news videotape of a rescue worker hacking at the cockpit window with an axe. Then the man with the axe explained to a television interviewer, "We got the copilot out. I tried to get the pilot out but he was already dead."

Jackie reached for Russ and Rob. Clusters of friends and family, all crying, rushed into the bedroom. Craig, weeping himself, fell into the arms of one of his father's best friends.

In the hallway later, a minister told Craig the family responsibility now was his: "You've got your mother but you're the oldest." With tear-rimmed eyes, the oldest son nodded and said he understood.

Rob, the youngest, wanted to grieve only with his dog, Otis. His grandmother led the third grader through a side door, away from the gathered people. She watched him hold Otis and cry.

All through the house, Jackie's father, Jake New, heard well-meaning friends asking, "How could God have let this happen?"

This worried him. So he pulled aside Craig, choked back tears, and told his grandson sternly, "Don't you let anybody make you believe that God did this."

23

1:45 P.M. A RINGING TELEPHONE brought Dr. Bobby Mitchell from a deep sleep at his home in Douglasville, Georgia. He heard an emergency room unit clerk say, "There's been a plane crash with twenty-eight to thirty people. We need you to come in right away."

"Yeah," Mitchell replied, not yet fully awake. "Okay."

Mitchell didn't say what he felt: *This is rude, pulling me in for a staged drill now.* Planes didn't crash in Carrollton, Georgia, after all, at least not planes with twenty-eight to thirty people.

He figured this had to be one of those rare major-disaster drills at the hospital with pretenders moulaged, or painted up, and acting traumatized, the ambulance service feigning a scene and emergency room doctors and nurses rehearsing triage.

Why now? Mitchell treasured his few hours of afternoon shut-eye. In another five hours, he was to start his night shift in the emergency room at Tanner Medical Center, a regional hospital near the Alabama state line.

But then he realized the ER clerk hadn't said anything about a drill. Dressing quickly, he turned on a television and heard a news trailer: "This has been a special report from ABC News. . . ." *Could this be real?*

Bobby Mitchell was a tall, handsome Mississippian, forty-one years old, still with an athlete's physique. His gracious disposition and eloquence gave him a splendid bedside manner. He moved through Tanner's ER like a man who belonged there. In ten years of small-town dramas, he'd seen locals pay a steep price for mistakes, naïveté, and recklessness

157

involving everything from bicycles to intoxicated country drivers. Some doctors didn't like the ER pace. Mitchell did. Stirred by "the concreteness of the urgency and the need," he moved from triumph to tragedy, working odd hours, at times missing his kids' ball games or birthdays. Sometimes he found comedy in the ER's wacky tales of patients intent on getting narcotics, of peculiar objects extracted from people's rectums. No wonder Dr. Mitchell starred at family reunions with his colorful stories.

Now in his Honda Civic, heading west on Interstate 20, he heard Atlanta radio reports about a plane crash near Carrollton. It was real, all right, and in less than fifteen minutes he would walk into the storm. *It'll be a bunch of dead people. No one ever survives these plane crashes.*

But when a report suggested survivors, Mitchell knew what lay ahead: *Burns. Burns of the worst nature.*

He drove into downtown Carrollton, a small though bustling place, marked by a county courthouse (with its requisite Confederate monument), lovely old homes, and a town square. Passing through roadblocks set up by police cars and fire trucks, Mitchell saw more flashing blue and red lights than he'd ever seen. Turning up Dixie Street toward Tanner, he slowed and a policeman tapped on his window: "Come on in, Bobby. They need you *fast!*"

At 2:20 P.M., he entered the hospital through a rear door to the doctors' changing room.

A minute later, emerging into a hospital hallway, Mitchell walked into a smell so powerful it seemed palpable, like gasoline, only much stronger. Jet fuel. So strong was the smell he expected to see fuel spilled on the floor.

In another ten strides that noxious smell gave way to an odor even worse, that of burned skin. Bobby Mitchell knew that reviling smell too well. He'd done burn treatment before; he knew the smell would get into his clothes and into his nose, and it would stay.

The hallway became an obstacle course of doctors, nurses, policemen, medics, members of the hospital's public relations staff, and dozens of unfamiliar faces. It was, to Mitchell, as if he'd come home and found people he didn't know in his house.

And then, down the hall, Mitchell heard a woman's wails: "Ohhhhhh, noooooo! Ohhhhh, noooooo!"

What is all of this?

At the physicians' desk, Dr. Tom Fitzgerald, the physician in charge, had an abrupt greeting for Mitchell: "I need you in there!" He pointed Mitchell toward Orthopedic Room A.

Mitchell stepped into that small room. It had been converted to a cramped four-bed emergency bay. Inside he saw five nurses and a doctor.

On the bed to the far right lay Robin Fech—"the flight attendant," a nurse told him. In the other beds lay three passengers covered in sterile towels, burn sheets, and absorbent abdominal pads to minimize the evaporative loss. Next to Fech was Michael Hendrix, and next to him, Bond Rhue. On the far left, nearest the wall, was Sonya Fetterman, whose wailing reverberated through the hallways.

Of the thirteen survivors brought to Tanner, Mitchell had initial responsibility for these four. The most essential task would be fluid replenishment, pumping in massive amounts of fluid intravenously, while monitoring urine output. Dressings wet with sterile saline would cool victims. Mitchell would check for respiratory distress and monitor vital signs. He would search for physical trauma and damage to major organs and the spinal structure. Above all, he would do what he could to comfort.

Sonya Fetterman drew his attention first. Nurses already had wrapped her face in bandages. "Mrs. Fetterman, I'm Dr. Mitchell and—"

"Ohhhhhh! Ohhhhhh, noooooo!"

Mitchell tried again, to no avail. He could not reach her. He prescribed morphine, five milligrams, and soon five milligrams more. Still, she screamed. Mitchell lifted her burn sheet and bandages. Her face was drawn, its muscles contracted. Her eyes seemed no longer a part of her face. They seemed to be looking through holes in a mask.

Sonya Fetterman had stumbled over the ASA Brasilia's threshold. Fuel splashed across her and her shorts caught fire. Alan Barrington heard her long, piercing shriek. Fetterman ran in a zigzag pattern across the field, her arms and legs burning. Barrington and David Schneider gave chase and knocked her down. She unbuttoned her shorts, which Barrington flung away. Fetterman pulled off her shirt and flapped her arms in a cooling motion; as others consoled her, she lay naked in the grass, arms flapping. Schneider thought to cover her, but with what? Tod Thompson gave Fetterman a shirt and shorts from his black bag. Across the field minutes later, Schneider saw her alone, hopping on one foot and falling into the grass. He rushed to her. "God, it hurts so much," she told him, half crying. Her voice gurgled slightly. Schneider saw blood in her mouth. She'd inhaled fire. He sought to comfort her, and patted her softly, below her right shoulder. "You're going to be fine," he said. Fetterman lifted her scorched arms at a 45-degree angle and again fanned them up and down. "Keep doing that," Schneider said. Fetterman was thinking about Amber, her toddler daughter back home in Texas. "My baby," she told Schneider. "She's so beautiful. She's so cute." Schneider said, "You're going to see her again." He thought her upper body looked relatively untouched by fire. He smiled at Sonya Fetterman and said, "We made it."

"Mrs. Fetterman," Mitchell said, leaning over her now, two nurses by his side, "are we helping your pain at all?" For the first and only time, Fetterman turned her eyes toward him. Almost immediately, she turned away and fixed her gaze on the ceiling. "Ohhhhhhhh! Ohhhhhh, nooo!" Mitchell thought she was trying to escape emotionally from where she was.

He turned to his right, to Bond Rhue. The federal attorney had been watching the doctor's exchange with Fetterman, saying nothing. His look was pure business, like that of a man with things to do, waiting his turn in line. Now Mitchell noticed Rhue's sharp face, his brows knitted with concern.

"Hello, I'm Dr. Mitchell. I'm going to look and see how—"

"What percent am I burned?" Rhue said.

The question startled Mitchell, not because it was an odd question—in fact, it was the most appropriate question of all. It was just so unexpected. Bobby Mitchell never had a patient ask such a question.

"Let me look and then I'll have an idea."

Mitchell was not a burn expert, though in a stint as medical director for the West Georgia Ambulance Service and for Carroll County Fire Rescue, he'd treated burn victims and trained firefighters in initial response to these victims.

Now he lifted the burn sheet from Rhue. His legs were horrible to see, third-degree burns and tight around the tibial plateaus. *If he survives, he may lose one of his legs.* Examining Rhue's torso, Mitchell said, "It doesn't look so bad up here."

At that instant, Rhue sat up, in Mitchell's face, like a jack-in-the-box, propping himself up with one hand. He demanded to know: "What percent am I burned?"

A foot away, Sonya Fetterman was screaming; loud noises came from the crowd in the hallway. Mitchell hesitated, then told Rhue, "Well, it looks to be about fifty percent." He had underestimated Rhue's burns, though not intentionally. Burns can be difficult to gauge initially, particularly their depth. Third-degree, or full-thickness, burns are not always apparent at first. It can take hours for blood vessels to coagulate and for skin to assume the lifeless, marbled appearance of such burns.

Bond Rhue, still sitting up, said, "Fifty percent?" He had a wild, anxious look. "Then I'm going to die," he said. "There's no way a man my age can survive that." He fell back.

Mitchell wondered how Rhue had learned about burns, though he wasn't about to ask. He didn't know that Rhue once had helped found an arson investigation division in Prince George's County, Maryland, or that he had taken a deathbed confession from an arsonist burned by his own fire, or that Rhue knew the "Rule of Nines," in which areas of a victim's body are assigned nine percentage points each for calculating the severity of burns. Using another burn standard, a victim's chances for survival were measured by adding their age and the percentage of total body surface burned; if the aggregate number exceeded one hundred, the victim almost certainly would die. Rhue knew about this, too. At age fifty-six, Rhue knew the meaning of an estimated burn percentage of fifty.

"There's no reason to give up," Mitchell said, trying his best to calm Rhue. "You've got some terrible burns on your legs, but even in your fifties, I think you can survive this."

Rhue said only, "Give me something to kill the pain."

In a crowded room, four beds pushed close together, Mitchell turned to his right, to Michael Hendrix. In the field the thirty-five-year-old engineer had walked to the Jeters' home and phoned his wife from their porch. Now in the emergency room chaos, Hendrix had an air of total peace.

A young, proud Southern man once made the mistake of trying to match wits with Michael Hendrix. "So, what was it that brought you Northern liberals down here to North Carolina?" the Southerner asked. Hendrix, a Marylander on a visit, paused—timing was his forte—and then raised a brow and said, "You ever hear of missionaries?" The room erupted in laughter. Even the Southerner gave his knee an aw-shucks slap. It was vintage Michael Hendrix: calm, self-contained, understated, droll. He wasn't much for religion, God, or high formality. At twenty, Hendrix had nearly died in a motorcycle accident. He spent two years in hospitals, undergoing multiple surgeries, including a reconstruction of his left elbow. From his hospital bed, he watched TV day and night, reruns of The Beverly Hillbillies *and* Gilligan's Island. *He knew the shows' theme songs, and*

years later, with a great sense of fun, he would playfully break into song:
"The weather started getting rough, the tiny ship was tossed . . ." His
humor had first attracted Linda Agar to him. She also liked his gentle
nature, not always seen in men six-foot-three. Other big men might stand
erect with chests puffed out, using size and heft as weapons of intimidation.
Not Michael Hendrix. Linda noticed on the day they married that he stood
back a step or two, legs apart, and made himself seem shorter. A gentle
giant.

Because Hendrix was wrapped in saline sheets, Mitchell could see little of his face. The physician introduced himself, told Hendrix he wanted to assess his condition. In a quiet, calm voice, Hendrix said, "Don't worry about me. I'm okay. Just take care of them." Through bandages Mitchell detected a hint of a boyish smile.

Mitchell was speechless. He'd just handled a screaming woman and a demanding man and now . . . *this.* "Well, I'm just going to look at you," Mitchell said. With the help of a nurse he uncovered Hendrix, only to discover that Hendrix wasn't okay at all. His burns appeared the most severe he'd seen: partial- and full-thickness burns across his body, 75 percent or more, only his chest spared fully, skin sloughing everywhere. Mitchell winced. *He's a dead man!*

Astonished by Hendrix's calm in the face of his injuries, Mitchell assumed Hendrix's nerves had burned through, or he had a Herculean tolerance for pain, or he had the most remarkable manner he had ever seen. Hendrix's body temperature had fallen to 96.3, not unusual for a burn victim once the integrity of the skin has been violated. His face, burned though not disfigured, was bright red, his hair singed. His legs had blanched white.

In talking with an emergency room nurse, Hendrix had spoken not of himself, but of his wife and their young son. He wanted to be sure his family was told that he loved them.

Now Mitchell asked, "Do you need something for pain?" Hendrix shrugged, so his nurse, Nell Ashmore, said, "He's been hurting quite a bit." Mitchell prescribed morphine.

Now, once more, Bobby Mitchell turned to his right, to Robin Fech. The flight attendant had only minor burns on her hands and feet, though she had bruises everywhere. Nurses had cut away not only her blouse and bra, but her pants as well, giving the nurses a chance to try to lighten her spirits by joking, "Wow, look at Robin's pink panties!"

Hearing Fetterman's screams, Fech asked Mitchell, "Can't you make her better?" He told her he was trying his best.

Fech asked about the pilots. "How are they?" Mitchell said he didn't know but would find out for her.

Fech complained of pain in her knees, hips, and arm. Nurses helped Fech up though she could hardly stand. They rolled her away on the bed for X rays.

Mitchell returned to his other patients.

Fetterman quieted for a period, then resumed screaming.

Rhue asked again about the extent of his burns. He wanted details: How much is second-degree? How much third-degree? Mitchell told him most of the burns were deep second-degree. It was clear to Mitchell that Rhue wasn't focused on pain. He was focused on living and dying.

Hendrix, still peaceful, asked if he had a chance to survive. Bobby Mitchell believed patients had a right to know their true condition, with one caveat—he would always leave them with hope. Years before, a local roughneck had arrived in the ER, shot once in the chest and bleeding profusely. He asked, over and over, "Am I going to die?" Bobby Mitchell wasn't sure. He replied, "Well, you could. But I think the surgeon can fix you." The roughneck, sensing the worst, asked for his mother. From the waiting room, she appeared. Mitchell heard the roughneck apologize to his mother for the tenor of his life, and then saw them weeping and embracing. Later the patient died in surgery and Bobby Mitchell realized that, while his candor hadn't helped his patient, it had helped his patient's mother, allowing her an important final moment with her son. He decided then: "Patients have a right to know."

So now he said to Michael Hendrix: "Yes, sir, you're young enough that possibly you can survive, but I'm not sure."

Hendrix's voice did not waver when he said, "I thought so."

"Burn centers," Mitchell added, "can do amazing things now."

Returning from X rays, Robin Fech was rolled back into the room. Another doctor stitched a laceration by her left temple. In a moment Fech heard a soft voice, as sympathetic as any she'd ever heard. "How are you doing?" She rolled her head to the right. It was the man on the adjacent bed, Michael Hendrix.

"I'm okay," Fech said. "How are you?"

"I'm okay," Hendrix said.

At 3:45 P.M. Fetterman, Rhue, and Hendrix were taken away for transfer to the Grady Hospital burn unit in Atlanta. Fech was admitted at Tanner for observation.

Bobby Mitchell followed Bond Rhue to the door of Orthopedic Room A. He told Rhue he was doing well, that he was headed to a very good burn center and had a good chance to survive. Rhue thanked him. Mitchell thought him polite and kind.

He followed Michael Hendrix out of the room, too. Hendrix remained calm, alert. "Good luck to you, Michael," he said. Hendrix thanked him for everything he had done.

Watching him rolled out, Mitchell wondered about Michael Hendrix's inner strength. Hendrix had drawn that strength from something but . . . what was it? His faith? His family? Mitchell had a reason for wanting to know. Admiration was only a part of it. He had a more personal and selfish reason: To learn the answer might make Bobby Mitchell a better, stronger, deeper man. To react so calmly to such burns, he knew, was not basic human nature. Mitchell had a passing thought of Jesus Christ, on the cross.

More than calm, Michael Hendrix had been extraordinary.

* * *

Hours later, Bobby Mitchell was called to assist with the autopsy on Ed Gannaway. It was nearly eleven P.M. when he stepped into Tanner Medical Center's morgue.

Several pathologists were in the room. They'd already received the "Tox Box," the toxicological specimen collection kit. Pilots are tested for the presence of drugs or preexisting medical conditions that might have contributed to a crash. The Tox Box, an eighteen-inch cardboard carton reinforced with Styrofoam, contains vials for blood and tissue samples. It also has space for dry ice, used to preserve samples during shipment to the FAA's Civil Aeromedical Institute in Oklahoma City for chemical analysis.

Standing over Gannaway, Mitchell said softly, "So this is the pilot."

He stood for a moment in silence, feeling sorrow and respect. The emergency room doctor's extraordinary day, unlike any he'd ever experienced, had started with the phone call at home, followed by radio reports, flashing red and blue lights, Sonya Fetterman's wails, Bond Rhue's questions, and Michael Hendrix's peace. Now, nearly ten hours after the plane's left wing tip struck the field, here, Mitchell thought, was the man who had held that plane's yoke in his hands.

Apparently, others in the room had learned from news reports some facts about Ed Gannaway's life. Someone mentioned that he was a runner. "And he used to be in some other job and then changed and became a pilot."

Standing beside the captain, Mitchell thought about the crash victims he'd seen earlier. They'd suffered burns, yes, but hardly any significant physical traumas.

"He sure did a good job getting them down," Mitchell said. "If all the force had gone *into* that field instead of *across* the field, then . . ." Mitchell felt he was about to cry. "I mean, if that nose had come down into the ground, there would have been no way . . ." He struggled to finish the point. "The credit for those people being survivors goes to him."

Mitchell felt tightness in his own chest. *What if Ed Gannaway hadn't changed careers? Would another pilot have done as well? The decision Gannaway made years ago is what saved those lives.*

"I hope, wherever he is, that he knows that he did a good job," Mitchell said. "I wish I could tell him that."

Then Bobby Mitchell decided to do just that. He placed his right hand gently on Ed Gannaway and said, "You're the hero."

24

JUST BEFORE TWO P.M., AS BOB GRUNBECK left a bank in Bangor, Maine, and stepped into his car, five messages waited for him on his cell phone. All five were from his office at the Fairfield Inn, where he served as general manager. Irritated, he called at once: "What *the freak* is happening? I told you I'd only be gone twenty minutes."

"Jennifer's been in an accident," came the reply. "You need to call this number immediately." He took down the number of Bowdon Hospital.

He ran back into the bank and asked to use a back office. From there he phoned Bowdon. "You need to be here," a hospital coordinator told him. "Jennifer's suffered severe injuries." She was about to be transferred to a burn unit in Birmingham, Alabama. "You need to get down here *now*."

Bob Grunbeck acted quickly. He phoned his boss, Patrick Walsh, in Bar Harbor, an hour away. Walsh's father owned the company that operated hotels and resort properties and employed both Jennifer and Bob Grunbeck. "Jen's been in a plane crash," Bob Grunbeck told him. He asked Patrick Walsh to look after his son, Johnny, still at preschool, and told him he was on his way to Birmingham. "I need to get to Jen."

Jittery and afraid, his heart pounding, Grunbeck burst through the front door of the Fairfield at 2:05 P.M. and began issuing orders. The Fairfield's management was, in effect, a one-man show, and Bob Grunbeck was that man. Running a hotel meant being in command of a thousand details. Grunbeck was a troubleshooting detail man. He worked hard and often, always had. When he'd proposed marriage to Jennifer in 1990, he was so overworked he gave her a diamond in a bag. Not a ring, just a diamond. "A really nice stone," Jennifer deadpanned, "just hard to wear."

Now, thinking of Jennifer, Bob Grunbeck told his front-desk clerk, "Call Delta and get me on a plane to Boston now."

Eight hours earlier he and Johnny had dropped off Jennifer at the Bangor airport for her 6:30 A.M. flight. Now Bob Grunbeck needed to get to Boston, and then to Birmingham. He stood fifth in line at the counter of Business Express, a regional airline with a revenue-sharing agreement with Delta. Its next flight to Boston would leave in twenty minutes. Grunbeck couldn't afford to miss it. He walked to the counter, around the rope barriers, ahead of others in line. He saw their angry glares. He waited to get the attention of the young man behind the counter.

Finally the man looked up. "Please go to the back of the line," he said.

"But there's been an emergency—"

"I'll get to you," he replied. "Please go to the back of the line."

Grudgingly, Grunbeck complied even as he thought again of Jennifer. He looked at the clock on the wall. From his cell phone, he attempted to call his company's corporate office but couldn't get through. A woman in line turned and said, "You can get in front of me." He thanked her.

When his turn at the counter came at last, Grunbeck told the man behind the counter that his wife had been on a Delta plane that crashed. The Business Express agent said, "We don't show anything."

"I'm telling you my wife was on a Delta plane—"

The agent said he knew nothing of an accident; besides, the plane to Boston was full. Seething and helpless, Grunbeck booked a flight at five P.M., two hours away. He would get to Birmingham at ten P.M.

He worried that would be too late.

"I want to be on this plane right now," he demanded. "Find me someone who knows anything about what's going on." The agent left the counter. Two minutes later, he returned with a phone number for a regional airline called ASA.

Grunbeck snapped, "Put me on standby for this flight."

The Business Express agent told Grunbeck he would be number nine on the standby list for a plane that only had thirty-five seats.

Grunbeck watched passengers board the Saab-340, a propeller-driven commuter. He'd been loud and obstreperous, and knew it. He wished he had been louder and more obstreperous.

He reached ASA on his cell phone and said he was Jennifer Grunbeck's husband. "Where are you?" the ASA official in Atlanta asked.

"Bangor, Maine," Grunbeck said. "There's a Business Express plane going to Boston now, but they won't let me on it."

The ASA official said, "Hold on." Grunbeck watched the last passengers board the plane. On the ramp, he saw the propellers spin. The ASA representative, back on the line, said he was speaking to Business Express, and said, "Hold on, we haven't forgotten you."

A Business Express representative approached. "Are you Mr. Grunbeck?" He nodded. "Come with me and we'll get you on this plane."

Bangor to Boston, 201 miles, seventy excruciating minutes to wonder about Jen. Bob Grunbeck sat through the flight in what felt like a catatonic trance. Early on he apologized to the businessman sitting next to him: "I'm sorry I'm not very composed right now. My wife was just in a plane crash and I don't really know what's happening."

On a pad, Grunbeck, the detail man, took notes: things to do, people to notify, arrangements for Johnny. A passing thought: Jen and I never even drew up our wills. He put that on his to-do list.

He felt alone. Everything and everyone seemed just out of his reach, his voice an echo. Yet now he found compassion in the seat beside him, a good Samaritan, kind and understanding. "Hopefully it won't be as bad as you think," the businessman said.

At Boston's Logan Airport, no one from Delta showed up, as promised, to meet him at the gate. His new friend escorted Grunbeck down the terminal into Delta's Crown Room, a private room for frequent fliers. There he spoke to Delta officials on Grunbeck's behalf. Grunbeck, meanwhile, phoned his corporate office again: The Walsh family had shut down headquarters to focus on helping him. The Walshes were attempting to charter a plane to fly him directly from Boston to Birmingham.

Bob Grunbeck phoned Bowdon. Now, he was told, Jennifer was being transferred, not to Birmingham, but to Chattanooga's Erlanger Medical Center. His businessman friend brought Delta agents to Grunbeck and told them, just before leaving, "If this man needs a flight, use my frequent-flier points. Just get him where he needs to go." When Bob Grunbeck thanked him for caring, the man gave him his business card and said, "Let me know how it all turns out."

Boston to Atlanta, 946 miles, and two hours and fifty-five minutes more to imagine Jen, dying.

From the plane, Grunbeck used his credit card to phone Chattanooga. Jennifer's situation was dire. She wasn't expected to make it through the night. Bob's brother, David, on a business trip to Atlanta, already had arrived at Erlanger, and instructed a priest to administer last rites. Jennifer's mother was en route from Washington, D.C. The message to Bob Grunbeck: "Get here as quickly as possible."

Seeing the lights of Atlanta below, Bob Grunbeck thought of his son. *How will I explain this to Johnny?*

And then a different thought: What do you call a man whose wife has died? He knew "widow" didn't sound right.

The plane touched down in Atlanta and taxied toward the gate. Then, a strange thing: A man's soft voice, saying, "You ready?" and Bob Grunbeck, turning to the aisle, saw a flight attendant.

"What do you mean?"

"Come with me," he said.

The Delta jet stopped short of the gate. The captain's voice filled the cabin: "If everybody will please remain in their seats." The captain said a passenger with a personal emergency needed to get off the plane. The flight attendant opened the plane's door. A cart with a staircase pulled beside the plane and now Grunbeck couldn't believe his eyes. *Doug Greene, Jennifer's boss, was standing there on top of the freakin' staircase!*

"C'mon, Bob. Let's go," Greene said.

Stepping onto the landing, Grunbeck saw a car waiting below. They hurried down the stairs and into the car, and breezed past the Atlanta airport terminals.

"Where we going?" Grunbeck asked.

"I got a helicopter," Doug Greene replied. They would take this chartered helicopter 106 miles to Chattanooga.

The Walsh family had delivered, big-time.

Rising into the darkness above Atlanta, Grunbeck heard the helicopter pilot say he had taken reporters out to the ASA crash site that afternoon. "The plane broke in three pieces," he said. He said a few people had been killed, but many had survived. "You wouldn't believe it. They crashed in the back of somebody's house. It was like a cow pasture. But it looked like those pilots did one hell of a job."

"Which way is Carrollton?" Grunbeck said. The pilot pointed to the west. "That way."

Again Bob Grunbeck thought, What do you call a man whose wife has died?

An hour later at the Chattanooga airport, Grunbeck and Doug Greene climbed into an Erlanger Medical Center emergency van. They sped through the city, siren screaming, lights flashing.

At 9:45 P.M., more than seven and a half hours after he'd gotten word on his cell phone in the parking lot of a bank in Bangor, Bob Grunbeck entered Erlanger. In the burn unit waiting room, he saw his brother, David, and Jennifer's mother. "It's bad," David Grunbeck said, choking back tears, "really bad."

Bob was taken into a small room where he met Dr. Phil Craft, head of Erlanger's burn unit and a consummate pro. The doctor presented a grim prognosis. Jennifer had been burned across more than 90 percent of her body. If she had suffered *only* these burns, Craft said, her chances for survival would be about 5 percent. But her back was broken, too, which cut those chances in half. One of her lungs had collapsed and she had a problem with her liver. Given the circumstances, Craft said, he could not operate.

"So you're telling me there's not a lot to do?" Bob asked.

"We'll just sit and wait," the doctor said, "and see what happens."

Bob put on a scrub suit and walked into the burn unit ward. There he saw the reality of a grim prognosis: a young woman, nearly her entire body wrapped in bandages, eyes swollen shut, lips swollen grotesquely, a tube in her throat, her long hair singed with black particles.

How do I even know this is Jennifer?

How do I know for sure?

Bob saw small placards beside her: instructions for nurses. "Log roll only," one placard read, meaning five or six nurses would have to work together to gently turn her, while being mindful of her broken back.

Now Bob Grunbeck moved beside a young woman who didn't resemble his wife. *How do I know?* He lowered his head, next to hers. Fighting back tears, he said softly, "Jen, I'm here."

Rolling her head slightly, Jennifer Grunbeck turned to her husband's voice.

25

THE FAA COMMUNICATION CENTER contacted the National Transportation Safety Board in Washington at 1:30 P.M., thirty-seven minutes after the Brasilia's left wing struck the field. An NTSB investigation was set in motion. At his home in northern Virginia that afternoon, Hank Hughes felt the vibration of his digital pager. The number was the direct line to the Aviation Survival Factors division chief. Hughes knew what that meant—and his adrenaline surged.

Hughes was on the NTSB's aviation go-team, which rotated each Monday. That meant if a plane went down in the United States—or, for that matter, anywhere in the world, be it mountains, ocean, or plains, so long as that plane had either American certification or American-made major components—Hughes would lead the NTSB's Survival Factors Group, an investigative unit assigned to study how and why passengers and crew survived or died.

Now, following procedure, he phoned his division chief, who told him an Embraer EMB-120, with twenty-nine aboard, had gone down in a field about an hour west of Atlanta, with fatalities and survivors. Then he provided launch details: The go-team would meet at Washington's National Airport at four P.M. and fly to Atlanta on the FAA's G-4, a twelve-passenger, twin-engine Gulfstream. Quickly, Hughes packed his "go-bag." He gathered his navy blue coveralls with the Safety Board patch, his investigation notepad, and an array of tools to use at the crash site, including a hundred-foot steel measuring tape.

En route to Atlanta, go-team members received additional information about the ASA crash. His division chief even passed along one bit of news directly to Hughes: "Hank, apparently there was a friend of yours aboard the plane, someone from Loudoun, somebody you used to work with. We don't know who it is yet, or his condition."

The news startled Hughes. *Somebody I used to work with?* Crash investigations weren't supposed to be personal, especially in Survival Factors.

Survival Factors required a certain personality. Crash sites were often gory. Over the years, a few survival factors experts had been unable to cope with the human carnage.

Investigating the hardware side of a plane crash was clinical. It tested your intellect.

Survival factors tested your soul.

Hughes almost invariably investigated human suffering. Once, at a crash site near Pittsburgh, he'd seen human body parts forty feet up in the trees. He always made certain to keep an emotional distance from his work. That distance was his protective armor.

Hank Hughes had been trained in forensic science, aerospace pathology, surveying, and civil engineering. He was an ex-cop, and still a cop at heart. He knew at least a dozen members at the Loudoun County, Virginia, Sheriff's Department. Most were former colleagues from his days on the Fairfax County, Virginia, police force.

Now, as he sat aboard the Gulfstream, their names began to run through his thoughts. *Sutherland, Barton, Danbaugh, Turner, Cooper . . . Who is it? And why were they flying to Atlanta?*

He thought about Charlie Barton, his mentor and old friend. They were scheduled to lunch together next week. He knew Barton was doing fugitive retrieval at Loudoun. *That would explain why he would be traveling.* Some twenty-three years before, Barton had been Hughes's training officer at Fairfax. The rookie Hughes had admired how Barton commanded respect, even from those he locked up. As partners, they'd driven together into racially tense areas. At the James Lee apartment complex near Seven Corners, Virginia, it was as if Wyatt Earp had arrived: Doors slammed, lights went off. The strapping Barton stepped out of the patrol car and walked the grounds; Hughes stayed behind, a lump in his throat. In the early years Barton shadowed and protected Hughes, big brother–like. He'd also taught Hughes the art and science of reconstructing fatal car accidents. Hughes thought it amazing how Barton could examine an accident's aftermath, interview witnesses, take photographs and measurements, and work backward, reconstructing the whole thing. Barton had been so proud in 1985 when Hughes told him he was going to work for the NTSB. All these years later, their friendship remained deep and abiding.

Now Hughes felt a sudden sickness. *Please, don't let it be Charlie.*

Hank Hughes was forty-seven, twice divorced, from small-town Pennsylvania, hard by the Susquehanna River. Almost from the beginning, his life had been shaped by violence, war, and human suffering. He hadn't resisted any of it: Instead, he'd steeled himself and dealt with it. His father had been blown off the back of a tank while fighting in the Pacific, and spent the rest of his life in and out of VA hospitals. He died when Hughes was a boy. In 1968, a soldier himself, Hughes was a twenty-year-old interrogator of Viet Cong POWs. He did what was needed to elicit information. He wasn't proud of his methods, but he believed his work was necessary to save the lives of American GIs. He returned home in 1970, disillusioned by the war experience, and then became a cop, spending fourteen years on the Fairfax force.

At the NTSB, he had investigated accidents in all five modes covered by the board: highway, railroad, pipelines, marine, and aviation. He'd interviewed a fourteen-year-old girl disfigured by a fire that swept through a church bus struck by a drunk driver. During that interview, the girl cried while Hughes tried hard not to. He stared at his notes and blinked back his own tears.

At one jet crash site, Hughes had spent more than a day searching the wreckage with bloodhounds for a toddler who had been traveling alone on the downed flight. He finally found the small boy's corpse and carried it out in his arms.

He never lost track of his purpose: His investigative work might keep others from dying.

At a crash site, Hughes took careful measurements and documented injury-causing mechanisms and restraint systems. He examined a plane's interior configuration, its safety appliances and emergency exit options. If there were survivors, he conducted interviews to chronicle the survival elements.

As a policeman, he'd investigated death one at a time. At the NTSB, death came to him by the dozens or even hundreds. Through it all, his head filled with ghosts. But Hughes determined that if he did his job well and with total fidelity, his ghosts would be friendly.

Good ghosts, he called them.

About the same time Hughes's pager vibrated in northern Virginia, Charlie Barton asked doctors at Tanner Medical Center about Tod Thompson. He wanted to see his young partner.

Doctors allowed Thompson only to walk slowly past the open door to Barton's room.

Later in the afternoon, Barton was transferred to Grady Hospital's burn unit in Atlanta, and Thompson followed later in a Carroll County Sheriff's Department cruiser.

At Grady, Thompson asked to see Barton. He was told that only family members were granted such privileges. Thompson already was feeling as if he'd broken the unspoken lawman's code: Don't come back without your partner. He wouldn't leave Charlie, not now.

"I'm the only family he's got here," Thompson said. The hospital staff agreed to let him in.

Thompson put on a scrub suit and mask, which concealed smudges of hay field dirt on his arms and face. Entering Charlie's room, he saw his partner surrounded by doctors and nurses, an array of tubes pumping fluids into him. His charred and swollen face was like nothing Thompson had ever seen.

He was unconscious. Thompson knew death was near. The young deputy was about to be admitted to the hospital himself for overnight observation. Wanting and needing to do something before leaving, Tod Thompson called out to Charlie one last time in his thoughts: *I'm here with you, buddy.*

"You have a passenger list?"

Urgency and tension marked Hank Hughes's voice. Arriving in the darkness at a Carrollton motel where the NTSB go-team was setting up its makeshift headquarters, Hughes met a captain of the local sheriff's department. The captain had a list.

"Who were the law enforcement people on board?" Hughes asked.

The captain searched his list.

Bond Rhue, from the Department of Justice, he said.

And two deputies from Virginia: Tod Thompson and Charles Barton. *Charlie.*

The captain said Barton was at Grady Hospital in Atlanta, alive but badly burned.

Hank Hughes needed to get to Grady at once.

The go-team's organizational meeting was scheduled for 9:30 P.M., but Hughes wanted out.

He found Bob MacIntosh, the methodical NTSB veteran who would lead the Safety Board's investigation team. MacIntosh, who had piloted heavy transports during a twenty-two-year air force career, had led several high-profile investigations in his seven years at the NTSB, including those of the United Airlines crash at Sioux City and, before that, the 1988 Aloha Airlines structural failure in which the roof of a 737 suffered metal fatigue and blew off in flight, causing the death of a flight attendant.

"Mac, one of my best friends was on the airplane," Hughes told MacIntosh. "He's in Atlanta, in bad shape." Hughes said he needed to go to Barton.

MacIntosh heard Hughes say only that he knew someone on the plane who had been burned and hospitalized. In the late sixties, MacIntosh had a similar experience, investigating the crash of an Air Force T-38 that killed his next-door neighbor. Sometimes, MacIntosh knew, crash investigations got personal. In transcribing cockpit voice recorders after a crash, the NTSB, as a rule, asked the airline to supply someone who knew the pilots and their voices. Listening to their colleagues' final living moments could be excruciating, but it was, to MacIntosh, a necessary part of the process.

MacIntosh asked Hughes to remain for the meeting. This surprised Hughes, who couldn't focus, let alone reply. Never before had an investigation been so personal to him. Hughes stayed.

In the meeting, MacIntosh, as Investigator-in-Charge, discussed the rules and procedures for the investigation. Already, he announced, ASA captain Ed Gannaway and three passengers (Jim Kennedy and Lonnie and Ludie Burton) were dead. He said the investigation would include various subgroups, and listed them by name and purpose, including Aircraft Performance, Flight Data Recorder, Cockpit Voice Recorder, Survival Factors, Air Traffic Control, Maintenance Records, and Meteorology.

The NTSB was a high-profile, overworked agency with a staff of four hundred plus five board members appointed by the President of the United States. Established by Congress in 1967, the board investigated and determined the probable causes of accidents in all transportation modes, and made safety recommendations to government agencies to prevent similar accidents. NTSB investigations used the "party system," which permitted any group that might bear responsibility for a crash to participate in determining its cause; in this instance, that included representatives of ASA, Embraer, and Hamilton Standard. Typically, the different parties, each mindful, and ever fearful, of impending litigation, raised competing theories about what caused a crash and argued their points under the auspices of the NTSB.

The organizational meeting lasted more than an hour. Hughes struggled to keep focus. The local investigator from the NTSB's Atlanta office had not yet recovered the flight recorders; they remained in the wreckage. MacIntosh was instructed by headquarters to retrieve the recorders at once. He left the meeting and ventured out to the floodlit hay field after eleven P.M. to recover them.

After the organizational meeting, Hughes gathered with several members of his Survival Factors Group, which ultimately would include one official from the FAA, two each from ASA and the Air Line Pilots Association, plus three from the Association of Flight Attendants. Hughes warned that theirs was a highly sensitive and, at times, emotionally debilitating task. He could never be sure which group members would hold up to the magnitude of the human horror. At previous crash sites, he'd seen 250-pound mechanics keel over in distress while tiny flight attendants held up. "It's okay, if you'd rather not do this," Hughes told his somber group members.

He didn't start out for Atlanta until after midnight. He got lost en route and stubbornly refused to ask for directions. He would find Grady Hospital on his own. He turned what should have been a seventy-five-minute ride into a two-hour odyssey.

He kept imagining Charlie, burned.

He thought about their scheduled lunch next week. He was furious with MacIntosh, an investigator he deeply respected, and furious with himself, for not having the gall to get up and leave the Carrollton meeting.

He walked into Grady Hospital past two A.M. and identified himself as an NTSB investigator. His sense of foreboding was confirmed.

Less than an hour before, Charlie Barton had died.

Hughes thought to ask to see Charlie's body. Recording a passenger's demise, after all, was part of his job. But this time he didn't do it. He couldn't bear to see what the flames had done to Charlie.

In the darkness, Hank Hughes made the long drive back to Carrollton. For the first time in ten years in studying survival factors, he felt himself breaking inside.

He wanted off this investigation.

26

SLEEPLESS, HANK HUGHES LED HIS Survival Factors team into the hay field at six A.M. Television camera crews that had spent the night along Burwell Road (and infuriated Paul Butler by repeatedly knocking on his door to ask to use his bathroom) stirred to life. By daylight, NTSB investigators from other groups were picking through the wreckage, studying scattered plane parts and ground scars and taking a thousand measurements to aid in their reconstruction of the crash of ASA Flight 529.

Hughes walked the field, retracing the plane's path. He looked back to the V-shape notched through the pines by the Brasilia. He saw the burned-out cockpit, grass browned from fire at a radius of about thirty feet, tiny pieces of twisted metal, scratched rocks, a dead blue jay.

He thought about Charlie. He wondered what Charlie was thinking as the plane went down.

He also realized a sad irony: He would investigate Charlie Barton's death by taking an accident's aftermath, interviewing participants and witnesses and working backward, reconstructing the whole thing. No one ever did such reconstruction better than Charlie himself.

In his field investigation notebook Hughes recorded the 4 percent upgrade of the terrain. He made notations about the left wing and engine, and burn patterns in the grass. He pulled out his hundred-foot steel tape and measured the distance between the plane's last tree impact and its stopping point (490 feet). He examined the relationship and location of debris, and checked the plane's oxygen system to see if it had contributed to the postcrash fire in the cockpit area (it had). He found a small, partially opened ditty bag in the twisted metal. Inside, he recovered an ID, featuring the name and photograph of a smiling middle-aged man with a mustache: "Bond Rhue." The DOJ guy, he thought. Hughes felt a kindred sadness whenever a law enforcement man went down. Meanwhile, from behind, TV cameras caught Hughes at work, half-bent, his field notebook tucked in the back of his pants, inside his belt. (His mother, home in Pennsylvania, would tell him later, "I saw *your better half* on TV again today, Hank.")

Since the 1960s, the U.S. aviation accident rate had dropped by 85 percent even as the volume of flights doubled. Hughes also knew that in more than four of every five accidents (with either structural damage or severe injury to someone on board) people on board survived. This was due, in part, to improved emergency training methods and enhanced crash-worthiness designs of aircraft, including the use of flame-retardant materials inside passenger cabins. Hughes abided by a well-established list of three criteria to determine whether an accident, in any transportation mode, was "potentially unsurvivable":

1. If the G-load, or force of gravity, exceeds the levels of human tolerance.
2. If the vehicle's occupant compartment is deformed by more than 15 percent.
3. If the crash environment is altered by water, toxic gas, or fire.

He knew the cruelest scenario of all had played out in Paul Butler's field: Passengers and crew survived the trauma of impact only to be overcome by fire.

Hughes studied the interior of the blackened ASA cockpit. Flight crews were trained, in emergency situations, to help passengers evacuate. But seeing the small hole in the first officer's right-side window, Hughes knew this first officer hadn't helped anyone.

Somebody had made an unbelievable effort to chip out his window, Hughes thought.

He pondered Matt Warmerdam's nightmare. *That poor bastard.*

Hughes assigned other members of his Survival Factors group to interview survivors at area hospitals, though, per procedure, he would interview any member of the flight crew able to talk.

In interviews, several ASA survivors said they had heard a loud noise out on the left wing. They described seeing torn-up metal stuck against the wing's front edge. In a press conference late Tuesday, NTSB board member John Hammerschmidt said parts of the propeller assembly might have lodged against the wing. "This is something we at the NTSB have yet to encounter, if this is in fact what occurred," he said.

Guided by Ed Gray, a go-team member drew a sketch of the propeller gearbox and assembly stuck against the leading edge of Flight 529's left wing. The sketch showed one of the four blades missing. Chuck Pfisterer provided a description nearly identical to Gray's.

The go-team's initial focus became the Pratt and Whitney of Canada PW118 engine and the Hamilton Standard 14-RF-9 propeller blades on the left wing.

Investigator Gordon "Jim" Hookey, an aerospace engineer, had joined the NTSB only four months earlier. Already he'd worked on several investigations, but this represented his first on-site work. Hookey was sitting in his Washington office Monday afternoon when a colleague stuck his head in the door and said, "We got one down." As a go-team member, Hookey was to serve as an understudy for one last investigation. That plan changed quickly, though, and Hookey emerged in a key role.

At the crash site early Tuesday, Hookey and other team members found pieces of the Brasilia's left wing forty feet past the trees.

Another 120 feet away, they discovered the left propeller assembly. It contained three intact blades and a broken stub of the fourth. The missing four-foot segment of that broken blade was nowhere to be found, the first indication to the investigators that it might have broken away before impact. (Survivor interviews confirmed the loss.) The NTSB would use a computer program to calculate the likely trajectory of the blade's missing segment, and then organize a search through the targeted area.

In the field now, Hookey examined the blade stub closely. Though dusted with dirt, the surface of the fracture showed signs typical of fatigue cracking—wavy parallel lines known to material scientists as "beachmarks" because they resemble rows of sea debris left on a beach by receding surf.

The stub also yielded an important clue—embossed on the butt of the blade, a serial number: 861398. A Hamilton Standard representative watched as Hookey oversaw the removal of the stub from the assembly.

Hookey took the blade stub to a mail packaging store in Carrollton. There, he identified himself as an NTSB member, though his blue coveralls with the Safety Board patch already had made that eminently apparent. Hookey pulled out the propeller stub and said he needed it bubble-wrapped and boxed for immediate shipment. Behind the counter, the man's eyes grew wide. He wrapped the blade. "How much?" Hookey asked, pulling out his wallet. The man shook his head and said he wouldn't accept payment. He said it was the least he could do.

Hookey drove the packaged blade stub to the Atlanta airport. From there it was flown to the NTSB laboratory in Washington, arriving late Tuesday afternoon.

Even before it had been cleaned, the stub of blade 861398 was examined in the NTSB laboratory Wednesday morning with a scanning electron microscope. A layer of heavy oxide deposits was discovered along the fracture surface. Further tests of the deposits revealed the presence of chlorine.

Over the previous eighteen months, three other Hamilton Standard blades had failed in-flight, and two (those in Brazil and Canada) had been traced to chlorine-based corrosion pits in the aluminum taper bore. Those blades had separated 18.5 inches and 14.5 inches from the hub.

The ASA blade broke at a similar location—13.2 inches from the hub. Using high magnification, NTSB material scientists saw how two microscopic cracks at adjacent locations along the blade's hollow inner surface had moved and then joined to form a single crack. That crack moved first toward the face side of the blade and then fanned out circumferentially around both sides of the hollow center, causing separation.

On the inner surface extending about one and a half inches from the fracture, NTSB scientists also noted a series of sanding marks.

Soon after his appointment by MacIntosh as head of the Maintenance Records Group, Jim Hookey began his paper chase. With group members, he drove to Atlanta and Macon to study maintenance records of the Brasilia (N256AS), its two Pratt and Whitney of Canada engines, and its Hamilton Standard blades.

Hookey had a particular interest in the history of blade 861398. Maintenance records indicated that a sanding procedure had been applied to that blade thirteen months earlier, at which time two-thousandths of an inch of material was removed. The procedure required that the surface of the sanded area be restored to its original finish, though, in this case, it appeared under the microscope as if a technician had failed to do that.

Specimens cut from the blade stub also were tested in the NTSB lab for tensile strength, conductivity, and composition. All values were consistent with the required composition for the aluminum alloy used.

The NTSB recommended that the FAA require immediate ultrasonic inspection of all Hamilton Standard blades that had accumulated more than 1,250 cycles since last inspected. The FAA did just that.

* * *

Each NTSB crash investigation has its own dynamics and complexities. Some take years to complete. In others answers come more quickly. Here, in a matter of seventy-two hours, investigators already understood, scientifically, why the ASA blade had failed and Flight 529 had gone down. Once the propeller snapped in two and caused the engine's destruction, the resulting mass of metal created a parasitic drag and rendered the Brasilia's left wing a killing liability.

The key question was: After warnings as recent as the year before, how could Hamilton Standard have allowed this to happen?

Hookey noted in the paperwork that the sanding repair had been made by a Hamilton Standard technician who signed his name: "CSB."

As investigators formulated a long list of possibilities, and a longer list of questions, Hookey early on placed one question at the top of his own list: "Who is CSB?"

27

FOR CHRIS BENDER, THIS TUESDAY in August 1995 began like any other. He rose before dawn, threw on his blue jeans and Hamilton Standard signature shirt, then headed to the repair shop in Rock Hill. He preferred to complete his tedious, technical work early in the day when his concentration was sharpest. On most days he accomplished plenty even before the seven-thirty morning meeting.

In the fourteen months since Bender had held blade 861398 in his hands, much had changed for him, and *in him*. He had undergone a personal transformation of sorts—two transformations, in fact. The first was in stature. No longer a rookie in the Ham Standard shop, he'd grown into his job nicely and earned the respect of his peers and managers. He'd worked on so many propeller blade taper bores he'd lost count. A thousand? More? A nice raise, to $12.50 an hour, allowed him to buy things he once only dreamed of, even a three-bedroom house, a 1940s fixer-upper in downtown Fort Mill, five minutes from his parents. He refurbished and repainted it. Eager to pay off the mortgage (he didn't like debt), he sometimes made double monthly payments.

Bender was doing handsomely, especially after a decision he'd made in the spring. He had visited his long-term girlfriend, who had left for an international Christian missionary academy based in Tyler, Texas— Youth With A Mission (YWAM). Though their relationship was ending, he liked what he saw and felt at YWAM. He thought of becoming a missionary himself. In church one Sunday, he heard the altar call. Not since childhood had Bender stepped forward to the altar of his family's charismatic church. But he rose and moved forward, somehow a different person. He soon decided he would leave his job and go to YWAM; he would enter Bible school and then spread the word of God. In July he told his bosses at Rock Hill, though he agreed to remain until December to help train a new technician.

Chris Bender's life was on the upswing, full of hope and purpose, when he walked into the Ham Standard cafeteria for the Tuesday seven-thirty morning meeting.

He stood in the back. "Some of you may have heard the news," a manager began. A mechanic waved his hand and said he had. Chris Bender hadn't. A plane had gone down, an ASA Embraer EMB-120. Several people were dead, others hospitalized. Details were sketchy and the cause of the crash unknown, though the manager said engine failure was possible. Then Bender heard the manager say, "Blade failure is also possible."

Bender knew ASA used Hamilton Standard blades. He'd even gone to Macon once to demonstrate for ASA workers how he did inspections. He knew Rock Hill had done the overwhelming majority of maintenance on Hamilton Standard blades used in North America. He also knew: *Every blade that has been inspected internally here, I've done. What if it was one of my blades?*

Bender said nothing during the meeting. His mouth went dry. He felt himself trembling. He sensed that no one wanted to look anyone else in the eye. A plane full of people had fallen from the sky, maybe because a Hamilton Standard blade had failed. Even as shop managers reaffirmed that details were unclear, Chris Bender became more afraid that it was blade failure, and that the blade was his.

After the meeting, Bender listened as a colleague said he'd heard that engine failure had precipitated a blade's destruction, that the pilots, trying to fly on one engine, had overstressed the blade.

Later Bender learned from a colleague that a 14-RF-9 had broken and that the NTSB had learned the blade's serial number and wanted the paperwork.

That afternoon, Bender and another colleague were asked by a shop manager to examine the broken blade's in-shop paperwork. Together they opened a packet marked "861398."

As Bender reached for the blade's taper-bore inspection record, his heart pounded.

The forms showed that, after failing an initial ultrasonic inspection, the blade had been blend-repaired.

Chris Bender's eyes moved down the page.

He saw three small letters, crowded together, and a date: "CSB, 6/7/94."

His handwriting.

His blade.

Word traveled quickly. A shop manager asked Bender, "Are you okay?"

Bender nodded, though he was not okay.

"If you want to go home or take the rest of the day off . . ."

Bender shook his head. He said he only needed to go outside for a little while.

He stepped outside, to be alone. He thought about the people in the plane, wondered who they were and what it must have been like going down, and feared the crash might have been his fault. Maybe it was the engine, he reminded himself. He tried not to cry.

Mechanics comforted him. A few tried to take his mind off the crash by talking about something else. Others related air force experiences in which they'd seen mechanics cry over crashed jets. They told Chris Bender things had gotten better for those mechanics.

That night Bender returned to the solitude of his own home. He phoned his mother and younger sister to tell them what had happened. He said Hamilton Standard had told everyone not to talk about the specifics, but a few people had died in the crash, and what if it was his blade? On the phone, he wept.

Later that night, he got before God. In prayer, he asked, Why did this happen? He prayed for strength. *Please help me get through this.*

Chris Bender could not imagine what he had done wrong. But he told himself that if the fault were his, he would accept full responsibility.

28

ON THE MORNING AFTER THE CRASH, Anne Gulia needed milk and cigarettes.

It had been a long and horrible night for Jim Kennedy's youngest daughter. Her sisters Meg, Monica, and Maddy and their husbands had left her house after midnight, all in tears. Now her mother, Nancy Kennedy, was on the kitchen telephone, calling relatives and friends, breaking the news, crying each time.

Nancy Kennedy had pulled into Anne's driveway near Newtown, Connecticut, Monday afternoon at about three-thirty. She walked in and said, "Dad's been in a plane crash."

"Don't be silly, Mom," Anne said.

Nancy Kennedy had been driving along Interstate 684 toward Connecticut for a visit with her daughters and grandkids when she heard a radio report. A commuter plane, Atlanta to Gulfport, had crashed, and at least two were dead. Right away, she knew. You're married to a man for thirty-seven years and have eight children with him, and you just know: Jim Kennedy was one of the two.

Typically, Nancy Kennedy raced to Newtown on the drive from their condo in Germantown, Maryland, but after hearing this report, she lowered her speed from seventy miles per hour down to sixty, and then, pulling into the slow lane, fifty. She'd kissed Jim Kennedy that morning at the subway stop in Rockville, Maryland. They were in a hurry, as ever:

bye-bye, kiss-kiss, and he was gone. He said he would get to his Gulfport office by three-thirty, Eastern Standard Time, and added, "Call me then." Nancy Kennedy didn't want to get to Anne's before her three-thirty call.

Her mother's fright was so contagious, Anne phoned a sister living nearby and said, "Maddy, Mom's freakin' out. She thinks Dad died in a plane crash." Maddy hurried over.

They turned on the TV and saw images of the burned plane. They made calls to west Georgia hospitals: no Jim Kennedy. Meg came over. On a computer, Jim Kennedy's daughters read breaking news stories quoting west Georgia sheriffs and rescue chiefs. They phoned those officials: no news on Jim Kennedy.

Maddy said, "Mom, Dad's probably a John Doe. Maybe he was hit on the head and can't identify himself. Or he's probably helping some elderly person trapped on the plane.

"Dad's strong, Mom."

At three-thirty, Nancy Kennedy had called her husband's Gulfport office, hoping and praying he would answer. He didn't. She left a message on his answering machine: "I'm at Anne's. There's been a plane crash and I think it might have been your plane. Please call me as soon as you can."

His secretary, Millie, called shortly after.

"Millie, I don't even know if he was on that plane," Nancy Kennedy said.

But Millie replied, "Yes, Nancy, he was." Millie said that another colleague, David Schneider, was also on the flight. Schneider had just phoned and said he'd seen Jim Kennedy on the plane.

Sometime after eight P.M., seven hours after the crash, Maddy's husband, Jim, reached an airline official in Atlanta, who said one passenger's body had been left at the crash site until NTSB investigators arrived, and that it was a near certainty the body was Jim Kennedy's.

Deep into the night, Anne heard her mother on the phone calling her other siblings in New York, Oklahoma, and California and saying, again and again, "I have terrible, terrible news." Each call was more difficult than the one before. Jim Kennedy, an incorrigible tease, had kidded, "I'm omniscient, I'm omnipotent, and I'm omnipresent." Only now were his wife and eight children realizing that they had believed him.

Heading out now for milk and cigarettes, Anne pulled out of her driveway, rolled down the car window, and reached inside the mailbox. From a stack of envelopes she pulled out one with familiar handwriting—her father's. A chill passed over her. A ghostly feeling, as if the letter had come from the beyond.

Anne backed up her driveway and ran inside. "Mom!" she said, all but shouting. "Look!" As she held the letter, her hand trembled. She pointed to the Germantown, Maryland postmark.

"Oh . . . my . . . God!" Nancy Kennedy said.

Jim Kennedy often sent notes to his children. Sometimes he enclosed newspaper clippings, other times small checks.

Opening the envelope slowly, Anne found pages clipped from a magazine—Delta's *Sky* magazine—with pictures of Labrador retrievers, and other dogs, dressed in handsome clothes, looking adorable and ridiculous. Her father knew that Anne, her husband, Steve, and fourteen-month-old daughter, Gina ("Gina Beena Thumbalina," to Jim Kennedy), adored dogs, and that they had two Labs of their own, Koala and Kelly.

All night Anne had been thinking about her father, and how, during her most emotionally trying times, he had made her pain disappear. He'd simply held her close, kissed the top of her head, and said, "It's okay, puddin'."

Now Jim Kennedy's youngest daughter felt as if her father was trying to do it one more time. She wept uncontrollably as she read aloud his handwritten note:

8/18/95

Just got in

Dear Anne—

Here are a few friends that I flew in with on Delta's Dog Pound
Special From Gulfport.

Anyone you know? If not, perhaps Koala and Kelly would recognize them—

I think the canine world is about to lead us all to the "Promised
Land" on all fours!

Heard you have a great garden. How come I never get any veg-
gies?! What am I, chopped liver?

Miss you and Gina Beena and Steve. Be good to him, he works
hard for you!

Love,

Dad

It was more than a daughter could take. Her father had written it Friday, three days before the crash. Anne read it a second time, and then
once more. She searched all eighty-five words for special, or hidden,
meaning.

To his children, Jim Kennedy had been capable of anything. He could
make their dark clouds disappear, and still their troubled waters. Suddenly, reading his note, Anne became certain that her father had known
he was about to die, or that his soul had known. How else to explain the
reference to the Promised Land? *Yes, Dad was always talking about the
saints, and the afterlife, and saying that if it was his time to go, he was
ready*. The note—full of wisecracks, silliness, and love—proved to a loving, grieving daughter that, at least on a spiritual level, her father was in
command until the very end.

29

FROM HER HOSPITAL BED, in a morphine dream, Robin Fech floated to the crash site. Shouting to passengers, "Get away from the plane," she noticed a man across the field. He wore a cowboy hat and boots. He watched the plane burn. Fech stared at him. She saw him pull out a cigarette and a match. "Please, no smoking, sir," Fech pleaded. *"Please don't light that cigarette."* Too late. He lit the cigarette. Another man rolled at her feet, a passenger whose name she did not know, a man on fire. Holding her right wrist, blood rushing from her left temple, Fech screamed, "He's burning. Oh, he's burning."

Claudette Underwood heard her daughter's voice and jumped up from her cot in the Tanner Medical Center room. She saw Fech thrashing in bed, jerking at an IV tube. She shook her: "Robin. Robin."

The flight attendant awoke. "Momma, I looked at him, and he was green. *He was green, Momma.*"

Hank Hughes arrived for his interview with Fech later on Tuesday. He had asked off the investigation so he could return to Virginia with Charlie Barton's remains and attend his friend's memorial service, but he says his request was denied. Grieving and angry, he considered going AWOL. Instead, he immersed himself in the work.

When Hughes arrived at Tanner, Fech wore a hospital gown. She had bandages on her head and arm. Her lip was bruised and swollen. He chatted with her and her mother for fifteen minutes, hoping to put the flight attendant at ease.

Fech confessed a sense of loss and guilt that she hadn't done more in the field to save lives. Already five were dead: Gannaway, the Burtons, Jim Kennedy, and Charles Barton. Hughes had heard similar emotions expressed by flight attendants in other crashes.

He introduced members of his Survival Factors Team. He asked Fech if a member of the Association of Flight Attendants could participate in the interview. Though Fech wasn't an AFA member—she considered union dues just another bill—she allowed the union official in the crowded room.

The NTSB's interview format was largely standardized; questions about postcrash smoke and fire were added, when relevant. At least two Survival Factors Group members participated in each survivor interview: One asked questions, the other recorded answers. The goal was to elicit factual information. Hughes instructed his interviewers to never interrupt a subject. Each interview began: "In your own words, and in as much detail as you can remember, tell us what happened." At that point, Hughes instructed his people, "Just zip it up and listen."

Fech told the interviewers she first thought the plane had collided with another aircraft. She told of the mangled heap on the left wing, how she had pulled down the left-side shades, reseated two passengers, and demanded individual demonstrations of the brace position. Hughes had a good idea what Fech would say; he'd heard descriptions from other survivors. Fech's narrative ended with the arrival of the rescue crews.

Though she didn't tell Hughes, Fech worried that she had done something wrong in the crash. She knew that Warmerdam had been burned severely and that she was the only member of the flight crew available to be interviewed, and it made her feel vulnerable, nervous. Hughes took note of Fech's sadness and humility. She expressed concern for Warmerdam, despair over Gannaway. "Let's take a break," Hughes said several times during the interview. "No, let's just get it over with," Fech replied. They talked for more than an hour.

Hughes considered Fech one of the most heroic flight attendants he had ever interviewed. He told her, "You and your crew did a wonderful job and so many survived because of what you did." He told her that passengers had praised her performance as "spectacular" and "exemplary behavior." They said, "She was like a drill sergeant," and "You couldn't do any more than she did."

Robin Fech cried.

A day later, a Tanner physician diagnosed Fech with "acute post-traumatic stress disorder." As Fech talked with the physician about the crash, she thought of her late father. "On top of this," the physician wrote in his report, "I believe this woman [h]as some unresolved grief related to her own father's death in May."

To break the flight attendant's cycle of agitation, he prescribed high doses of sedatives.

On Thursday, three days after the crash, Fech was released from Tanner. She was among the first survivors sent home. One more reason, she thought, to feel guilty. To begin her emotional healing, a doctor suggested that Fech, on her way home, visit the crash site.

Before leaving Tanner, Fech wanted to see other passengers. Already Claudette Underwood had spoken with several. When she introduced herself as "Robin's momma," Alan Barrington, his arm in a sling, got up from his wheelchair to embrace her. In Kevin Bubier's room, Underwood heard well-wishers celebrate her daughter.

Local newspapers reported the praise of Fech. Back home in Omaha, survivor Chuck Lemay spent two hours with an NBC television crew, talking about Fech's heroism and how she had prevented a panic among passengers before impact, material for the network's nightly news show and a future newsmagazine program. The attention concerned the guilt-ridden Fech; she feared someone would resent it.

Now Underwood pushed her daughter's wheelchair toward Dawn Dumm's room.

Fech wanted to thank Dumm for the way she had urged her mother, Mary Jean Adair, to crawl from the burning fuselage.

Dumm was receiving treatment when they arrived. The flight attendant and her mother waited in the hallway.

Doctors used pins and rods to reattach Dawn Dumm's injured foot. The resulting pain was intense and unrelenting. In addition, her back had been scalded by hydraulic fluid.

Dumm's mother had been taken to the Grady Hospital burn unit. The last time Dumm had seen Mary Jean Adair, she lay near the burning fuselage, too exhausted to move. Larry Dumm, her husband, had left their two sons with his parents and driven fourteen hours from Baltimore, stopping at Grady to see Adair, before arriving at his wife's bedside at Tanner.

Mary Jean Adair wasn't convinced her daughter had survived, even as relatives insisted on it. Adair said to one relative, "I know you will tell me the truth. *Where is Dawn?*" Adair wanted proof. She wanted to hear her daughter's voice.

Julia Eason had come to see Dumm the night of the crash. Eason had left her home near the crash site to hold Dumm's hand in the field. She saw pain in the young woman's face as her husband, Elbert Eason, tended to her. Julia Eason had promised Dumm she would visit her in the hospital, and when she left home after dinner Monday, she told her husband, "Elbert, I don't know when I'll be back."

Just out of surgery that night, Dawn Dumm looked up from her bed, saw Eason's kindly face, and heard her soft voice: "Do you remember me?" Dumm smiled through the pain. "Yes, you were with me in the field."

Julia Eason spent that night in Dumm's room. She read to her from the New Testament and prayed aloud with her. She became a steady, healing presence, a candle in Dawn Dumm's darkness.

Claudette Underwood wheeled Robin Fech into Dawn Dumm's room. Fech was struck by Dumm's attractiveness, lovely dark brown hair set against her soft white skin.

But now Fech thought Dumm treated her coolly. From her bed, Dumm told Fech how she had peered out of an opening in the burning fuselage, her mother in tow, and screamed for help. She said she saw Fech standing on the other side of the wing with two men, one holding a briefcase, the other wearing only underwear. Dumm said she made eye contact with Fech.

Dumm asked: Why didn't you come back to help us?

Fech didn't remember seeing her. She didn't know what to say.

"Robin," Underwood said finally, "could you not hear them screaming?"

"Well, no," Fech replied. "There were so many screams I heard." Then, turning to Dumm, Fech said, "I guess I didn't hear you."

Fech was stunned, confused. She did not understand what she was hearing. She didn't know what to think or say. After so much praise . . . this, a confirmation of her self-doubts. She wanted to run, to get away. Her mother led her out of the room.

Several hours later, Kevin Bubier was wheeled through Tanner's front doors. Outside the media waited. Using Bubier's exit as a diversion, hospital officials escorted Fech and Underwood down a back hallway and out a side door. Stepping into a black Suburban, the flight attendant and her mother were driven to the crash site.

Some media members remained on Burwell Road, behind yellow and orange police lines. Their cameras caught Fech, hobbling with a walking crutch, her right arm in a sling. She wore dark glasses, a baseball cap, and a white terry cloth robe.

Fech walked past the cockpit. She looked at what remained of the fuselage. The plane looked not at all as she remembered it. The horror had been so large and now the plane, burned away, seemed so small.

Fech talked to no one in the field, and didn't stay long. Underwood had asked for an ambulance to drive her daughter to Athens. (Robin begged off, saying her last ambulance ride was a bad memory.) Short of that, Underwood wanted ASA to provide a limousine, something comfortable and big enough to allow Robin to recline, and also to carry home the many flowers that had come to the hospital. Her daughter needed rest and, besides, Underwood thought this was the least the regional airline could do, given what her daughter had done.

ASA produced a black stretch limo, and TV cameras caught mother and daughter leaving the field in it.

The black stretch limousine stopped at a small-town pharmacy outside of Atlanta. Underwood went inside to fill her daughter's prescriptions, while Fech rested in the backseat.

Inside, Underwood overheard a shopper talking about the ASA crash and the heroic work of the flight attendant.

The beaming mother said, "Yeah, you're talking about my daughter. *And she's sitting right out there in that limousine.*"

The shopper asked to meet Fech, and right away. Underwood escorted him to the limo. Seeing the flight attendant slumped in back, the shopper stuck out his hand and said, "We're so proud of what you did. Thank God for you." He asked if he could touch her.

Robin Fech half-smiled and shook the man's hand. When the limo pulled away, the flight attendant looked at her mother, shook her head, rolled her eyes, and said, "My number one PR agent . . ."

30

ON A LONELY COUNTRY ROAD in northern Virginia, a long line of flashing blue lights followed the hearse carrying Charles Barton. From Tod Thompson's view, the lights went on forever, from one rolling hill to the next, from Purcellville to Leesburg, far as his eyes could see.

Charlie deserves this, Thompson thought. Twenty-nine police motor-cycles and ninety police cars served as honorary escorts. Barton had become the first Loudoun officer killed in the line of duty in the county's 238 years.

A middle-school auditorium was too small for the five hundred people at the memorial service. Barton's widow, Macil, told friends she always knew that when Charlie walked out the door, he might not come back. She said he died doing what he loved, being a lawman.

Thompson felt all eyes on him, as if the room had gone dark and he stood in a white-hot spotlight. The young deputy felt certain his friends and fellow deputies blamed him for Charlie's death. At the memorial service, he heard whispers and assumed people mocked him. *How could Tod come back without Charlie?*

Thompson wanted to speak at the service about Charlie and himself, how he'd done everything he could to help in the field. Too nervous and shy to speak to the assembled mourners, Thompson instead explained to a colleague giving Charlie's eulogy what had happened following the crash, the way Charlie had taken charge in the back of the fuselage and told other passengers they had to go through the fire.

Thompson's wife, Pam, also sensed people staring at her husband. But she believed people looked at him not because he came back alone, but because he came back at all. His survival was a miracle and everyone knew it.

The young deputy took it all hard.

Just being at Charlie's memorial service shamed him.

Hank Hughes took it hard, too. He didn't make it to Charlie's service, he says, because the NTSB hierarchy had denied his request to be relieved of crash investigation duties. Hughes finished his on-site work Friday morning and released his Survival Factors team. He realized then he had come to a turning point in his professional life: He no longer respected NTSB management.

Hughes needed to be alone, so he remained in Carrollton for one more night, in his motel room, still grieving, still angry. He'd retrieved Charlie's personal effects, including his gun and badge. He intended to return those, and the honor they represented, to John Isom, the Loudoun sheriff.

So here, then, was Hank Hughes's own private memorial service for Charlie Barton: He stood at the bathroom sink of his motel room, warm water rushing over Charlie's silver badge. Hughes picked at the nylon and leather that had melted onto the badge.

For this moment, Hughes had bought a fifth of Old Crow. Charlie had always been there for him. But Hughes hadn't been there for Charlie. He'd failed to reach Charlie on his deathbed, and now he'd missed his memorial service.

He turned on the television, though he wasn't watching, and cranked up the volume so no one would hear him cursing and crying. He finished the bottle of whiskey and used his toothbrush to clean Charlie's gun and badge. He would stop scrubbing only when both shined.

31

I N MAINE, GEORGIA, AND VIRGINIA, thoughts of Jim Kennedy haunted three men who had left him behind. Even as friends and family said they had been chosen by God to survive, Kevin Bubier, Alan Barrington, and David Schneider imagined darker truths. They saw Jim Kennedy on his back inside the burning plane, semiconscious and trapped. Kennedy became a symbol to these men, a symbol of their failure, perhaps their cowardice.

At home in Waterboro, Maine, Kevin Bubier still felt Kennedy's limp hand in his own palm. Yet he didn't know if the trampled man had gotten out of the plane. Bubier didn't remember letting go of his hand. *Did I carry him out?* In nightmares he stared into a conflagration, fire surrounding him, closing in.

One night Bubier awoke in the darkness, heard his wife, Christine, and felt her loving touch, only to see the fire still. Even awake, he returned in a frenzy to the trampled man.

Before paramedics took him from the hay field, Bubier noticed in the burned grass outside the plane a white sheet covering a dead man's body.

Was this the same man whose hand he'd held?

In Roswell, Georgia, two nights after the crash, Alan Barrington sat at the kitchen table, his dinner growing cold, his wife, Beverly, on the phone across the room, agreeing once more, Yes, it is a miracle Alan survived.

Barrington thought about those who had died, people he did not know but might have saved, including Jim Kennedy. He realized the funerals were a day or two away. His thoughts transported him to grave sites. He imagined a grieving family asking, *Did you do everything you could to help save my father/my mother/my son?* He played out the sequence: He'd tried to rouse Jim Kennedy but was distracted by another passenger calling for help. In the field he'd pulled off Sonya Fetterman's flaming shorts, then used his bare hands—throwing dirt and grass—trying to suffocate flames consuming another passenger. Now, at his kitchen table, Barrington told himself, Unless you died in the attempt, you did not try hard enough. He said aloud, "I'm alive," and so the answer had to be, No, I did not do everything I could have done.

He wept. He'd accepted his own death during the plane's descent and prayed that Beverly would have the strength to raise four small children alone. But now he realized his own weakness.

He fell from his chair to the floor.

As his children slept upstairs, thankful for his existence, Barrington cried for an hour. Beverly stroked his hair and embraced him. She had never seen him like this. Her husband was not an outwardly emotional man. He was strong, self-contained. She called his mother in Texas and pressed the phone to his ear. On the kitchen floor, Barrington went quiet as he heard his mother's prayers.

Arriving at the funeral home on Main Street in Newtown, Connecticut, late Friday, David Schneider was on a mission.

When first told his colleague was dead, Schneider imagined that he had been the last person to speak with Kennedy, even if Kennedy hadn't responded. Schneider felt despair, and obligation. In coming to Kennedy's wake, Schneider would do his duty by "carrying his soul home," to his family.

He waited in a line to express condolences to Nancy Kennedy. Standing next to her, in order of birth, were her eight grown children: Kate, Gene, Clare, Meg, Monica, Maddy, Anne, and Tom. Schneider, wearing a bandage on his right hand, was struck by the size and attractiveness of the Kennedy family. Several colleagues stood with him, and Schneider was grateful for their presence, though still he felt profoundly alone.

Finally he stood before Jim Kennedy's widow. "I'm David Schneider," he said, head bowed. His voice stumbled: "I don't know if you know that I was in the plane crash?" Nancy Kennedy nodded.

"Do you want me to tell you about it?" Schneider said.

Nancy Kennedy's voice cracked. Yes, she said.

"I saw Jim," Schneider said. "I tried to pick him up." His voice choked with emotion. The Kennedy children craned their necks to listen. "'Jim. Jim Kennedy. C'mon, we've got to get out of here,'" Schneider said, recalling the moment. He heard a small explosion and screams. The fire had intensified.

"Maybe I should have tried to carry him out." Schneider shook his head as tears came. "I'm sorry. I hope he didn't die because of me."

Nancy Kennedy and David Schneider could not have known all of the facts and eyewitness accounts, or even that Jim Kennedy had risen on his own and made it outside the fuselage.

Nancy Kennedy put a hand on Schneider's shoulder. She mentioned the autopsy listing the cause of death as "thermal burns." It also reported no soot found in her husband's breathing passage. Maybe, she told Schneider, he wasn't breathing when the flames got to him.

Hearing this, David Schneider thought once more about what had transpired inside the burning fuselage: *Jim didn't blink at me. His eyes didn't move. That's why he didn't get up! He was already dead!*

Schneider felt relief. He was thankful that Kennedy had not died in anguish, and that his own inability to help had not caused his death.

He believed Jim Kennedy's soul had returned home. In the funeral home on Main Street, David Schneider felt the heavens move.

32

CHRIS BENDER TRIED TO CONCEAL HIS NERVES. Nine days after the crash, the NTSB's Propeller Maintenance Group came to Rock Hill. He shook hands with each group member: three from the Safety Board, two from ASA, and one each from Hamilton Standard, the FAA, the Air Line Pilots Association, and Embraer.

The group came to better understand the work done on blade 861398. Shop managers conducted a "walk the process" tour.

The NTSB's Jim Hookey, in charge of the maintenance records group, asked Bender to demonstrate his work on taper bores—the inspection and repair process he applied to the ASA blade as well as any new methods being used.

His demonstration lasted more than five hours.

He removed lead wool from a taper bore four different ways.

He inspected the bores of scrapped blades with a white-light borescope (as he had the ASA blade). He also used fluorescent penetrant and ultraviolet light (a newer method). Several group members took the borescope in their hands to see what Chris Bender had seen.

Bender demonstrated his sanding procedure. First, he said, he always matched the serial number on the paperwork with the number on the blade. Then he opened the *Component Maintenance Manual* to the appropriate repair and used it as his working document.

During the demonstration, Bender was peppered with questions. Hookey offered various scenarios, asking, "What would you do in this situation, Chris?" If he had any questions or uncertainty, Bender said, he always went to his shop managers.

Never, Bender said, would he make a decision on his own.

Bender also sat for a lengthy interview, as did two Rock Hill managers. In his interview, Bender talked about his initial training by Hamilton Standard. He said it took at least six weeks of borescope inspections before he felt confident he would not miss anything suspicious. He also said he had never seen a crack in a taper bore—in fact, he said he'd never seen a picture of a crack.

Hookey thought, What? How could a technician look for something he'd never seen?

If Bender found damage in a taper bore, he said, he sanded it, per instructions.

Chris Bender said that, during the tense moments at Rock Hill in spring 1994, he sometimes worked sixty hours or more in a week, though his managers never asked him to speed up his work.

Hookey spent two days at Rock Hill, impressed by Bender's working knowledge and his sincerity. Alone with the technician on the second day, Hookey asked, "Do you have any questions for me, Chris?"

Bender asked about the people in the plane.

Hookey told him what he already knew: a few had died; others were badly burned and hospitalized. Some, with minor injuries, were luckier.

Bender bowed his head. "Was it my fault?"

Hookey said he still had unanswered questions, but he believed that ASA Flight 529 had crashed because of the failure of the blade Chris Bender had worked on.

Bender stared at the floor, saying nothing.

Before leaving, Hookey thanked Bender for his patience and candor. He gave him a business card and his pager number.

"Call me, Chris," Hookey said, "if you just, you know, want to talk."

* * *

Two weeks later. An egg farmer named W. F. Stillwell drove his tractor and bush hog near Pine Hill, Alabama, thirty-five miles west of the crash site. In the tall grass beside his barbed-wire fence, Stillwell spotted a silvery piece of metal.

He got off his machine to take a look.

There he found a nearly four-foot segment of an airplane propeller blade.

He knew what it was.

Only a day before, the NTSB's high-profile search for the missing blade had been called off in the northeast corner of Randolph County, which borders Carroll County on the Alabama-Georgia line.

After falling eighteen thousand feet, the blade segment had sheared off a limb from a small cedar tree. It landed softly—so softly it had not left an indentation in the earth—and within a hundred yards of the primary search zone identified by the NTSB, an area previously canvassed by helicopter.

Stillwell had heard the warning: "If you find the blade, don't touch it." Immediately he phoned the sheriff. The blade segment was shipped to the NTSB laboratory and put to the microscope.

The findings on the taper-bore surface were familiar to NTSB investigators: heavy oxide deposits, traces of chlorine, and sanding marks.

33

THE PHONE CALL HAD TAKEN days to arrange. Finally, from intensive care in the Grady Hospital burn unit in Atlanta, Mary Jean Adair heard her daughter's voice.

Adair cried and gave thanks.

She told Dawn Dumm she had only wanted to be certain she was alive. Now she had her proof.

Adair had been told about Dumm's condition. "Why didn't you tell me about your foot?"

Dumm said, "I didn't want to upset you any more." She reassured her mother she was receiving wonderful care at Tanner.

She thanked Adair for freeing her from the fallen kitchen galley inside the burning plane.

Adair, in turn, thanked Dumm for helping her escape from the wing and the flames that scorched her.

Mother and daughter said a prayer and once more expressed their shared devotion.

In Milstadt, Illinois, Gateway Baptist Church members had been stunned to learn that the Reverend Steve Wilkinson's plane had gone down on his return from preaching trial sermons to their congregation. Burned across two-thirds of his body, Wilkinson had fallen into a coma in the Grady burn unit.

T. M. Thompson, secretary of Gateway's pastor search committee, wrote a letter to the thirty-five-year-old minister:

September 10, 1995

Dear Brother Steve,

After much prayer, discussion and seeking the guidance of the Holy Spirit, our committee has decided you are the one we wish to present to our fellowship to become our next pastor. We are all in agreement. . . . We all feel that the four sermons we have heard from you are all powerful and true messages. . . . Steve, we realize that the path to recovery that you are on is long and unpredictable and that this must and should take priority in your life right now. As a committee, we have all agreed and plan to inform our fellowship that we wish to wait for you. . . .

On September 14, twenty-four days after the crash, Michael Hendrix died at Grady Hospital. Bond Rhue, who knew how to calculate burn survival rates, died there four days later. The sixth and seventh deaths caused by the ASA crash struck Dr. Bobby Mitchell hard. Mitchell had thought often of the men since they'd left his Tanner Medical Center emergency room. Rhue knew what he was in for, Mitchell thought. He felt a personal attachment to Hendrix, and so did nurse Nell Ashmore. They'd admired Hendrix's selflessness and inner calm. Hearing of his death, Ashmore cried until she could no longer function at work, and went home.

The Reverend Steve Wilkinson was near death at Grady, too. Several years before, Wilkinson had preached a sermon about tragedy and the struggle to understand whether it was God's work or Satan's. "We can stop flattering Satan," Wilkinson said from the pulpit that day. "The sovereign God who sits on the throne of the universe is able to take even our worst experience and make it an instrument of his sovereign purpose.

God is in control." Of God's discipline, Wilkinson added, "That temporary pain will yield an eternal victory if we learn to accept it."

Steve Wilkinson had shown only one moment of awareness at Grady. He recognized his mother at his side. He squeezed her hand and smiled. Allene Wilkinson read to him a letter from the family's first minister, who wrote that he'd always known Steve would become influential in the Baptist Church. As she read the letter, her son was intubated and unable to speak, but Allene Wilkinson saw a tear move down his cheek, and she knew that he'd heard.

She spoke to him and read to him every day, but with no further sign that he heard her. On September 18, hours after Rhue's death, Steve Wilkinson, with his mother and sister at his bedside, died.

By coincidence, Dawn Dumm and Mary Jean Adair were released from Tanner and Grady hospitals on the same day, September 20. Adair was to return to her home near Pittsburgh and Dumm to Abingdon, Maryland, near Baltimore. Their family tried to arrange for the mother and daughter to depart from the same airport so they could see each other for the first time since the crash.

It didn't work out. They took separate air ambulance flights, accompanied by relatives. Adair left from Atlanta and Dumm from West Georgia Regional, the small airfield Gannaway and Warmerdam had attempted to reach.

Neither Dumm nor Adair wanted to board another plane; medication eased their anxiety. Dumm had undergone multiple surgeries on her left foot. A piece of bone was taken from her back and placed at her ankle; a muscle was transferred to her lower leg to improve circulation to her foot. Boarding the air ambulance, Dumm told the pilot, "I really have to trust you to get on this plane."

Julia and Elbert Eason stood outside the aircraft, saying their goodbyes. "There's one more open seat," Dumm told Julia Eason.

Julia Eason had visited Dumm all thirty-one days she'd been at Tanner and often spent the night in her room. Dumm was virtually the same age as Eason's own children. They'd formed a bond akin to mother-daughter.

Now, watching the jet ambulance rise over Carroll County and disappear, Eason felt mixed emotions. Though she was sad to see Dumm leave, at the same time she was ecstatic to know the young woman she had helped in the field had made it, and was going home.

In the weeks that followed, Dumm and Adair spoke every day. They talked about family, especially Lucas and Zeke, Dumm's sons, who called Adair "Mom-Mom." Dumm and Adair talked about their recoveries and also the crash experience. Adair wanted details. She was confused about what had happened in the field. "What did you do?" she asked Dumm again and again, a question invariably followed by, "And how did you do *that?*"

It was almost as if they had swapped roles: Dumm became the mother, providing answers, support, and comfort. "You took care of me, and wouldn't leave me, no matter what, even if the plane blew up," Dumm told her. "I'm really proud of you."

Dumm suffered nightmares. They had a common theme: Usually she was trapped in small space, once inside a church, another time in a hall with a stage, crushed beneath seats. She also had nightmares about her foot. In one, a doctor said he intended to cut off her toes and reattach them on the side of her foot for better balance.

September became October. Dumm and Adair discussed getting together. They weren't ready yet for travel.

By Thanksgiving they'd meet.

Christmas at the latest.

On October 14, a Saturday night, fifty-four days after the crash, Dumm phoned Adair. They'd spoken earlier in the day.

Two of Dumm's sisters were visiting Adair. They'd just finished dinner. On the phone with her sister, Dumm heard a loud thump in the background. Adair, sixty-four years old, had collapsed. A nursing aide rushed to help. So did Dumm's sisters. Paramedics arrived to take Adair to a local hospital.

Mary Jean Adair died of a heart attack. In Westmoreland County, Pennsylvania, the coroner's office later would rule that Adair's heart failure had stemmed from physical stress caused by the crash. "Even though we can't come out and say the burns caused her death . . . you have to look at the beginning, middle, and end of this," the chief deputy coroner said. "The beginning was the plane crash."

Dawn Dumm took another jet ambulance to Pennyslvania for her mother's funeral. She stayed a week in Adair's home, attended by the same nurses and sleeping in the same hospital bed Adair had used during the previous weeks.

At the funeral, Dumm, in a wheelchair, paid tribute to her mother. She had given a tribute at her father's funeral little more than a year earlier. She prayed her parents were together again, happy and content.

When we have needs, Dumm said, we should pray to them and ask for their help.

My mom was such a hero to me, she said, adding, Otherwise I would not be here in front of you today.

34

JIM HOOKEY'S INVESTIGATION DISCOVERED no reason that the taper bore of blade 861398 should have been sanded. It did not have the rough surface typical of shotpeening, and Chris Bender's own notes reported that he hadn't found any tool damage. Yet the young technician at Hamilton Standard had sanded the blade that came apart at eighteen thousand feet and put twenty-nine lives at risk.

Sanding blades was routinely done at Bender's shop, most often on blades subjected to the shotpeening process in which steel shot or glass beads are blown against the metal taper-bore surface to strengthen it. A perplexing by-product of shotpeening was an uneven surface that often caused ultrasonic inspection to report flaws. Almost always, these were only superficial irregularities that could be removed by a routine sanding of the surface area in question.

However routine sanding may have been, NTSB material scientists came to believe that Bender's sanding marks suggested the answer as to why the ASA blade broke in two. The sanding marks made by Bender's tools may have hidden a metal-fatigue crack by creating, in effect, a surface that acted as a mask.

In ultrasonic inspection, the transducer's sound wave works by reflection: It must go to the blade's smooth inner surface and come back with just as much strength as it had entering the blade. But when the wave hits a roughened surface, it is diffused, and its reflection comes back less distinctly. It's analogous to light: Light will reflect off a smooth mirror, but not off the rough surface of a badly scuffed mirror.

In October, six weeks after Hookey's first visit, he returned to Rock Hill with members of the NTSB's Propeller Maintenance Group. They interviewed Bender and his superiors with emphasis on Hamilton Standard's work in the spring of 1994, the company's crisis point when hundreds of propeller blades needed immediate inspection and repair.

Bender answered the group's questions directly. Yes, he said, he'd been instructed that sanding was the appropriate corrective action when a mechanic found roughness or peaks on the taper-bore surfaces of blades that had been shotpeened. That roughness, he said, might cause an ultrasonic rejection when it was no more than a harmless surface irregularity.

But blade 861398 had not been shotpeened. Hookey knew that. He also knew mechanics were not permitted to sand, or "blend," such a blade unless damage from tool marks was visible. And yet he'd read, in Bender's own writing, "No visible falts found, blend rejected area."

So Hookey asked Bender, "Why did you sand this blade, Chris?"

Bender said he'd been trained to do it. He said a question about sanding an unshotpeened blade had come up in the shop and, as he understood it, the answer was the same—it was permissible to sand the blade.

He admitted it was uncommon for an unshotpeened blade with no visible damage to fail an ultrasonic test. He'd seen it happen maybe ten times, and each time he had done exactly what he'd done on 861398. He'd gone in and sanded the taper bore.

One of Bender's managers told the NTSB in an interview that he was unaware in the spring of 1994 that unshotpeened blades without visible damage had failed ultrasonic tests, and that this subject "was not considered or questioned." But, the manager said, Rock Hill was pumping out hundreds of blades per month during that time and he wasn't always aware of everything that happened, and not everything was brought to his attention, even though he encouraged technicians to keep him fully apprised.

Beginning in early April 1994, and lasting for four or five months, the manager explained, Hamilton Standard headquarters had daily phone discussions with its repair shops about blade repair procedures. During this period, the Rock Hill manager said he asked headquarters if sanding was permitted to remove an ultrasonic indication in both shotpeened and unshotpeened blades. He was told that it was, confirming Bender's understanding. Even so, the manager explained to the NTSB that he never told his Rock Hill technicians they could sand unshotpeened blades without visible damage. He told Hookey's group he didn't know why Chris Bender had done it.

A fruitful day of interviews, Jim Hookey thought. It was now clear that Chris Bender was not a renegade mechanic freelancing blade repairs on his own. To the contrary, Bender was scrupulously careful and conscientious; even his managers said that.

That Bender had inappropriately applied a sanding procedure to 861398 was also clear. But his instructions were, at best, imprecise and confusing. He could not have seen a fatigue crack that had grown deep inside the blade, not with his tools or training. Bender even said that he'd had to blend some unshotpeened bores without visible damage more than once in order to make the "indication" go away.

Jim Hookey and his group members had no further questions for Chris Bender.

They had plenty for Hamilton Standard.

35

ON THE NIGHT AFTER THE CRASH, in a Chattanooga burn unit, doctors asked Bob Grunbeck if, in the most dire circumstances, he wanted to keep his wife alive by using "extreme measures" such as life support or shocking her heart.

He would ask Jen.

A tube in her throat, eyes swollen shut, her body layered in sterile burn sheets and bandages, Jennifer Grunbeck could not speak or see. On morphine, she could not even feel.

But she could hear as her husband stood by her bedside and said, "You're hurt bad, Jen. You're on the edge. Do you want the doctors to go as far as they can go?"

She heard these words glide past. She was thinking about Johnny, their four-year-old, wondering where he was.

"Do you want the doctors to do everything they are capable of doing?" Bob asked. "Do you want them to use extreme measures? Do you want to fight this, Jen, or not?"

Anyone who knew Jennifer Grunbeck knew she could dig in and make a stand. That much was made clear long ago, when she last saw her father. An only child, she lived with her mother in Florida. Her parents had split before Jennifer's second birthday. One day, a decade later, her mother told Jennifer her father was in town on business. "He's coming over." He was a big man; his presence filled their doorway. "So this is my little girl," he said with a smile. Jennifer looked up at a father she barely knew and said, curtly, "I used to be." She got up and walked out the back door, leaving her father holding his smile and a clear sense of his little girl's resolve. She was a fighter, all right, and now, grown up, she heard her husband ask, "Do you want to fight this or not, Jen?"

Just then, Bob saw a subtle movement. Jennifer moved the index finger on her right hand, ever so slightly, up and back, up and back. *Freakin' unbelievable!*

Ninety-two percent burned—certain to be dead, by Bond Rhue's formula—Jennifer Grunbeck would fight.

In the Erlanger burn unit waiting room, a nurse told Bob Grunbeck: "Mr. Reeder wants to meet you. He's in charge of this hospital."

A minute later, with an entourage of staff, Skip Reeder, president and chief executive officer of Erlanger, introduced himself, said how sorry he was about the crash, and stressed that the hospital's every resource would be made available to Bob Grunbeck and his family. Then Reeder became emotional, losing his composure. He said two of his relatives, the Burtons, "Uncle Lonnie and Aunt Ludie," had been on the plane, and since had died. But Reeder did not explain any other personal details, such as how he learned of their demise. On the afternoon of the crash, awaiting word on the Burtons' fate, Reeder had been notified that Aunt Ludie had been airlifted from the crash site, and was arriving by helicopter, at that very moment, on Erlanger's roof. ("Where are you taking me?" Ludie Burton had asked a paramedic in the helicopter. "Chattanooga," the paramedic replied. "Chattanooga?" she said. "Erlanger," he said. Just as paramedics placed an oxygen mask over her mouth, Ludie Burton said, "Skip?") Reeder had found the whole emergency room staff waiting for him outside the ER. Aunt Ludie was dead on arrival, he was told. He asked to see her. A doctor advised against it. Her burns, he said, were disfiguring. Reeder insisted: "It's my last time. I have to." When he came out, tears in his eyes, he wished he'd taken heed. Later that night,

Reeder had had another difficult moment, in Atlanta's Grady Hospital, with Uncle Lonnie. Reeder had thought surely Uncle Lonnie would survive. Though sixty-nine, Uncle Lonnie seemed so large, healthy, and formidable, Reeder imagined him living forever. But his appearance was every bit as bad as Aunt Ludie's. At his bedside, Reeder's wife, Adrienne, whispered: "He's only hanging on for Aunt Ludie, Skip. You need to tell him that she's gone but that everything is okay." Skip Reeder spoke softly. "Uncle Lonnie, Aunt Ludie is gone. She came to our hospital." Reeder's voice choked with emotion. "You don't have to worry about her. She is waiting for you on the other side." Minutes later, Skip and Adrienne Reeder were watching, and weeping, when Uncle Lonnie died.

To the Grunbecks, Reeder explained none of this. He only said he felt a powerful connection to Jennifer Grunbeck and every other person on the plane, including the copilot, Matt Warmerdam, who was in another intensive care unit room down the hall. Reeder said he would be out of town for the next two weeks to attend the Burtons' funeral and take care of family affairs. He offered Bob Grunbeck his home on nearby Signal Mountain.

Before leaving, Reeder called for everyone in the waiting room, family and staff, to hold hands and bow their heads. They formed a circle and Reeder led them in prayer.

By early Wednesday morning, Bob Grunbeck had not slept for nearly two days. Marlboro Lights had turned his fingertips orange. He'd paced the hallway outside Jennifer's room so many times, he'd started counting floor tiles—there were thirteen, every time thirteen.

Bob Grunbeck hailed from a large working-class Catholic family, the fifth of nine children. It was a tightly knit family, a far cry from Jennifer's in her formative years. Already his three older brothers had arrived at Erlanger. His sister Ann was formulating family hospital shifts on a calendar, while his parents, back in Connecticut, took care of Johnny.

In the wee hours of Wednesday morning, Jennifer's oxygen level and blood pressure plummeted. Nurses had allowed Bob to stay in her room, but now they asked him to leave. One nurse told him the situation was severe.

Bob paced the hallway, counting tiles, smoking, sipping coffee, putting more quarters in the vending machine, praying. In a few hours, he awakened his brothers. "It doesn't look good," he said.

"What should we do, Bobby?"

He took a deep breath and told them to plan for the worst.

They started to arrange Jennifer's funeral.

Bob had never thought about where his wife might be buried. He went to the waiting room to discuss it with Jen's mother; she deferred to him. He decided Jennifer would be buried in Northford, Connecticut, his hometown. His brothers, Danny, John, and David, addressed the details. They set up flights and arranged for a plot at the family cemetery.

Then, early that afternoon, a nurse burst out of Jennifer's room, excited. "Jennifer's bouncing back," she shouted.

Bob buried his face in his hands and wept. He spent the next hour by Jennifer's side. He knew he needed to learn more now about the burn experience; nurses gave him reading material. Barring major complications, a burn victim can expect to stay, on average, one day in a hospital for every percentage point of body surface burned. This would be a long haul.

With his brothers, Bob checked into a nearby hotel that afternoon, took a shower, and got some rest.

Though she couldn't talk, everyone in the family knew what Jennifer was thinking—she was thinking about Johnny. He was still in Connecticut, and no one had told him about the crash, a fact that began to weigh heavily on his father.

Bob knew he needed to give Jennifer a sense of Johnny's presence in her room. A photograph would do it. A picture of Johnny would serve as a ray of hope, a reminder that her son was waiting back home.

In New England, his sister-in-law 'Berta Grunbeck remembered a picture she and her husband, David, had taken the previous weekend, Johnny sitting on a rock wall on the 1,530-foot summit of Cadillac Mountain. A towhead and all boy, in his shorts and sneakers, Johnny had been leaping from one rock to another, no time to stop. Finally 'Berta and David got him to sit on the wall, like a four-year-old king upon his throne. In the backdrop Maine's rocky coast looked heavenly: an azure August sky caressing Cadillac Mountain, the first place the sun rises each day over America. As soon as the camera shutter whirred, 'Berta and David knew their picture was a beauty, Maine's coast and Johnny at their best, a great picture for Bob and Jennifer to use for a Christmas card or perhaps some other special occasion. Now 'Berta developed the film and Johnny looked every bit as wonderful as she remembered. She enlarged the photograph, big as a poster, and shipped it to Erlanger, via overnight mail.

Bob placed the poster in Jennifer's room. When she opened her eyes days later, the first thing she saw was Johnny.

Each time nurses turned Jennifer, Bob moved the poster, placing it where she could see it best.

During the first few days, burn victims receive inordinate amounts of fluid to restore evaporative losses that have seeped from their burns. Jennifer Grunbeck's weight, normally 135 pounds, soared toward 200. Her burns were cleaned daily, her saline dressings changed. But Grunbeck was only twenty-eight, and youth was her ally. Dr. Andrew Munster, a leading burn specialist at the Baltimore Regional Burn Center, has written that, among burn victims, aging begins at thirty-five. A 30 percent burn for an eighty-year-old victim, Munster has written, is as life threatening as an 80 percent burn in a twenty-year-old.

A week after the crash, Dr. Craft oversaw the skin grafting process for Grunbeck and also Warmerdam, who was 42 percent burned. Burned areas must be covered with new skin to prevent infection and to limit scarring. In the initial procedure, doctors removed slivers of healthy, unburned skin from Grunbeck's head and attached it, using staples, to other areas destroyed by burns.

Since she was 92 percent burned, the majority of it third degree, Grunbeck did not have sufficient skin graft donor sites of her own. So over time Erlanger doctors would remove small pieces of healthy skin from Grunbeck and send them to a laboratory in Cambridge, Massachusetts, where skin cultures were grown in layers in petri dishes. Such skin cultures are fragile and expensive and need three weeks to grow. They possess one distinct advantage: Since they are grown from the patient's own skin, they won't be rejected by the body.

Burn treatment is a long and, at times, excruciating process: the removal of staples, the horrific pain from baths and twice-a-day debridement when dead skin, old creams, and secretions are excised from burn wounds, the seemingly ineradicable soreness and itching, the strain of physical therapy, the failure of pain pills, the loneliness of the struggle. The process tore at the will of burn victim Mary Ellen Ton, who, in *The Flames Shall Not Consume You,* wrote, "Death became very alluring—quite beautiful, in fact, when seen as an escape from pain."

As Jennifer Grunbeck underwent her first grafting, Johnny was en route to Chattanooga. Bob wasn't sure how to break the news to a four-year-old. He counseled with a pediatric psychologist at the hospital, who advised that he not tell Johnny too much, that he leave room for the boy to create his own sense of what happened, that he allow him to ask questions, and that he ask Johnny why he had asked certain questions, in case there were underlying issues. Above all, Bob Grunbeck was to reassure him.

The father was nervous when he sat down with Johnny in their Chattanooga hotel room.

Mommy's airplane had an accident, he began. And Mommy was hurt really bad.

How bad? Johnny asked.

There was fire and she got burned, he said.

Johnny remembered the lesson from firefighters visiting his preschool and asked, Did Mommy remember to stop, drop, and roll?

Bob smiled: Yes, she did. And you telling her that probably saved her life.

Can I see Mommy?

No.

Why not?

Hospital rules.

Father and son sat together for some time.

You need to be strong, Johnny. And so do I. And I will be here for you, okay?

Bob already had made up his mind: They were going to take this on as a family, and he, Jennifer, and Johnny were going to win. Still, matters weren't made any easier the next morning when he spotted an article in a Chattanooga newspaper. It quoted Dr. Craft talking about Jennifer, saying, "We do ask for divine intervention and we need it."

Bob placed Johnny in a preschool in Chattanooga. His sister Ann wrote notes each day about what Johnny did and said; her reports were read aloud to Jennifer. By now the Grunbecks were a team. Ann devised a schedule so two family members were always on hand to help Bob. Bob's parents, siblings, brothers-in-law, and sisters-in-law used vacation time to come to Erlanger.

Two weeks after the crash, the Reverend Gus Koch came to Chattanooga. In blue jeans and a leather jacket, he rode up from Carrollton on his motorcycle. He didn't see Jennifer at Erlanger, though he shared dinner with the Grunbecks. He told his narrative about the hay field, and how Jennifer talked about Johnny and his love for hot dogs and macaroni and cheese. He told them how courageous Jennifer was, for kicking her way off that plane. There wasn't a dry eye at the table.

Out in the burn unit waiting room, Bob Grunbeck met Amy Warmer-dam. They saw each other every day, sometimes read medical reports together. Bob even tried to help her learn to play Game Boy.

Robin Fech and her boyfriend, the ASA mechanic Chris Price, visited Erlanger six weeks after the crash. Amy Warmerdam allowed them into Matt's room. They barely recognized him. His face had swollen from water retention; his hands were bandaged; his entire left side was burned to the crown of his head; his left ear had been virtually seared off.

Fech sat at his bed and asked to touch him. Warmerdam said yes. She put her arm on his.

Medicated, Warmerdam asked Price what caused the crash. Price sensed the first officer couldn't tell if the crash somehow had been his fault, or if he and Gannaway had done everything just right. Price reassured him that they had done excellent work, and that everyone knew that.

When Jennifer Grunbeck spoke her first words in late October—"I want to see Johnny," she said—Skip Reeder learned about it within minutes. He rushed down to the Erlanger burn unit, where the staff was giddy and using the word *miracle*.

But doctors wouldn't allow her to see Johnny, for fear of infection.

Johnny had asked for Jennifer, too. He couldn't sleep one night. He told his father, "I want that song that puts me to sleep." Bob raised an eyebrow. "You know," Johnny said, "the song that Mommy sings to put me to sleep." Because he had no idea what Johnny was talking about, that prompted a deeper realization: He'd been working too much, and needed to be home more.

At the hospital the next day, he asked Jennifer about it.

"'Keep on Singing' by Helen Reddy," she told him. "It's in the CD player. It's track nine."

Only Jennifer could answer her son's question and put an end to his doubts.

Johnny's request convinced Bob that his son wasn't certain his mother was alive.

Jennifer experienced crash nightmares. "Extreme dreams," Bob termed them. Usually they occurred during her first hour of sleep, and for a time they moved in sequence, starting each night at the precise point at which the previous night's dream had ended, and advancing, like a movie, a few frames. The intensity of the dreams scared her husband: As Jennifer dreamed of smoke, she coughed heavily; as she dreamed of escaping the burning plane, she kicked and thrashed about. He tried to calm her by asking questions that penetrated her sleep.

"What's happening, Jen?"

In a semi-dream state, she told him a woman had put out her flames and was rescuing her. The woman was carrying her out of the fuselage, along the wing, and then laying her gently in the soft grass.

"Who is she?"

Jennifer saw an older woman, gray-haired, strong, devoted, and loving.

"Who is she, Jen?" Bob asked.

"Nana," Jennifer said.

Nana? Never had Bob heard his wife speak this name. Later he asked Jennifer's mother, "Who is Nana?"

The question surprised her: "What do you mean, 'Who is Nana?'" Jennifer's mother explained that Nana was her own mother—Jennifer's grandmother. Nana had stayed with them briefly when Jennifer was a second grader. Unable to care for herself, Nana was placed in a nursing home, and later died.

An old restored picture of Nana had been on the living-room wall throughout Jennifer's childhood.

How remarkable, they thought, that Nana returned to Jennifer now, and in such a meaningful way.

The mother-son requests were piling up. After more than two months apart, Jennifer and Johnny desperately wanted to see each other. The picture of Johnny from Cadillac Mountain was no longer sufficient. Doctors held the line, though, insisting Jennifer had come too far to risk a setback. Jennifer received new skin grafts every ten days. Her body, meanwhile, produced too much calcium; the resulting condition, known as heterotopic ossification, caused her elbows to lock.

In November, Bob came up with a plan. In a Thanksgiving fund-raiser, Johnny's preschool had collected nearly sixty dollars. Several students would present the money to a charity in a televised ceremony at a local supermarket. Bob talked to the preschool director. He asked if Johnny could be a presenter. He said he didn't want Johnny's name mentioned. He only wanted Jennifer to have a chance to see him. In return, Bob said he would contribute five hundred dollars. The preschool director agreed.

At the prescribed hour, Bob walked into Jennifer's room. "Turn on the TV, quick," he said. "Johnny's going to be on."

"What?!"

"Don't worry," Bob said with a smile. "Just watch."

Nurses filled the room. In a moment, Johnny appeared on the burn unit TV screen, with two classmates by his side. He was dressed as a Native American. He wore a paper vest and a single feather on his head.

Tears welled in his mother's eyes. Jennifer said, "He looks so different and so . . . old!"

No longer a picture on the wall, Johnny had advanced into a moving image. He was on the screen, giggling and talking with his little friends. Bob's plan had worked, but only to a point. It produced an unexpected result: "I need to see him *now*," Jennifer said.

"You can't," a nurse answered.

"'No,'" Jennifer replied firmly, "is no longer an option."

"But he could have a cold—"

"Then cap-and-gown him," she said. "Or put me in a bed on wheels and wheel me out. You either get him in here or get me out there. I *need* to see him."

A nurse walked into Jennifer's room on Thanksgiving Day and told her Matt Warmerdam was being wheeled down the hallway and had asked to say a quick hello.

"Well, if he's going by, sure," she said.

Nurses pushed Warmerdam's bed into the room, placing his head close to her.

"Hi, I'm Matt, your copilot," he said, managing a small smile.

The last time she'd heard his voice, Flight 529 climbed toward thirteen thousand feet and he'd said, "Ladies and gentlemen, good afternoon. Welcome aboard Atlantic Southeast Airlines . . ."

Warmerdam didn't look at all as she had imagined. He'd nearly died during the first weeks at Erlanger. Potentially fatal infections threatened him. His weight plummeted from 208 to 139. One week he went off the ventilator, but his lung collapsed the next week, and so he went back on the ventilator. To his wife, Amy, his recovery then seemed minute to minute. But he was stabilized now. Warmerdam's face was full and heavy, undoubtedly from fluids, and he appeared so young. Grunbeck figured a pilot would be much older.

"You guys did a hell of a job, from what I've been told, with what you were given," she told him. "Thank you."

"I'm sorry I couldn't have done more," Warmerdam said.

"It wasn't your fault," Jennifer replied.

"I guess we both have a lot to be thankful for," she added.

Warmerdam nodded and said, "Yeah."

In a few moments, nurses wheeled him back out into the hallway.

Bob arranged for Johnny to visit Jennifer. First he counseled with an Erlanger psychologist about the variables. The Grunbecks had spent nearly ninety days at Erlanger and there was talk that Jennifer might soon be released. He knew that a major setback for her, or for Johnny, would be devastating. The psychologist agreed the meeting carried risk. "Johnny may go running from the room," the psychologist said, "and Jennifer may plummet."

Bob cleared out Jennifer's room, removing even her bed. He sat his wife in a reclining chair in the middle of the room and placed another chair beside her, for Johnny. Jennifer could not move her arms, which remained locked at the elbows. More than five hundred get-well cards, and several pictures of Johnny, were taped to the walls. Someone had sent Jennifer a blue teddy bear, and Bob suggested she give it to Johnny as a gift.

Bob had told Johnny, "Mommy's in rough shape, but she really wants to see you. Mommy looks different now. You might not recognize her. She has no hair, lots of bandages, and she can't move a whole lot. She's just beginning to talk. But trust me, it is Mom, and she really wants to see you."

He helped Johnny into a scrub suit—an adult's, much too big—and placed a mask over his mouth. Only his eyes were visible.

Bob led him into the room. Johnny did not make eye contact with his mother. He walked toward her, then past her, to the window.

Jennifer was crying. Happy to see him, she was also afraid that her son wouldn't look at her.

"Johnny, come over here and sit down in my lap," Bob said. "We need to talk to Mom."

Johnny didn't move. "Come on over here," Bob said. The boy sat in his father's lap.

Jennifer told him she had been keeping up with his progress in school (thanks to Ann Grunbeck's notes). "Have you eaten any vegetables the last three months?" Jennifer asked.

"No, hardly any. Grammy's been making me eat grilled cheese," Johnny said, still not making eye contact.

She said, "Aunt 'Berta's been telling me different." And he nodded and said, "Yeah, Aunt 'Berta makes me eat vegetables."

She gave Johnny the blue teddy bear and the boy looked up at her. Suddenly something clicked. He stared into her teary eyes and said, "It really is you, Mommy. I can tell by your eyes."

She wanted to see Johnny's face. She asked him to take off his mask and then his cap. Bob helped remove them. Johnny had never looked so gorgeous, so perfect.

Jennifer wanted to hold him but couldn't because of her locked elbows. Johnny approached her. He reached out and touched her hand, gently. He stroked her fingers, moving over the knuckles and down to the tips. Jennifer Grunbeck watched her boy. This was the moment she had lived for.

Part VII

The Value of a Human Life

36

IN MISSISSIPPI, HOURS AFTER THE CRASH, Renee Chapman's godmother, Vivian Rigby, phoned an attorney friend. She told him what had happened and said Chapman was laid up in a west Georgia hospital. "You call that hospital, find that child, and bring her home now," the attorney said, his voice urgent. "And tell her to stay away from ministers. They won't be ministers. They'll be runners for some attorney or an insurance company." This sounded preposterous to Rigby, but her attorney friend's concern had precedent. In 1987, after Northwest Airlines Flight 255 crashed in Detroit, killing 156, a man posing as a Roman Catholic priest, wearing a cleric's collar and carrying a Bible (albeit a Protestant edition), comforted victims' grieving families. After gaining their confidence, he reportedly solicited them as clients for a Florida attorney. Rigby phoned Tanner Medical Center and told Chapman to stay away from ministers. Chapman said two ministers already were in her hospital room. They'd offered to drive her home to Mississippi, a six-hour trip. "Don't go with them," Rigby warned. She told Chapman her mother already was bound for Carrollton.

Nancy Kennedy arrived from Washington a day after the crash to claim her husband's body. At the Atlanta airport, she was ushered into a room. A man entered, said he was from AIG Aviation, a member of American International Group Inc. (AIG), the global insurance giant. He expressed condolences. Nancy Kennedy thought him compassionate and genuine. Then she heard him ask, "How much did Mr. Kennedy earn a year?" She replied, as if talking to a friend: "He was making six figures." He asked several more questions, which Mrs. Kennedy considered impertinent and intrusive. She'd been a widow for twenty-four hours after thirty-seven years of marriage to a man who had just died by fire. She felt victimized. This is dirty pool, she thought. Nancy Kennedy, well-read, Fordham graduate, good Catholic, mother of eight, grandmother of eight, didn't like the man or his work. Rising above it all, she took his business card and held her emotions in check.

Linda Agar-Hendrix also arrived in Atlanta on Tuesday. Her husband, Mike, burned across most of his body, was in intensive care in Grady Hospital's burn unit, his survival uncertain. While she was en route to Grady, her car suffered a flat tire. She finally made it to the hospital, where she saw her husband bloated by fluid resuscitation. Escorted into a hospital conference room, surrounded by people she didn't know, she heard all of them talking to her simultaneously, a clutter of voices. She asked an ASA representative, "Why did the plane crash? What happened?" No one knew yet, came the reply. The clamor of voices continued. Agar-Hendrix said, "Who are you? Who do you represent?" A man said, "AIG," to her an unknown acronym. She asked him several questions more and learned AIG Aviation was the airline's insurer. He wanted to meet with her, alone, to talk. She asked everyone around her, "Give me your cards, *please.*" A woman pulled her aside, out of the room, away from the clutter of voices, into a quiet place. There the woman, a hospital chaplain, told Linda Agar-Hendrix, "You can scream in here if you want."

* * *

David McCorkell had met an AIG Aviation representative on the porch of the Bowdon hospital within the first two hours after the crash. He was offended by his presence so soon, though the man seemed tactful enough. McCorkell returned home to Minnesota determined to keep his life from disruption. He made his previously scheduled business trip on September 3, flying to Montreal. Another AIG Aviation representative phoned him in Montreal and offered to fly to Canada to meet with him. McCorkell put him off, but the man was persistent. McCorkell agreed to a meeting at the Minneapolis–St. Paul airport upon his return. At the airport, the AIG Aviation representative offered him $35,000 to sign a piece of paper that would keep him from filing a lawsuit over the crash. McCorkell wondered, Is this normal? Is this right? To him, $35,000 seemed a lot of money just for being in a plane crash. Besides, McCorkell wasn't assessing blame. It wasn't his nature. Accidents, after all, happened. But to a thirty-seven-year-old computer trainer for a grocery chain, $35,000 was nearly a year's take-home pay. He thought to sign but wavered. Everything he'd gotten in his life, McCorkell told himself, he had earned. Suddenly the offer rose to $40,000. These were numbers McCorkell had never known. He realized AIG Aviation was willing to spend a lot of money. The two men talked for an hour. McCorkell did not sign. Later he spoke with Jason Aleshire, who told him about an attorney he'd hired in L.A. McCorkell hired him, too.

The first lawsuit from ASA 529 was filed ten days after the crash in U.S. District Court in Houston, on behalf of Sonya Fetterman, intubated in Grady Hospital's burn unit. Fetterman's suit against ASA, Delta, Embraer, Hamilton Standard, and its parent corporation, United Technologies Corporation, charged gross negligence and sought $135 million in damages. Reading a newspaper report of the suit, Dr. Bobby Mitchell recalled Fetterman's emergency room wails and thought, My God, if anyone has suffered, it's Sonya Fetterman. Fetterman's husband and three children were listed as co-plaintiffs.

In airline crashes the true defendants are the airline's insurers. After a crash, insurers take the lead in contacting victims and their families, often providing money to meet their immediate needs, such as travel and lodging. But in previous airline disasters insurers also attempted to contact "walk-away" crash survivors in hopes of settling claims quickly and limiting exposure to liability. Almost immediately after a crash, airline insurers set up individual files for those aboard the downed plane. After the 1987 crash in Detroit of Northwest Flight 255, plaintiffs' attorneys placed ads in local newspapers warning families of crash victims to be wary of airline insurers: "While it may seem that they can offer you comfort or assistance, you must be aware that they do so for reasons of their own self-interest—not yours."

Plaintiffs' attorneys have been every bit as quick to seize upon aviation crashes, and sometimes quicker. (After the 1985 crash of Delta Flight 191, a newspaper cartoonist depicted them as vultures from the law firm of "Pickem, Pickem, Scavage and Bones.") In representing crash victims and their families, plaintiffs' attorneys look to file suit in a court whose laws on recoverable damages and liability seem most advantageous to their client. Over time, they will identify fact witnesses (to describe the circumstances of the crash), as well as expert witnesses (to address either mechanical aspects that define liability or medical issues for which a plaintiff seeks damages). They'll create damages brochures, or demands, placing a monetary value on their client's life. In so doing, they'll employ an economist or actuary to analyze the present value of their client's lost future earnings. They'll also seek damages for their client's shattered family life, pain, and suffering. Some will present demands to the insurer in several pages, others in several hundred pages. A maimed or badly burned survivor stands to receive a larger settlement than the family of someone killed in a crash because the survivor's suffering and medical bills will continue. Insurers also know that a courtroom appearance by a maimed or burned survivor has a profound effect on a jury.

Plaintiffs' attorney John Greaves, whose firm represented five ASA survivors (Aleshire, Barrington, Bubier, Brumfield, McCorkell), says, "It's all very crass, but we can't bring people's lives back. All that the law allows is for money to be paid, so that's what we do."

Ascribing monetary values to human lives is a drama in its own right. Says Greaves, "Take a man at forty, doing as well as he can, a $35,000-a-year guy, with a wife and three kids. He spends all his time with them. He takes them hunting and fishing and gives them life skills and advice. Now take the executive who is never home and makes a million dollars a year but doesn't spend time with his wife and kids. With the first person you'd focus [the damages brochure] on noneconomic loss and his value to family; with the second you'd focus on the economic loss. But who is to say whether the loss to the lower-earning man is less? What's his death worth to his kids?"

Few lawsuits resulting from airline crashes go to trial. After intensive investigations, crash liability usually is uncontested. The issue for trial becomes damages. Defendants in air crashes tend to be risk-averse. Airlines would rather not have their names dragged through a long public trial. Furthermore, air crash trials present Herculean challenges for defense attorneys, who must convince jurors to look beyond the natural sympathy for victims to issues of liability. Defense attorneys will attempt to personalize their corporate client and remind jurors that a corporation is but a collection of people, and therefore entitled to fair consideration.

In the matter of ASA 529, United Technologies/Hamilton Standard retained Mark Dombroff of Dombroff & Gilmore. Glib, talented, and blunt as a bludgeon, Dombroff had spent fifteen years (1970 to 1985) heading a U.S. Department of Justice section that defended civil suits against the government, before moving to the private sector. He counted several major U.S. airlines among his clients. If the ASA 529 case went to trial, it would be Dombroff's to try. Until then, the firm's day-to-day attorney on the case would be Jonathan Stern. A licensed pilot and former air traffic controller at Washington National Airport, Stern, thirty-six, had worked briefly for Dombroff at DOJ and later joined him in private practice. Stern had left Dombroff to form his own firm in 1994, but Dombroff brought him back in October 1995, specifically to handle the ASA matter.

Stern attended each of more than two dozen liability depositions. He logged sixty-five thousand air miles in the first year, interviewing Hamilton Standard employees and former employees, from Connecticut to California to Rock Hill. He followed the trail of paper, and the trail of Hamilton Standard people, seeking to understand everything and everyone who had anything to do with the 14-RF-9 blade, 861398.

Jennifer Grunbeck, in mid-November 1995, wasn't interested in hiring an attorney. She didn't want to see anyone or talk to anyone. But her sister-in-law, Ann Grunbeck, a lawyer herself, was insistent: "You need to do this." Ann thought it imperative to hire an attorney before Jennifer was released from Erlanger. That way, she thought, the attorney would have an easier time gaining access to Jennifer's hospital records.

"This is about Jennifer and what happened to her. It's not about anything else," Bob advised his sister early in the attorney selection process.

Ann Grunbeck did her research, phoning noted plaintiffs' attorneys. She produced ten prospects, then whittled the list to three. She arranged for all three to come to Chattanooga, one at a time, on three consecutive days. Each would have dinner with Ann and her brother David. Ground rules would be established for their meeting the following day with Bob and Jennifer.

Two of the attorneys, in suits and ties, showed up at Erlanger at the prescribed times, accompanied by several colleagues. To Jennifer, these groups seemed like entourages. In their separate presentations, the two attorneys talked about their qualifications, the legal victories they, and their firms, had scored, and their proposed strategies for the Grunbecks.

Both talked settlement. One said he knew the insurers personally and projected a $30 million settlement within thirty days. The other made no predictions, only that "You'll never have to worry again." (Hearing this from her wheelchair, Jennifer thought, I'm pretty sure I will have to worry again.) Bob sensed both attorneys addressing their pitches primarily to him, Ann, and David, not to Jennifer. He saw one turn his back to Jennifer, and it offended him.

The third attorney was different. Mich Baumeister dressed casually. He came alone. He made no mention of a settlement; he said only that he would take Jennifer's case to court, if she wanted. "But you're just getting out of ICU," Baumeister said. "This isn't the right time for you to make that decision." He talked directly to Jennifer.

Mich (pronounced MITCH) Baumeister liked to describe himself as an "in-your-face New York attorney," an underdog fighting for "the little guy." Raised in the city, his father a fireman, Baumeister came of age during the sixties and fused that decade's social fervor with his own Gotham-styled resourcefulness and grit. He'd come home from Vietnam in 1969 and gone to law school at Seton Hall, on the GI bill. For a time, he worked for Kriendler & Kriendler, arguably the granddaddy of all plaintiff firms in aviation law. He toiled in the background in those early years, preparing cases, but his ambition and ego demanded more. He wanted to be out front as a trial lawyer, so in 1976 he took a 50 percent pay cut to work as a prosecutor for Robert Morgenthau in the Manhattan District Attorney's office. There Baumeister did it all: He tried assaults, rapes, murders, and usually won. He moved in 1978 to the U.S. Attorney's office in New York, trying white-collar cases, including securities fraud.

He returned to Kriendler in 1980. When the firm split, Baumeister cut out on his own. In 1988 he reconfigured his own firm to create Baumeister and Samuels, with offices in Morristown, New Jersey, and New York. (Bob Grunbeck asked, "Who is Samuels?" and Baumeister's answer surprised him: "My wife," tax attorney Lynn Samuels.)

In 1992, Baumeister had been one of the six attorneys in the Pan Am 103 trial who proved that airline guilty of "willful misconduct" in failing to discover a terrorist bomb placed aboard its 747 jetliner, London to New York, in December 1988. Pan Am had failed to match luggage with individual passengers. The bomb that exploded over Lockerbie, Scotland, and killed 270 people was hidden in a Toshiba radio inside a bag that didn't belong to a passenger. In that trial, Baumeister cross-examined Pan Am's chairman, Thomas Plaskett; he worked with the enthusiasm of a mastiff that had come upon a soup bone. He sensed Plaskett being defiant on the witness stand, taking him on. Okay, Baumeister told himself, all bets are off. Baumeister slammed down one of his props—a dictionary— on his podium. Then, his voice rising, his tone and his questions combative, Baumeister used his leg for leverage, steadily inching the podium closer, closer, closer to Plaskett. "Counsel has got . . . the podium . . . halfway up to the jury box, and he's practically in the witness's face," the defense attorney charged. At the judge's instruction, Baumeister moved the podium back. Then, minutes later, facing his witness anew, Baumeister pushed the podium forward again as the defense attorney roared, "There he goes again!" Replied Baumeister, "Just a nervous habit." Said the judge, "Move it backwards." It was vintage, New York in-your-face Mich Baumeister.

When Baumeister told the Grunbecks he'd represented victims in the Pan Am 103 case, it struck a chord with Jennifer. She had a friend who had lost someone close in that crash. She also appreciated that Baumeister stayed in touch with that family as well as with other past clients. To her, he seemed less businesslike, more personal, than the other attorneys.

Baumeister noticed Jennifer's wide, sympathetic eyes. Her head had been shaved, her hair only beginning to grow back, and her body was covered in bandages. Baumeister marveled at her resilience and sense of humor. He decided during this first meeting that the triggering-damages event wasn't merely Jennifer. Rather, it was *the story of Jennifer,* and her ability to fight through odds that would have crushed most people. "Jennifer combined all of the worst physical injuries," Baumeister said, "with all of the best human qualities." He believed a jury would see her as an absolute hero.

Jennifer told Baumeister she wanted only three things: (1) to know the truth about what caused the crash; (2) to make certain it never happened again; and (3) to regain her former life.

Before leaving Erlanger, Baumeister said, "Jennifer, I'm very tactile as a trial attorney. People often accuse me of getting in the jury box." He asked to touch her. "But I don't want to hurt you. Is there any part of you that doesn't hurt?"

"The top of my head," Jennifer replied.

"Can I touch you there?" he asked. She nodded. Baumeister touched the top of her head, softly, then said, "It would be an honor to represent you."

On December 6, after 106 days of treatment, Jennifer was released from Erlanger. Burn unit nurses and doctors embraced and cried over a triumph once unthinkable. Skip Reeder hugged Jennifer and whispered, "We love you." The Grunbecks flew to Boston, where Jennifer spent a few days at Massachusetts General Hospital, before moving to a physical rehabilitation facility in nearby Woburn.

The magnitude of her victory was underscored three days before Christmas when Sonya Fetterman died at Grady Hospital, cradled in the arms of her younger brother, Nathan Villarreal, who told her, "Go to God now, honey." The last of the ten ASA victims, Fetterman had survived a grueling 122 days in what seemed a slow, silent scream.

That week, Mich Baumeister arrived in Woburn, Massachusetts, and was hired as the Grunbecks' attorney. Jennifer signed her name to the agreement with only an "X."

The following July, in U.S. District Court in Boston, Jennifer and Bob Grunbeck formally filed suit against United Technologies/Hamilton Standard, Embraer, ASA, and Delta. Their suit contended that Jennifer was "rendered with permanent and disfiguring scarring over 90 percent of her body; was rendered sick, sore, lame and permanently disabled; suffered severe emotional distress, shock, fright, fear of impending death and mental anguish." From each of the four named corporate defendants, the Grunbecks sought $150 million in liability, $100 million in punitive damages, and $50 million for Bob Grunbeck's loss of consortium. Total damages sought by the Grunbecks: $1.2 billion.

November 6, 1996. In the Washington, D.C., law office of Dombroff & Gilbert, Mich Baumeister extended his hand and said, "So I finally get to meet Mr. Bender." Chris Bender, nervous, shook hands with the lawyer.

Bender was a Bible student at Youth With A Mission in Tyler, Texas, having left Hamilton Standard eleven months earlier. He was engaged to a fellow missionary, Amy Emrich; he'd proposed beneath a summer Texas sky filled with shooting stars, and gave her a cubic zirconium ring purchased at K-Mart for twenty dollars. Bender had just returned from an evangelical outreach program in Missouri. He arrived for his deposition wearing a shirt, tie, and slacks. He had been forewarned that Mich Baumeister was, as Bender would say later, "this multimillion-dollar lawyer who was going to let me have it." Jon Stern had prepped Bender months earlier in a lengthy session during which Stern conducted a mock deposition with another attorney portraying Baumeister. Bender was advised that Baumeister had been playfully mocking him as "Bender the Blender," a pejorative he might use again.

To expedite the cases and increase the efficiency of litigation, the ASA lawsuits, filed in multiple federal jurisdictions, had been grouped in Multi-District Litigation (MDL) in Atlanta, in Judge Orinda Evans's U.S. District Court for the Northern District of Georgia. Attorneys formed a Plaintiffs Steering Committee, pooling their time and resources, resolving universal issues in the case, dividing roles and responsibilities. Baumeister would depose witnesses.

Now Bender sat at a long table before nine attorneys, a video camera, and a court reporter typing soundlessly. It was all foreign to him. When he left Tyler, Bender's fiancée had promised to pray for him.

Before important depositions, Baumeister felt an adrenal rush, and here, sitting before him, was the technician who had touched the ASA blade. Baumeister's excitement stemmed from discovering where the story line would go: Had the witness been prepped to deny it? Would there be a stupidity defense? He'd found variations and contradictions in depositions of Hamilton Standard managers. Several plaintiffs' attorneys sensed Hamilton Standard trying to turn Bender into a scapegoat. Baumeister already had seen Jim Hookey's filed reports, which detailed what Bender and his managers at Rock Hill had said to the NTSB about the repair and inspection process. The purpose of this deposition wasn't to develop trial testimony or to find "smoking guns." It was to secure certain admissions and to understand relationships at Rock Hill, such as who reported to whom, and for Bender to explain, on the record, why he had sanded the blade on June 7, 1994.

Baumeister quickly recognized Bender as "a scared kid, who felt deeply about the tragedy," and that, best of all, "Bender was there to give it up."

Deep into a six-hour deposition, with a defense attorney objecting to his "argumentative" tone, Baumeister asked Bender, "Can you tell me what authorization, either oral or written, that you had on June seventh, 1994, that would have allowed you to blend the inside of that ASA 529 taper bore when there was no damage or pits noted?"

Bender: "Okay, I was told if you had a rejected blade and there was no damage or pitting but if you had ridges . . . you could blend . . ."

Baumeister: "Who told you that?"

Bender: "That was told to me by a multiple—a couple different people."

Baumeister: "Give me the names of each and every person that told you this procedure which you say allowed you to blend the taper bore of ASA 529."

Bender mentioned the name of one of his managers.

Baumeister: "Who else?"

Bender mentioned two more names of workers at Rock Hill.

Baumeister: "But there is no document that says you can do that, correct, that was in existence on or prior to June seventh, 1994?"

Bender: "That, I don't know."

Later Baumeister asked, "And you learned, unfortunately, much later on that by blending you could almost mask those difficult-to-see cracks and pits; isn't that correct?"

Bender: "That's correct."

Sitting in the room, Jon Stern heard no surprises. Stern and other defense attorneys knew defending the case would be problematic. They had concluded months earlier that United Technologies, Hamilton Standard's parent corporation, was liable for the ASA crash and would be responsible for compensating victims. Along with a representative of Associated Aviation Underwriters, the New Jersey–based insurer for Hamilton Standard/United Technologies, Stern already had entered settlement talks with plaintiffs' attorneys, though some (including Baumeister) were holding out, waiting for the NTSB's final accident report.

When the deposition at last ended, Chris Bender was exhausted. Baumeister congratulated him on his impending marriage, shook his hand, and departed, pleased with his day's labor.

Stern told Bender he had handled himself admirably and that if this case ever went to trial, the videotaped deposition would be all that was needed from him.

Chris Bender returned to Texas and immersed himself in the Bible.

Three weeks later, in a board meeting in Washington, open to the public, go-team investigators presented a draft of the ASA 529 accident report to the NTSB's five board members.

Vying attorneys and representatives from Hamilton Standard, Embraer, ASA, and Pratt & Whitney sat elbow to elbow in the small, five-row gallery. The room was crowded and stuffy, and white-hot lamps provided for television cameras intensified the cramped feeling. Such board meetings often are ceremonial, little more than pro forma announcements of investigative findings staged for the media.

But this was different. Board members were inflamed by what they heard. An exasperated Jim Hall, the NTSB chairman, asked investigators: "I'm just trying to understand why after the two accidents [and] the procedures developed [by Hamilton Standard], it took the third accident to determine that the procedures that had been developed [were] essentially ineffective?" Plaintiff's attorney Keith Franz noticed Hamilton Standard representatives sweating during the hearing, particularly when Bob Francis, the NTSB's vice chairman, called for tougher language in the final accident report against the propeller manufacturer. Francis said, "What I'm trying to get at here is a little more accountability from the management of Hamilton Standard in the probable cause of the accident." He wanted the word *corporate* added so that blame would be placed at the highest level. The final report read: "The fracture was caused by a fatigue crack from multiple corrosion pits that were not discovered by Hamilton Standard because of inadequate and ineffective corporate inspection and repair techniques, training, documentation and communications."

Bob MacIntosh and Jim Hookey sat at the front table and led the investigative team's presentation. An overhead picture of the burned-out fuselage, with Jim Kennedy's corpse covered by a white sheet in the foreground, was shown. "The accident scene, as we found it," MacIntosh said in his opening remarks. Investigators also showed a four-minute videotape demonstrating how the ASA blade was inspected with a borescope and then sanded.

During the meeting, Chris Bender was not identified by name, only as "the technician" or "the inspector" or "this gentleman."

The NTSB, in its final report, concluded that although the sanding repair was "inappropriate" and had camouflaged a deeper crack in the propeller blade from being detected in a later inspection, Chris Bender had done essentially as he was instructed. The final report called the inspection and repair tools used by Bender "inadequate." That included the borescope, which left Bender to search for microscopic corrosion without any optical magnification, and the dowel rod/comparator he used in an attempt to restore the sanded surface to its original polished finish. Much later, in an interview, MacIntosh would say of Hamilton Standard, "They could have used a combination of processes. Obviously they could have used better optical tools. [But] they chose to visually make sure the corrosion was out of [the taper bore] by using one-to-one [same as the naked eye]. They then chose to use a little dowel rod to make the final finish. They did not seem to understand the criticality of it." MacIntosh would term Bender's polishing tools "primitive."

The NTSB determined that Hamilton Standard's internal documentation and communication "created confusion" that led to the "misapplication of the blending repair." One investigator told board members in the hearing that he'd heard different versions from Rock Hill employees as to why the blade was sanded: "We talked specifically to the inspector who did the work [Chris Bender] and he indicated that he was unclear when he got to this point and he asked for guidance from management. We talked to management to try to see what guidance he got and we got a sense that perhaps they had not given him the guidance to go ahead as he did. There is a point of ambiguity where we were unable to establish exactly what happened and perhaps never will be able to."

The board also concluded that Bender's training had been "inadequate" and "ineffective." MacIntosh told board members: "The gentleman who was doing this specific blade had been acquainted with the automobile industry, where you are looking for . . . red rust. He had to be retrained to find the corrosion and the pits . . . and indeed it's a different situation."

Though Bender was required to restore the sanded surface to its original finish, the NTSB, in its final accident report, noted, "the sanding marks in the blended area of the accident blade were much rougher than the original surface finish. The sanding marks left by the blending appeared to have smeared some of the corroded surface, suggesting that the sanding took place after the corrosion had formed. Although some of the fatigue initiation area was along the sanding marks, the fatigue cracking initiated from corrosion pitting damage that extended below the taper bore surface to a depth much greater than the sanding marks. Therefore, the Safety Board concludes that the sanding marks left by the . . . blending repair did not contribute to the initiation of the fatigue crack in the accident blade. However . . . the sanding marks may well have allowed the cracked blade to pass the ultrasonic inspection following the . . . blending repair."

The report added, "[The] accident blade was again ultrasonically inspected, and this time, neither a rejectable nor a reportable indication was generated. This allowed the blade to be returned to service, and it was installed on the accident airplane."

The NTSB final accident report covered an array of issues in the crash of ASA 529. Though air traffic controllers at Atlanta Center had waited until the crippled Brasilia fell 4,500 feet before turning over communications to Atlanta Approach, that was not a contributing factor in the accident, the NTSB ruled. However, the Safety Board believed that if Atlanta Center controllers had called for emergency services as soon as Matt Warmerdam made the request—more than six and a half minutes before the crash—rescue efforts might have been "more timely and therefore more effective."

The NTSB also recommended that a sturdier, more functional crash ax replace the type used, to little effect, by the trapped Warmerdam.

Investigators praised the work of the ASA flight crew, terming their responses to the crisis "reasonable and appropriate."

"Mr. Hughes," board member John Hammerschmidt said during the hearing, "could you describe for us the actions of the flight attendant during the emergency situation?"

Sitting at the second row of tables, with other go-team group chairmen, Hank Hughes told of Robin Fech's efforts during the nine minutes, twenty seconds and in the field. When Hughes finished, Hammerschmidt said, "Sounds to me like that was truly an exemplary performance." Another board member, George W. Black, went a step further: "I feel obligated to say that this flight attendant—so many times we have a criticism of the actions [of a flight crew member]. This is a situation where a person went above and beyond the call of duty."

Listening from the gallery, Keith Franz liked what was he was hearing. Franz represented ASA survivor John Tweedy as well as the families of Bond Rhue and Michael Hendrix. Franz had put off settlement overtures. He wanted to hear first from the NTSB, "an independent tribunal whose credibility would be unassailable in front of a jury," he thought. Now that the NTSB had been heard, and had come down hard on Hamilton Standard, Franz was ready to talk settlement. The NTSB's final accident report would form the cornerstone for how he, and other plaintiffs' attorneys, would proceed.

A majority of the twenty-nine cases already had settled, and in the months that followed, talks accelerated to settle the rest.

"We must do what is, at best, unseemly and, at worst, impossible—we must put a price on a life," Jon Stern, attorney for United Technologies/Hamilton Standard, later wrote in his article, "Defending Damages in Death Actions," in the American Bar Association's *Litigation* magazine (Summer 1997, vol. 23, no. 4).

Still, Stern wrote, the law requires zealous advocacy on behalf of both sides, and in his article he suggested ways to cut through what are often exaggerated claims by plaintiffs: "There are only so many hours in the day. The decedent could not have been a workaholic on the verge of earning promotion after promotion, a housekeeper who devoted half a day to those duties, and a nurturing parent who helped kids with their schoolwork and hobbies." A plaintiff's quality-of-life claims, Stern wrote, call for a defense attorney to search carefully for "hallmarks of dissatisfaction and displeasure" in the decedent's life, such as career dissatisfaction and "marital or familial strife (for example, marital separation, divorce, children with drug or alcohol problems)." He noted the fine line a defense attorney must walk in pursuit of truth: "Points will rarely be scored, either with the factfinder at trial or in settlement negotiations, by acts of insensitivity to the feelings and emotions of the survivors."

As part of settlement talks, Stern met some family members of those who had perished in the crash. In particular, the captain's wife, Jackie Gannaway, had made a powerful impression upon him. She exuded pride and dignity and Jon Stern couldn't help but feel the magnitude of her loss.

Attorneys for Jennifer Grunbeck and Matt Warmerdam were among the last to settle. Mich Baumeister told the insurer that Jennifer Grunbeck, twenty-eight years old and 92 percent burned, faced surgeries for the remainder of her life. As part of his strategy, he'd had videotapes made of her new life in Woburn that showed how she needed help getting dressed, eating, and showering. "This isn't about me saying X and you saying Y," Baumeister told the Associated Aviation Underwriters representative. "This is about you and your company saying, 'We're going to do something that is unprecedented.'" Baumeister researched national standards for settlements of burn cases. He looked to appellate courts to gauge sustainable values for damage verdicts. He talked with other plaintiffs' lawyers.

As settlement talks unfolded, Jennifer asked him: "Will Hamilton Standard admit fault, publicly?"

"No," Baumeister said.

"Will they ever admit it?" Jennifer asked.

"Don't even bother with that," Baumeister told her. "That's not what this process is about."

By spring 1997, the confidential settlements were complete. In all, Hamilton Standard's insurer paid in the area of $125 million to the victims of ASA 529. Individual settlements ranged from slightly more than $100,000 to more than $20 million.

Soon after settling Jennifer Grunbeck's case, the firm of Baumeister & Samuels published in a brochure the notice that Mich Baumeister "had the distinction of recently concluding the largest personal injury settlement ever recovered in an aviation disaster."

Later Baumeister told Jennifer Grunbeck he hoped to dance with her one day at Johnny's wedding.

Part VIII

Revelation: A Mosaic

37

NOW AND THEN, A CAR STOPS on the road near Paul Butler's house and sits there while its occupants look at the hay field where ASA Flight 529 came to rest. Strangers have knocked on Butler's front door and asked to walk in his backyard. He has allowed them in even as he wondered, What is it they're looking for?

As I researched the ASA crash for this book, it became clear why I returned to Butler's hay field time and again. There was death, yes, and there was work to do explaining how it happened. But of the twenty-nine people aboard the ASA Brasilia, nineteen survived. In their stories was a miracle of life.

How does anyone live through a plane crash? This is as compelling a laboratory of humanity as any, and provides a window that allows us to see why people do what they do when put to the greatest stress, the stress of panic and fear. It shows what moves some people to heroics, what moves others to cowardice or shame.

From afar, we may believe we know what a plane crash is like. Yet until those abstract concepts are made real, we cannot know. The ASA survivors know it through every sense given them. They felt the plane's tremblings, heard its wings breaking off treetops, saw fire and smoke, and smelled burning flesh.

They'll tell you they aren't heroes, that all they did was live. I understand their thoughts but respectfully disagree. Heroes act to sustain life and give life meaning. That, these people did. Gannaway, Warmerdam,

Fech, Grunbeck, Hendrix, McCorkell, Adair and Dumm, and others were ordinary people who did extraordinary things. It was nothing they had planned. It was simply their response to the conditions they encountered. This was the revelation of ASA 529, ordinary people revealing the extraordinary power of the human spirit.

Children realized that and one day crowded into an elementary-school gym in Bowdon, four miles from the crash site. A student placed a long-stem rose in a glass vase.

"Captain Ed Gannaway," a classmate announced.

There came the mournful wail of bagpipes, and then another student with another red rose.

"Mary Jean Adair."

Three summers before, children had rushed to Butler's hay field, a few on bicycles, to see the little plane that had fallen from the sky. Now they brought forward ten roses, one for each of the dead, and when the children finished their memorial, Robin Fech and Alan Barrington took the roses to the hay field, now familiar to them in ways only they could understand.

They knew where the broken fuselage had been. Several firefighters returned to the field with them and pointed to the spots where each of the dead had first been found. At each spot Fech and Barrington placed a rose, and with each rose they pronounced a name.

"Bond Rhue," Fech said.

"Sonya Fetterman," Barrington said.

"Lucille Burton," Fech said.

"Charles Barton," Barrington said.

In a field once on fire, now there were flowers.

I began contacting survivors two and a half years after the crash. A few replied to my interview requests immediately; most took weeks or months; a couple took more than a year, and one (Jean Brucato, Kevin Bubier's "guardian angel" in the flowered dress) did not respond at all.

The interviews typically were conducted in survivors' homes and lasted three hours and more. Settlements with Hamilton Standard's insurer had been completed, allowing people to speak more freely.

Most survivors had undergone counseling, and their thoughts about the crash had crystallized. A few couldn't remember certain aspects; Ed Gray turned to hypnosis to try to recall how he got out of the plane. Under hypnosis, Gray saw, through a hole in the fuselage, gray sky edged by flames, but no other new information emerged.

Memory is imperfect. Yet studies suggest that memory of a life-threatening experience often is more accurate and reliable than memory of an everyday event, particularly with information that is central, not peripheral, to the experience. The ASA survivors' narratives provided a confirmation of those studies; memories seldom conflicted.

ASA survivors have had limited contact with one another. They have recovered apart, and in some cases, alone. Nevertheless, they feel a powerful connection to those they know only by name or the clothes they wore on August 21, 1995.

During interviews, survivors asked many questions, the most common, "How are the others doing?" Almost without exception, they cried. Several asked if the two passengers who swapped seats during the descent had survived, wondering if the change had altered their fates. (It hadn't. Both Ludie Burton and Bond Rhue died.) Many survivors expressed guilt, for in the broken fuselage they had made decisions based not on ethics or morality but on adrenaline-driven survival instinct. They were afraid their lives had been purchased at the cost of others'. Whatever they did in those decisive seconds, they now live with it. Some have made peace with their actions, some haven't. John Tweedy escaped from the burning fuselage and never went back to it. For a time he suffered guilt. But then he reconsidered what had transpired: Maybe he hadn't been wrong, after all. For one thing, Tweedy later realized he had been saturated with fuel, and so returning to the flames might have cost him his own life. And what about his children at home? He had a responsibility to them, too, didn't he?

Occasionally, I offered survivors pieces of the puzzle they never knew existed. In his northern Virginia condominium, David Schneider demonstrated his movements after the plane had skidded to a stop. He unstrapped an imaginary seat belt, took two steps across his living room, and bent to help Jim Kennedy. Then he leaped toward his sofa, acting out his leap into the flames and out of the plane, leaving Kennedy behind.

Since attending Kennedy's wake and meeting his widow, Schneider had clung to the belief that his colleague had died inside the fuselage, before the flames got to him. He fell silent when I told him Kennedy somehow had made it out of the fuselage.

Kevin Bubier worried that he'd break down if we talked about Kennedy in a restaurant. In the security of his home in Maine, Bubier stared into the distance, eyes tightening at the corners as he tried to imagine Kennedy. He asked, "Did the guy have shorts on?" Yes, Kennedy wore blue-jean shorts. "All of a sudden I remember seeing bare legs under the [seat] cushions," Bubier said. "That's weird. I never really thought of that until now."

He remembered Kennedy's sneakers. "And I remember white sports socks. They might have even had a red stripe on them."

Bubier shook his head. "I remember that better than his face. Sometimes you'd like to go under hypnosis to see if you could figure it out. But that might be even worse of a nightmare than you'd want to deal with, know what I mean?"

Tod Thompson knew what Bubier meant. A portrait of his dead partner, Charlie Barton, hung near the entry to the Loudoun County Sheriff's Department, framed with a plaque and letters from Bill Clinton and Virginia's governor. Because of that portrait, because of Barton's friends in the department, and because he felt a survivor's guilt, Thompson worked outside the office when he could. No officers mentioned Charlie's name to him and he thought, Maybe they're afraid to bring it up.

From time to time, Thompson saw Barton's only son, Rick, a shy, lumbering hardware store clerk. They'd exchange stiff, brief small talk, nothing more, and Thompson would walk away from each conversation feeling more guilty and sad. He wondered if Rick blamed him for Charlie's death. He once saw Charlie's son from a distance and changed directions to avoid him.

Since the crash, Thompson and his wife, Pam, have had two children. A friend told Mrs. Thompson, "God had a purpose for Tod staying on this earth—to be a dad."

Four other children have been born to crash survivors, daughters to Dawn Dumm and Angela Brumfield, sons to Alfred Arenas and Jason Aleshire.

Angela Brumfield felt indebted to Robin Fech. On the morning of the crash, Brumfield had accepted an offer to become an ASA flight attendant. She closely watched Fech during the nine minutes, twenty seconds. Once she was safe in the field, Brumfield's first thought was: I wonder if the flight attendant survived?

Brumfield had left Atlanta that day intent on starting a new life without her boyfriend, Rob Mills. But when she returned to the New Orleans airport after the crash, Mills was waiting for her with a wheelchair and a dozen red roses. That night, with tear-streaked cheeks, Rob told her, "I almost lost you." They married in 1997; their first child, a girl, was born two years later.

They named her Robin.

Rob Mills said, "One day I'll tell my daughter, 'You are the namesake of the lady who saved your mother's life.'"

When Robin Fech visited Angela and Rob and saw their baby asleep, she reached into the crib and stroked her hair. "It's so soft," Fech said. Then she ran her fingertips along the fleshy folds of the baby's legs and said, "Look, she's got big thick legs. Just like me."

She picked up the baby. "She's beautiful, so beautiful." Robin Fech closed her eyes.

A mosaic of the human spirit is made of imperfect pieces imperfectly fitted and yet beautiful in its whole. We might seek a piece that suggests honor and find nothing more substantial, or less substantial, than the NTSB investigator Hank Hughes returning Charlie Barton's gleaming handgun and badge to Loudoun County.

Or we might find Matt Warmerdam. In the spring after the crash, Warmerdam and his wife, Amy, drove to Ed Gannaway's home to meet with Jackie and the three boys Ed so often talked about. Warmerdam wanted to answer questions from Ed's sons and affirm to them that their father was a hero.

Jackie Gannaway, a social worker, knew and studied psychology. She wanted her sons to know only the truth about the crash. She had taken them to the hay field. There, the oldest, Craig, sixteen, studied the terraces that broke the fuselage. He wondered if his father might have survived if not for those terraces.

Jackie flew with her sons in an ASA Brasilia, Macon to Atlanta, to make certain they didn't develop a fear of flying. She showed them the transcript of the cockpit recordings. Reading the transcript, Jackie was proud of Ed's coolness. She sensed fear in him only when he stuttered during the final communications. "Ed never stuttered in his life," she said. Even four years later, Jackie knew from memory her husband's final words: "Help me, help me hold it, help me hold, help me hold it."

She told her sons there was a meaning and purpose to their father's death: Because Ed Gannaway was captain, "a lot of people were able to walk away from the crash."

Only in the captain's absence did Craig Gannaway fully realize how much his mother and father had loved each other. He felt helpless seeing his mother alone, crying.

Now, in the living room, he saw Matt Warmerdam's severe scars and disfigured hands, and it made the intensity of the crash more vivid and horrific.

The Gannaway boys asked Warmerdam powerful questions: Was their father scared? Did he know he was going to die? Did he suffer?

Their father was too busy to be scared, Warmerdam said, and he believed they would land the plane safely. Warmerdam told the boys that as soon as he regained awareness in the burning cockpit, he shook their father but he was unconscious. That comforted Craig Gannaway, who took the information as confirmation that his father did not suffer.

Warmerdam became emotional about Ed Gannaway. With a catch in his voice, he told the captain's sons, "You should be very proud of him."

Is there redemption in a second chance?

Alan Barrington left his middle-manager's job and moved his family back to his native Kansas City, where he founded his own one-man ministry. Ed Gray and Barney Gaskill retired early to spend more time with their families. Kevin Bubier left the shipyards, built a new house on a pastoral twenty-four acres near his hometown of Turner, Maine, and now dreams of taking a trotter to the Hambletonian, the Super Bowl of standardbred horse racing.

As ASA 529 fell, David McCorkell had been furious with God for allowing him to die alone. Survival brought a new resolve. McCorkell quit his job and accepted a new one in Alaska. There he would fish in big streams and watch gorgeous sunsets. He would become a freer man, a new Dave. Three months after the crash, he climbed into a three-seat plane piloted by a business acquaintance and flew over Newfoundland. Fear of flying was illogical, McCorkell decided: "If you were in a car crash, you'd probably get in a car again."

Then, surrounded by the natural grandeur of Alaska, McCorkell realized he was still alone. So he left Alaska and found his way back to Chicago and his ex-wife, Lila. Soon they talked of trying marriage again. It took five years, and a move to South Carolina, before Dave and Lila walked into a chapel, exchanged vows, and made it official.

David Schneider, wracked by survivor guilt early on, listened as his priest said, "God understands that you want to save yourself." Still, Schneider demanded to know why he had been saved when others beside him had died. That answer, his priest told him, might come "tomorrow or it might not happen until you are seventy-eight. Or it might not happen at all."

During the nine minutes, twenty seconds of ASA 529's descent, Schneider's confidence and focus had helped Fech do her job. But now he was cut loose, adrift. He considered joining the Peace Corps. Maybe he'd become a veterinarian. He thought of moving to a cabin in Montana's wilderness.

His marriage collapsed. Later he poured himself into a new romance, "stuff out of *Romeo and Juliet*." But he admitted to loving this woman with such intensity that he frightened her away. Depression set in. Schneider was thirty-two years old and felt fifty. He changed jobs and waited for an epiphany he feared would never come.

Dr. Bobby Mitchell knew death, as doctors know death, but he never knew it quite like he did on the day he met Michael Hendrix.

So in the spring of 2000, Mitchell accepted an invitation to the dedication of the Michael D. Hendrix Burn Research Center at the Johns Hopkins Bayview Medical Center in Baltimore.

He wanted to meet Hendrix's wife and tell her what he'd told friends and colleagues, that he'd learned "one of the greatest lessons of my career" from her husband in ER almost five years earlier. An extraordinary man, Mitchell said of Hendrix. "Not a selfish bone in his body. At a time he was facing eternity, he was so calm and at peace."

That peace intrigued the doctor. *What was its source?*

Linda Agar-Hendrix donated $500,000 in her husband's name to the Baltimore Regional Burn Center, the largest single gift in the center's history. At the dedication, candlelight flickered in front of a small framed picture of Mike Hendrix as his widow, in her brief tribute, paraphrased the first law of thermodynamics: "Nothing or no one is ever lost, but just changes form."

Afterward, Mitchell approached her and said, "Your husband was at peace with us, and he was with friends."

Mrs. Hendrix explained her husband's uncommon grace. He had considered the possibility of death, she said. He had just changed jobs and knew he would be traveling regularly; he had increased his life insurance. He was an engineer, pragmatic, fatalistic. Their marriage had been strong. Her husband wasn't a religious person, but he was comfortable with who he was and what he believed in.

Bobby Mitchell understood that life has shades of truth. Now he understood that Hendrix accepted life's most certain truth, death. He had prepared for death financially and emotionally. He understood a plane crash could happen. When it did, he accepted it. Hendrix hadn't lived his life in fear and he wouldn't die afraid. He knew his place in the universe.

Such a life, the doctor knew, deserved respect and honor.

Distraught over her father's death, Clare Kennedy stepped into a small office near New York's Central Park. There she watched a spiritual healer close her eyes and raise a hand to feel and read the energy of Jim Kennedy. "Conscious channeling," the healer called it, and she warned Clare that such channeling often produces frightening results. A friend of Clare's had arranged this session, explaining to the healer only that Clare's father had died in a fiery plane crash. Now the healer told Clare that she saw and heard Jim Kennedy. He was in a hospital-like setting attended by other souls. Through the healer, Jim Kennedy told Clare that everything around him—color, time, and speed—was beautiful and enhanced and without physical barrier. The healer asked Clare, "Did your father have a bud or buddy? A big round guy?" Clare replied, "That was my uncle Bud. My father loved his brother." The healer said Uncle Bud had helped Jim Kennedy get "across to the other side" and they would spend time together now. Then she described the Jim Kennedy she saw: very tall, short hair, broad shoulders, handsome. She said the last image he saw before death was the face of his wife. Clare Kennedy scribbled notes on a pad. She filled two pages, then three and four, sobbing. Jim Kennedy told the healer he was proud of the way his family had handled his funeral. "And your father is saying how cute you were as a little girl with pigtails." Clare wiped her eyes. Jim Kennedy always had bragged about his seven beautiful daughters. The healer's voice became dry and raspy, Jim Kennedy's voice, saying, "I know they are looking for my papers"—the family was searching for his will—"Tell them there are some boxes in my office." (The family later found boxes stuffed with papers, none the will.) Finally Jim Kennedy said he was tired and would leave. He told Clare to look after her mother. "I'll be back," Jim Kennedy said. "What does that mean?" Clare asked. The healer said it might mean she would see him in a dream or, perhaps, in a different realm. Energized and exhausted by the session, Clare took a taxi home to the Upper East Side. She called her mother by cell phone from the taxi's backseat and, in the city's traffic, talked for forty minutes. She told her mother the healer's words and also her father's words. She believed Dad was at peace. Mother and daughter wept.

A spring rain fell on Newtown, a lovely Connecticut Yankee village. In Nancy Kennedy's front yard, a maple tree's leaves, brilliant red, stirred in the wind. The life story of Jim Kennedy's widow has the rich texture of triumph and tragedy: eight children, thirteen grandchildren, thirty-one years of marriage around a midlife six-year separation, then a plane crash.

After her husband's death, Nancy Kennedy would sit on her daughter's porch, smoking cigarettes and looking at the nearby hills, suddenly becoming angry, angry with her husband for leaving. Over time, her anger shifted to ASA (the plane), to Delta (ASA's affiliate), even to Atlanta (the flight's originating city). She refused to watch the 1996 Olympics on television because the Games were conducted in Atlanta.

Her trust in God "ebbs and flows, waxes and wanes." Still, she found in the tragedy an affirmation of goodness. She knew now that several passengers delayed their escape and faced fire in an attempt to help her husband get out of the plane. "That says a tremendous amount about the human spirit," she said.

She confessed to wondering how she would have responded to such a test. "I hate to get too truthful, but I would've hightailed right out of there."

She sold their "honeymoon condo" in Maryland, returned home to Newtown to be closer to the kids and grandkids. Around Newtown, in grocery stores and shops, she saw older couples and felt envious and cheated. She hated widowhood: "It's the most horrible, nonperson type of role to play."

She missed her husband's sense of humor. "Every morning he'd say something and he knew I would bite." Remembering those moments, Nancy Kennedy smiled beautifully. "And he did it just to get my blood circulating." Laughing and crying and loving him still, she said, *"He was such a bum. . . ."*

"If there is a meaning in life at all, then there must be a meaning in suffering," Viktor E. Frankl, a Holocaust survivor, wrote in *Man's Search for Meaning*. "Without suffering and death human life cannot be complete."

In the summer of 1996, every part of Jennifer Grunbeck's body hurt. Her skin hurt the most. Her plastic surgeon demanded that she wear pressure garments twenty-four hours a day to minimize scarring. An occupational therapist (for her hands) and physical therapist (for the rest of her) wanted Grunbeck for three hours apiece each day. She had a suitcase full of splints of different shapes and sizes. Her lawyer, Mich Baumeister, had told her it would take five years before she felt grounded.

The first year would be lost to a fog; the second year would be devoted to surgeries and therapy.

The summer of '96 began that second year. She fell into a deep depression, sometimes expressing it sarcastically. "I'm a size eight," she told her plastic surgeon, "so why have you given me size six skin?" She felt imprisoned by her skin, and she felt the skin as pain.

She watched TV news each night and wondered, Why is it that the mother always gets killed and the child molester is doing fine? What is the purpose of it all?

Bob Grunbeck left his job to devote himself to his wife and son, Johnny. He cooked for Jennifer and bathed her. She mourned the loss of her old life and appearance. When she went out in public, people stared; so she stayed home. Her world shrunk and she took out her anger on Bob. "Leave me alone," she would say. "Just leave. You deserve better than this."

Bob would have none of it. "Don't tell me what to do," he said.

Mired in a physical and emotional abyss that summer, Jennifer once wanted to die. She planned an overdose of the painkiller Percocet. When Bob failed to talk her out of it, he slammed the plastic pill bottle on her bed table and said, "You want to do it, then do it. I don't want any part of this."

He stormed out of the house, but not before making sure the bottle cap was tightly closed. He knew the burn damage to Jennifer's hands wouldn't allow her to twist it open, anyway.

An hour later, coming out of a rainstorm, he returned only to find Jennifer gone. He saw the pill bottle unopened. He thought, Where is she? And he remembered a pond down the road. *She jumped in the freakin' pond.*

As he turned to leave the bedroom, Jennifer walked in.

Drenched, she'd only gone for a walk.

* * *

It's a fine thing, to go for a walk, fine also to laugh.

When Matt Warmerdam first left Erlanger in the spring of 1996, he and Amy rented an apartment in Chattanooga. Late one night in a Winn-Dixie supermarket, Amy pushed Matt's wheelchair with one hand, a shopping cart with the other.

They passed a lobster tank.

"Wait! Stop! Stop! Stop!" Matt said. For twenty minutes they watched lobsters step on one another's heads.

"Hey, look at this one over here!"

"I'm going to come and get you!"

"Oh, no! Don't step on my head! *Oh, noooooooooooo!*"

They laughed and carried on and it was fair to ask what sort of grown-ups roll a wheelchair through a grocery store and stop to imagine themselves as lobsters. "Just being dorks," the first officer said, and at that moment he was a happy man.

Happy to be alive, happy to be with Amy.

The mosaic has darkness.

Back home in Madison, Connecticut, after the crash, Chuck Pfisterer was toasted by friends as a true survivor. They bought him drinks, which he rarely declined. The cruel irony was, they considered him a man lucky to be alive while he was uncertain that was a lucky thing at all.

Pfisterer avoided flying, and once drove on a business trip forty-two hours from Connecticut to Michigan and back, chiding himself all the way, "Come on, Chuck, you're more at risk on this highway than you would be in the air."

He flew several times, but always with someone, and panic typically set in a week before the flight. He feared losing control. He'd think, I can't believe I'm going to get off the ground again. To make flying easier, his daughter gave him a teddy bear with a *Good Luck* sign; Pfisterer set it next to a shot of Jack Daniel's. He brought his tranquilizers, too, and wore the same brown loafers he'd worn on the ASA flight. They had singe marks on the sides. He called them "my lucky shoes."

He drank as "a result of my wanting to forget certain things," not only from the crash, but from life. In the summer of 1999, he bottomed out.

Driving home after work and his usual stop at a bar, Pfisterer unwittingly cut in front of a van on the road and then noticed the van following him. He saw its driver talking on a car phone. Pfisterer pulled onto side roads, hoping to lose the van, but the van followed, its driver still on the phone.

A Middletown, Connecticut, police car appeared, lights flashing. Pfisterer pulled to the side. The policeman gave him a Breathalyzer test. His alcohol level registered above the legal limit. Handcuffed and put in the police car, Pfisterer was driven to the local precinct station, where he called his wife and daughter. The policeman said Chuck Pfisterer was one of the nicest people he'd ever met, but his daughter wasn't so kind.

On the way home, she read him the riot act: How could you do this, Dad? Why are you drinking so much?

Pfisterer knew she was right, which made it worse—and made it better. He soon quit Jack Daniel's.

"If I didn't have my family, I never would have made it," he said. Thinking about the hay field, he said, "There were things that happened that day, like the guy with the burning sneakers melting on his feet and asking for help, and I couldn't do anything. I mean, that will be with me until the day I die. I'm not saying there was anything I could do to help him, but don't you think I wanted to beat those flames out? . . . There are so many times I say to myself, Why didn't I have the wherewithal to maybe just run around and push people to the ground? There's survivor guilt, believe me."

Chuck Pfisterer shook his head. "Down the road you are alone. You have to face your thoughts and how you feel about everything that went down. You have to deal with it day to day. That's just life, you know. I have to deal with it myself."

* * *

Chris Bender and his wife, Amy, attended a church play in 1997. He didn't know until he reached his seat that this play was about the crash of a small plane.

Early on, the audience learned about the passengers' relationships with God. Just before impact, some passengers onstage repented, others cursed God—and the stage lights suddenly went dark.

The playhouse filled with sounds suggesting a crash. Then screams echoed around the church. When the lights came up, the audience found out which passengers went to heaven and which to hell.

"Are you okay?" Amy Bender asked her husband. He had spoken of his role in the ASA crash with virtually no one outside of his family. Now, even as he told his wife he was fine, Chris Bender thought of the people aboard ASA 529.

What was it like as they were going down? What were they thinking? Did they cry out? Hold each other? Were they cursing God? Repenting?

Bender imagined, incorrectly, one thing to be certain. There would have been screaming.

The day of ASA 529's crash, fear moved in plain sight. Now, for the Reverend Gus Koch, fear moved in the shadows of memory.

The ASA crash took him where he'd resolved never to go again: Vietnam, 1969, a day when he rode in the back of an army jeep.

He was a medic. He saw a South Vietnamese school bus erupt in flames. Children, on fire, were screaming. He urged the jeep driver to stop. The driver refused and said the burning bus was probably a Viet Cong trap. Koch thought to reach for the driver's gun, but didn't. As the jeep drove away, he looked back at the bus and the children.

He'd never forget the fading screams of those children he left in a burning bus. But he consciously willed himself to disremember. He would not see that bus again, would not sit in that jeep, would not allow himself to be driven away.

Then, on an afternoon a generation later, he found himself in a hay field and there was fire and there were screams.

For Gus Koch in 1995, the ASA crash was only part of a year of hardship and heartache. A hurricane sent a hickory tree through the roof of his church's sanctuary; he was diagnosed with diabetes; and the health of his wife, Edie, suffering from multiple sclerosis, deteriorated.

Come Sunday mornings, he sermonized about the courage and conviction of his four heroes: Albert Schweitzer, the Reverend Martin Luther King Jr., Dietrich Bonhoeffer (a Lutheran minister in Germany who decried Nazism and was executed days before the Allies could save him), and Arland Williams, famous as "the man in the water" after the 1982 crash of an Air Florida jet in the Potomac River at Washington, D.C. Live television showed Williams, a passenger on that plane, helping other passengers to the safety of a rescue helicopter before he disappeared beneath the black, icy water.

"From Arland Williams," Koch told his congregants, "we learn that even strangers are worth all that we can give."

In Paul Butler's hay field, Koch had given more than he knew. By closing a door against the Vietnam memories, he had gained a kind of peace, uneasy perhaps, but a peace nonetheless. That day of the crash, he himself had opened that door by rushing to help the suffering victims of ASA 529, and now he suffered for it.

Almost a year later, there came a telephone call. Jennifer Grunbeck, he was told, was in despair and on the brink of giving up. She needed encouragement. Maybe Gus Koch, who had found her in the hay field and comforted her and told her there was reason to live, could provide it.

Koch couldn't call her. He was afraid. He had absorbed so much pain. Taking on any more might break him. "It was like all of my insulation had worn off," Koch said. "I had no defense against the pain of other people."

He did all he could do for Jennifer. He prayed for her. He was awed by her resilience in the face of so much suffering.

He counted her as his fifth hero.

Robin Fech tried to get back into an airplane. But she made it only as far as the flight attendant's jump seat near the door. She kept that door opened and left through it when fear overcame her.

Her psychotherapist's plan was to slowly desensitize Fech to an airplane so she could fly again. First she did nothing more than park at the Macon airport to watch planes take off and land. Next she walked into the terminal. The first time she moved onto the tarmac, she cried. It was so unlike the person she had been, full of sass. But each step toward recovery revived the terror. She couldn't use a curling iron without being reminded of the smell of fire.

A year and a month passed before Fech could step into an empty Brasilia identical to the crash plane and stay awhile. Alone, she did a necessary thing. She sat in each of the seats. Closing her eyes, she tried to become the passengers who fell from the sky with her. She wanted to know what they had felt during the nine minutes, twenty seconds.

At home, she had diagrammed the seat assignments. She knew Jennifer Grunbeck was in 4B, Jean Brucato in 4C. She'd drawn squiggly lines where the fuselage had broken in Row 5, where Jim Kennedy and Bond Rhue sat.

Sitting in 4A, she became Ed Gray, the Connecticut businessman. She looked out the window at the propeller assembly, trying to see what Gray had seen. Now, alone in Row 8, she saw again the young David Schneider, bursting with confidence. He promised to open the emergency door once the plane was on the ground.

Sitting in the back row in 10B, she saw an older African-American woman standing beside her seat, turning in a circle. Ludie Burton had been confused. From her diagrams, Fech knew most passengers in the back had died.

She closed her eyes and saw them all again, alive and afraid, just as they were before the pine trees and the field.

* * *

The crash became Robin Fech's life.

With Ed Gannaway dead and Matt Warmerdam in recovery, Fech was the only crew member who met the press. The public face of the disaster, she was celebrated as a heroine on *The Oprah Winfrey Show,* and she posed by a Brasilia for *People* magazine. With her mother, Claudette Underwood, she stood before Georgia's legislators, who gave her a standing ovation.

Letters of praise arrived. One person wrote, "You showed more courage in thirty minutes than most people do in a lifetime!" Another: "I revere you, Robin Fech!" A flight attendant wrote to thank her "for making us look like something more than a glorified waitress." Alan Barrington said of Fech's efforts: "If someone told you that you had less than ten minutes left to live, are you going to do your job? I'm not going to do mine."

Fech kept in touch with a handful of survivors, a few of whom thanked her for her work in the air that day. Others sent Christmas cards ("You were instrumental in saving many lives. Happy Holidays! Love, Tod and Pam Thompson"). Chuck Lemay's e-mails called her "Momma Hen." When a Comair plane crashed in icy conditions near Detroit in 1997— another Brasilia, also with twenty-nine aboard, killing everyone—Fech called a few ASA passengers to see if they wanted to talk.

As genuine as her enthusiasm for the community of survivors was, it had limits imposed by her own struggles.

Chuck Pfisterer visited the crash site in 1996 and left a phone message for her, but Fech didn't respond; Pfisterer felt snubbed. Similarly, it was left to Clemmie Jordan, Fech's sister, to call Jackie Gannaway and say Robin wasn't strong enough to speak to her. Ed Gannaway's brother, Bob, wondered how Fech could do magazine and TV interviews but didn't have the strength to call the widow of the pilot who had saved her life.

Her friends heard every detail of the crash so often, they all but told her to shut up. One said, "Get on with your life." Her boyfriend,

Chris Price, said, "I want that fun, carefree, footloose person that she was then, and that she's not now. I can't blame her for it. I can't blame anyone for it."

Her brief conversation with Dawn Dumm at Tanner Medical Center three days after the crash continued to confuse and hurt Fech. Robin asked Clemmie, "Why is she so angry with me? What did I do? What didn't I do?"

At the heart of Fech's darkness: She desperately wanted the praise of others even as she felt unworthy of it. She wondered if more lives might have been saved. She believed that others had embellished her work, particularly what she did in the hay field. "An emergency worker said I was directing them," Fech said. "I have had a lot of guilt about this. These passengers know I didn't do all this wonderful stuff that has been said about me."

There is no embellishment, though, to the nine minutes, twenty seconds in the passenger cabin. Those moments were hers. For the first time in Fech's life, she felt she had made a difference. She had done her job and done it well. Flight attendants work the front lines of any aircraft disaster, trained rigorously on safety procedures. Those who break down in crisis fail not only themselves but their passengers. A few years after the ASA crash a commercial jet dropped and rolled, injuring several passengers before leveling off. "Probably the worst part was the stewardess," a passenger on that jet said later. "She just couldn't compose herself. She was telling us everything was going to be okay, yet she was crying."

Fech knew she had passed the sternest test of her life. Never before had she acted with such confidence. Had panic swept through ASA 529's passenger cabin, it's possible no one would have survived. She knew that as well.

If only her father, Duane, the old naval aviator, dead of cancer three months earlier, could have seen what she did. One more time, she thought, that I can't make him proud of me. *Damn him for dying!*

On antidepressant medication, she sought out therapy and was diagnosed with post-traumatic stress disorder. Once called "shell shock" and later "battle fatigue," PTSD was first listed in the *Diagnostic and Statistical Manual of Mental Disorders* of the American Psychiatric Association in 1980. Its symptoms include fear of recurrence, unresolved grief, sleep disturbances, loss of memory and concentration, and survival guilt. Virtually all the ASA survivors suffered some of these symptoms, none more demonstrably than Robin Fech. She returned to work at ASA's Macon office in November 1997, not as a flight attendant, but as a receptionist of sorts, answering phones, part time. That week she made her first flight since the crash, to Atlanta and back. She did the trip again a few days later. The flight attendants were friends, and they chatted all the way, so Fech didn't consider it a real test of her airworthiness.

She worked in the office only briefly; nervousness forced her to give up the job.

She didn't fly again for two more years.

A psychologist evaluating Fech in 1997 concluded that it was unlikely she would ever return to work as a flight attendant.

They went to a mall together, the mother and son, Jennifer Grunbeck and Johnny, now eight years old.

The boy who once couldn't look at his mother in a hospital room noticed two kids staring at her.

So he confronted them. "It's my mom," Johnny Grunbeck said. "She was in an accident. You have any other questions, or not?"

The kids froze. Then they shook their heads and walked away.

Matt Warmerdam's recovery was long and excruciating. In one cosmetic surgery, doctors put a tissue expander beneath the first officer's scalp and inflated it with saline twice a week. They did the procedure for months, giving him what he called a "big bubble head." Much later he underwent surgery on his disfigured left hand to reposition the thumb and reduce web space between it and the index finger.

As Warmerdam slowly reclaimed parts of himself, he also reclaimed parts of his plane. From a salvage yard in Georgia, he retrieved the soot-streaked cockpit window with the hacked-out odd-shaped hole in its center. He also obtained the small crash hatchet. He kept both in his garage. He wanted to get the busted propeller blade, too. More than souvenir hunting, this was how the first officer regained an important part of who he was. Warmerdam said he intended to fly a Brasilia again one day. He'll do it with a single purpose: "Me kicking its ass instead of it kicking mine."

On August 21, 1996, the first anniversary of the ASA crash, Amy Warmerdam pushed her husband's wheelchair onto the tarmac of a small New Mexico airport.

They boarded a Cessna, Amy in a back seat, Matt in the right front seat, next to a flight instructor hired for the moment.

Warmerdam wore his burn stocking and had just undergone the first of several surgeries on his left elbow. To him, this first flight since the crash was ceremonial; he knew he'd fly again, sometime, somewhere. It might as well happen in New Mexico on a family visit.

So he said, "Okay, let's get this over with. This will be fun."

They flew for fifteen minutes. For a while, the plane answered to the man in the right seat. He last touched the yoke of a plane as it went down through trees. Now he put his scarred and splinted left hand where he'd always wanted it to be. The feeling was merely sensational.

His head shaved to stubble, a sixty-five-pound pack strapped on his back, Chris Bender stood in the morning fog atop Springer Mountain in north Georgia in the summer of 2000. He would lead eight college-age "disciples" on a twenty-three-day, 230-mile hike along the Appalachian Trail.

Bender began with a prayer: "Father, we anticipate that we will strengthen our relationship with you as we walk with you. We expect, Father, that you will teach us discipline and that as we grow closer to each other we will grow closer to you."

Then, looking to his Youth With A Mission group members, he said, "This is going to be cool."

Cool? One YWAM disciple banged his head against a bridge. Another fell off a log into a river. Rainstorms struck suddenly and temperatures dropped below freezing. Muscles rebelled, and members longed for the food back home: steak, ice cream, Cajun food.

Chris Bender loved it all. He led discussions about the need to restore morality in America. He prayed for the country's future. He met hikers on the trail and performed "friendship evangelism."

At last he had found his place in life. He and his wife had traveled to Israel the year before to lead a month-long YWAM outreach program. They participated in a "Reconciliation Walk," retracing the steps of the crusaders and asking the forgiveness of Jews and Muslims for atrocities committed against them in Christ's name.

On the streets of Jerusalem and Tel Aviv, Bender handed out pamphlets in Hebrew and Arabic. He stood before the River Jordan, where Christ was baptized, and the Sea of Gallilee, where Christ walked across the water.

There he understood how he had moved from a technician's job to an evangelist's. It was God's wish, and he simply obeyed.

Three years after the crash, Hamilton Standard, in a written statement, said that Bender had not been to blame: "All associates involved in the manufacture and subsequent inspection and repair of the blade that fractured during the accident followed written company processes and procedures. Our investigation following the accident determined that certain of these processes and procedures were inadequate. . . . Hamilton Standard accepts full responsibility for the fracture of the blade which caused the crash."

Even so, it was not as if Bender had left behind the ASA crash. He often thought of contacting survivors and families.

"But what would I say?" Bender said. He answered the question: "Let them know that I do care and that I haven't forgotten about them. I still do pray for them. I still pray that something good can come out of something so awful. And, um"—his voice quavered—"if there was anything that was possible for me to try to do—I don't even know what."

He decided against such conversations. "I don't know how they would take me. I mean, I figure some people would probably be bitter about it, and probably hateful toward me. And that's something I would totally understand."

On the Appalachian Trail, he told his YWAM members about his role in the ASA crash and said he had grown from the experience. Whether the task at hand is the repair of a propeller blade or reading the Bible, "You must always understand why you are doing what you are doing."

He was asked about the crash: Where did it happen? How many people died? Were there lawsuits? He answered every question.

Then a group member offered a prayer. He thanked God for delivering Chris Bender to a better place.

Atlantic Southeast Airlines was bought in full by Delta Air Lines.

Hamilton Standard became Hamilton Sundstrand in a merger with Sundstrand Corporation. The newly constituted corporation, with annual sales of more than $3 billion and a worldwide workforce of about eighteen thousand, immediately announced itself as the aerospace industry's third largest supplier of systems and components, including propeller blades. Its propeller inspection and repair process, meanwhile, has long since been overhauled, replaced by procedures that not only meet FAA requirements but, in some instances, exceed them. Now a mechanically positioned borescope is used, which allows for high-magnification images; those images appear on a full-sized color TV monitor. Chris

Bender's blend-repair is no longer allowed. A precise machining process repairs visible damage to the bore, and the follow-up inspection uses eddy current, a highly sensitive, electromagnetic technique.

In the fall of 1996, President Clinton signed the Aviation Disaster Family Assistance Act, providing a thirty-day waiting period that forbids attorneys on either side from unsolicited contact with crash victims or their families. Later that waiting period was extended to forty-five days.

Survivors from ASA 529 returned home to pick up their lives: Renee Chapman went back to Mississippi, John Tweedy to Maryland, Chuck Lemay to Nebraska, Alfred Arenas and Jean Brucato to Georgia. Basic Airman Jason Aleshire resumed his career at Keesler Air Force Base in Biloxi.

On Mother's Day, Dawn Dumm sends a card to Julia Eason, who with her husband came from their house to Dumm's side in the field. "We really formed a bond," Julia Eason said. "She almost became my daughter."

Mich Baumeister, Jennifer Grunbeck's attorney, represented a total of more than forty families of victims from TWA Flight 800 and Swissair Flight 111.

Bob MacIntosh, NTSB investigator in charge at Carrollton, called the ASA 529 accident investigation "very successful." He said, "The metallurgy that was developed by our laboratory put the manufacturer on notice that fifteen thousand propeller blades had to be modified. In a nutshell, our business is to prevent similar accidents from happening again."

More than five years later, he said, "And another propeller hasn't failed."

ASA Flight 529 was a short-hop, turbo-prop flight with none of the big-jet, transcontinental mystique that draws media attention. That does not diminish the power of Paul Butler's question, "What is it they're looking for?"

Maybe strangers come to Butler's hay field simply to see the very place where an airplane hit the ground and burned. Maybe the morbidly curious stop along that road in western Georgia because they want to walk where people died.

All I can know, really, is why I wanted to be there. I felt a connection to the people who in life and death consecrated this place. I first walked in that hay field to learn the literal lay of the land. That knowledge was necessary for the journalism I would do. I last walked there with Robin Fech and Alan Barrington and in the walking discovered the real reason I was drawn there, drawn by a story of human resilience, grace and hope. Learning what it was like for the people inside that little Brasilia, I also might learn about myself: To what would I cling? To whom would I call out? How, *in extremis*, would I react?

There's no way to know answers to those questions, not until the abstract is made real, but this much is certain: what happened inside that plane revealed in ordinary people extraordinary possibilities.

In the summer of 2000, Matt and Amy Warmerdam parked their mobile home in front of Steve Chadwick's house.

It had been four years since the first officer had seen the man from the Carroll County fire rescue team. Warmerdam had come to Carrollton then to thank Chadwick for pulling him from the burning cockpit. That day he had urged Chadwick to ask any question he wanted: "You won't hurt my feelings. Just ask."

Chadwick saw Warmerdam's heavy scarring and asked, "Did we do you a favor?"

"Hell, yeah," Warmerdam replied. He said he planned to live another seventy-five years because he had so much to live for, a wife and, perhaps one day, kids. "And let's face it," Warmerdam said, smiling, "the world is a fantastic place with me in it."

In the years since, Chadwick had quit the fire department. "Too much sadness," he said, part of that sadness the ASA crash. Now he saw the Warmerdams emerge from a mobile home, preceded by a bouncy golden retriever named Runway.

Warmerdam told Chadwick he'd been back up in small planes in California and that he intended to return one day to ASA, perhaps to fly regional jets.

Chadwick admired the man for that.

I visited Warmerdam in his new home on a hillside overlooking San Francisco Bay. He said, "There's a whole lot of life left for me, and this hasn't ruined me." He said his values and ideals were not changed by either the crash or his settlement with Hamilton Standard. "I don't want to be 'Matt the Millionaire.'"

He wanted to be Matt the Pilot. "Now that I don't have to [fly], I want to. It's what I do, you know? It's unfinished business. If I'm going to quit, I want to quit when I say I want to quit."

We sat in his kitchen, Matt looking across a table at Amy. "And, of course, I'd like to thank the wonderful love of my life over there, who is the reason I still want to be here and the reason this life is okay still."

In *Twilight of the Idols,* **Friedrich Nietzsche, nineteenth-century** German philosopher, wrote, "He who has a why to live can bear with almost any how."

Jennifer Grunbeck knew her why. She was Johnny's mother.

Amy Warmerdam once called to say Matt sometimes was too dejected to keep up with therapy. She asked Jennifer, "What makes you go?"

"Johnny," she said. "It's all him. I mean, I made a promise to him that I would be back on Friday and I was three months late."

Grunbeck's anger at Hamilton Standard, and at God, was tempered by her resolve: "If I waste all of my energy on being angry, I'm not going to get well."

Her goal remains August 20, 1995, the day before the crash. As nearly as possible, she hopes to regain the life and appearance she had that day.

In the first years after the crash, Jennifer and her husband, Bob, sought to keep their struggles and sadness from Johnny. But at least once, in the summer of 1997, Johnny heard it all.

Bob's father was about to undergo major surgery and his family planned a get-together at his brother David's house. Jennifer, depressed, refused to go. A loud argument ensued in front of Johnny.

"C'mon, Jen, let's go," Bob said, trying one last time. She wouldn't budge. So Bob and Johnny left without her.

Almost immediately, Jennifer knew she'd made a mistake. After all this family has done for me, she thought, how can I do this to them? She showered, dried, and dressed—three things she hadn't done for herself since the crash.

Unable to put on socks, she wore slip-on shoes. She made it downstairs and picked up her car keys. She had driven only once since the crash, in a parking lot, a year earlier. Ever since, her red Dodge Intrepid had sat out front, like a piece of street art.

Now, as she shuffled toward her car, Justin, a neighbor's six-year-old boy, said, "Should you be doing that?"

"Just stay in your driveway, Justin," she said. Jennifer told herself, If I make it to the end of the subdivision, then I can make it to the main road. If I can make it to the main road . . .

She drove to the main road, and on, and she drove for an hour, and when she pulled up to the house, one of Bob's brothers spotted the red car and thought, Why do I know that car?

When Jennifer stepped out, he said, in disbelief, "Son of a bitch!"

Bob had felt uneasy since leaving the house. He'd called Jennifer several times, but no one answered. He'd considered returning home. Now, seeing her walking toward where the family had gathered out back, Bob called to her: "What are you doing?"

Then he asked, "How did you get here?"

Jennifer held high the car keys.

"You didn't," Bob said. "Did you?"

Jennifer nodded.

Mad as hell and crying tears of joy, Bob said, "I'll be damned."

That night, Jennifer drove back home. Johnny rode with her.

Almost five years after the crash, still in a malaise, Robin Fech decided, Enough. She had tried "the therapy thing and the medication thing." Now she would try her own thing.

She sold her new home in Macon and moved to Atlanta to be near her mother, and her sister and her family. She quit therapy. She no longer initiated crash talk. She made no appearances and speeches.

She would no longer worry about life and death. She would live in the moment, spontaneous, letting fun come to her as the old Robin had.

She bought a Jet Ski and zipped across north Georgia lakes. In the Florida Keys, she hired a speed boat to take her parasailing and told the driver to step on it: "I've already fallen from eighteen thousand feet, so falling from five hundred feet won't bother me."

Then, in perhaps her greatest test, she walked through Hartsfield Atlanta International Airport, as she'd done the morning of August 21, 1995.

She was not totally at ease. She carried some pills in case she needed them. She had phoned her psychotherapist to tell her what she was about to do. Her psychotherapist told her to remember her breathing exercises. When you get there, the therapist said, give me a phone call.

As Fech had done on that day a lifetime earlier, she walked outside and boarded an ASA Brasilia, climbing a set of narrow steps and lowering her head slightly to pass through the low doorway.

The Brasilia's destination: Gulfport, Mississippi.

Fech took the last vacant seat in the back of the little plane—seat 10C. She knew 10C was Lonnie Burton's seat. She listened to the flight attendant's pre-flight speech and detected a few minor changes from the one she'd memorized years earlier.

The flight was a breeze: ninety minutes, smooth, uneventful, another of the thousands of such flights made every day. Fech might have been in her living room, she seemed so serene.

When the Brasilia bumped against the Gulfport runway, she raised her arms overhead, the way a football official signals a score.

Again the imp she once was, she said, "Touchdown!"

Then she turned to a man who had been reading the latest Tom Clancy epic and asked, "That a good book?"

In the terminal, Fech called her therapist and left a happy message.

She said, "The Robin has landed."

To commemorate the fifth anniversary of the crash, a small memorial was created on a lovely walking path behind the Shiloh United Methodist Church.

The memorial plaque's inscription, written by the Reverend Gus Koch:

They fell to Earth, and found friends.

Acknowledgments

THIS BOOK EXISTS ONLY BECAUSE of the wonderful cooperation from those who experienced the ASA crash first-hand. Over three years, I conducted nearly five hundred interviews with the extended ASA crash community, traveling to nine states, including Alaska, California, Maine, Texas, and Louisiana. Some people graciously sat with me on several occasions. Many follow-up interviews were conducted by telephone, usually to discuss and/or corroborate newly learned facts and details.

Collectively, these interviews form the backbone of this narrative. In writing about events in the field and hospitals, I've used multiple interviews to reconstruct the actions and statements of people who could no longer speak about them. A few discrepancies in recollections could not be reconciled, and the conflicting versions have been noted.

As part of my research, I studied the 1,200-page investigative file of the National Transportation Safety Board and testimony taken during litigation. I am especially grateful for the time and candor of NTSB investigators Bob MacIntosh, Hank Hughes, and Gordon "Jim" Hookey.

In *Young Men and Fire* (The University of Chicago Press, 1992), the story of the 1949 Mann Gulch forest fire that claimed the lives of thirteen U.S. Forest Service "smoke jumpers," author Norman Maclean wrote, "If a storyteller thinks enough of storytelling to regard it as a calling, unlike a historian, he cannot turn from the sufferings of his characters. A story-teller, unlike a historian, must follow compassion where it leads him. He must be able to accompany his characters, even into smoke and fire, and bear witness to what they thought and felt even when they themselves no longer knew."

Two men died by fire in Paul Butler's field—Captain Ed Gannaway and Jim Kennedy. As I *accompanied them,* through research and inter-views, into smoke and fire, I came to know their wives, Jackie Gannaway and Nancy Kennedy. I visited their homes in Georgia and Connecticut. Mrs. Gannaway and Mrs. Kennedy treated me only with kindness. Because they allowed me inside their worlds, I came to know Ed Gan-naway and Jim Kennedy—the essence of who they were, defined in part by the loved ones they'd left behind. Jackie Gannaway and Nancy Kennedy have never met, though I hope one day they will; they share dig-nity and grace.

My work on the ASA 529 crash began with a seven-part series in *The Atlanta Journal-Constitution* published in November 1998. The series was edited by Thomas Oliver and Jim Walls. I'm grateful to them, my col-league Rich Addicks (who, with his camera, accompanied me most of the way) and also to *AJC* editors Ron Martin, John Walter, and Hyde Post for their support, which was, and still is, as good as it gets. My newsroom buddies Bill Rankin and Henry Unger provided helpful suggestions as the series evolved into this book.

The story of ASA 529 draws upon many academic disciplines and technical fields: from psychology to physiology, and from the mechanics of flight to the mechanics of metal fatigue. I turned to expert readers, ask-ing each to hammer away at my early drafts, identifying factual inaccura-cies and/or false assumptions.

Thanks, then, to: Dr. Charles Figley, psychologist and director of Florida State University's Traumatology Institute; Dr. Andrew Munster, retired director of the Baltimore Regional Burn Center and professor of surgery and plastic surgery at The Johns Hopkins University; Captain Scott Miller, a Canadair Regional Jet pilot and instructor for a regional airline based in Memphis; William Langewiesche, correspondent for *The Atlantic,* licensed pilot, and author of *Inside the Sky: A Meditation on Flight* (Pantheon, 1998); and Dr. David McDowell, Regents' Professor, and Carter N. Paden, Jr., Distinguished Chair in Metals Processing in the mechanical engineering school at the Georgia Institute of Technology.

I received other critical assessments from several former Emory colleagues: David J. Garrow, Pulitzer Prize–winning historian and Presidential Distinguished Professor at Emory's law school; Dr. Robyn Fivush of the psychology department; and Pat Wehner, post-doctoral fellow at Emory's MARIAL Center. My friends Joyce Justicz and Ben Lefkowitz also gave helpful suggestions.

A number of books provided understanding and context. Though all are not cited by title in the text, several were especially helpful, including: *Aviation, An Historical Survey from Its Origins to the End of World War II* by Charles Harvard Gibbs-Smith; J. E. Gordon's *Structures, Or Why Things Don't Fall Down;* Viktor E. Frankl's *Man's Search for Meaning;* and Dr. Andrew Munster's *Severe Burns: A Family Guide to Medical and Emotional Recovery.* In a broader sense, three books served as models: Maclean's *Young Men and Fire,* John Hersey's *Hiroshima,* and Thornton Wilder's *The Bridge of San Luis Rey.*

A project of this nature leaves a writer in need of the help, kindness and patience of others. I received more than my fair share. Dr. Laurence Jacobs, a professor in the school of civil and environmental engineering at Georgia Tech, demonstrated ultrasound techniques (using a transducer and oscilloscope) in the school's lab. Jackie Bullard of Emory's journalism department handled any administrative need with a smile. My former Berkeley professor, Leon Litwack, a Pulitzer Prize–winning historian who has helped me for years in ways even he couldn't know, lent me his on-campus office for a summer, and then wouldn't even let me buy him lunch. Randy Gue and Andrew Larrick conducted research. Elizabeth Wilson transcribed taped interviews.

My literary agent, David Black, is among the best in the business. He is the Lenny Dykstra of literary agents, all nails. David will go to the wall for his writers—and then through the wall. I'm also indebted to Susan Raihofer, Gary Morris, Joy Tutela, and Leigh Ann Eliseo of the David Black Literary Agency for their counsel and friendship.

When Steve Ross, editorial director at Crown, first read my book proposal, he became emotional. Steve saw this story as I saw it—a book not about a plane falling, but the human spirit rising. Steve has been my editor now for two years, and I still feel his passion. He's been my ally, advocate, and friend, what every writer longs for in an editor. His assistant, Kate Donovan, could not have been more kind or efficient.

Almost daily, Dave Kindred has taken the meaning of friendship to a new and higher level. During this project, I spoke with him merely ten thousand times. One of the finest, most compassionate journalists I know, Dave's old enough to be my father, young enough to be my best friend. He calms my nerves and my prose.

Sometimes, in the dark of night, I think of the people aboard ASA 529. I get out of bed and sit in a rocking chair. The crash sequence and the fire in the field play out in my head. Invariably I find myself walking down the hall to my children's bedrooms. I look in on my sons, Ross and Win, and my daughter, Leigh. Then I return to my wife, Carrie. It's a simple act that has a powerful calming effect on me. Carrie and the kids are my sun, moon, and stars. Knowing they are with me, and that I am with them, gives me peace. Tomorrow is not promised but my fidelity to them is.

Survivors of aviation disasters and serious burns have an acute need for specialized support and assistance, as do their families. The following four nonprofit organizations do important work in these areas, and are dependent on donations:

National Air Disaster Alliance/Foundation
2020 Pennsylvania Avenue, NW, No. 315
Washington, DC 20006-1846
www.planesafe.org

Mission: To raise the standard of safety, security, and survivability for aviation passengers and to support families of air crash victims.

Wings of Light, Inc.
PMB 448
16845 N. 29 Avenue, No. 1
Phoenix, AZ 85053
www.wingsoflight.org

Mission: To provide three distinct air crash support networks for: 1. crash survivors; 2. families of victims, and 3. rescue/response personnel, including fire fighters, NTSB investigators, and emergency medical personnel.

The American Burn Association
625 N. Michigan Ave., Suite 1530
Chicago, IL 60611
www.ameriburn.org

Mission: To promote the art and science of burn-related research, teaching, care, prevention, and rehabilitation.

The Phoenix Society for Burn Survivors, Inc.
2153 Wealthy Street SE #215
East Grand Rapids, MI 49506
www.phoenix.society.org

Mission: To uplift and inspire anyone affected by the devastation of a burn injury through peer support, education, collaboration, and advocacy.

About the Author

GARY M. POMERANTZ served for the past two years as Distinguished Visiting Professor of Journalism at Emory University in Atlanta. His first book, *Where Peachtree Meets Sweet Auburn*, was named a 1996 Notable Book of the Year by *The New York Times*. A graduate of the University of California, Berkeley, he has written on staff for *The Washington Post* and *The Atlanta Journal-Constitution*. For his seven-part series in the *AJC* on the air crash that is the subject of this book, he captured in 1999 the Ernie Pyle Award for human-interest writing and the Society of Professional Journalists' Sigma Delta Chi award for feature writing. Pomerantz lives with his wife and three children near San Francisco.